Ayabacholization Classroom In My Life: The Longest Shortcut To University Education

Peter Ateh-Afac Fossungu

Mwanaka Media and Publishing Pvt Ltd,
Chitungwiza, Zimbabwe
*
Creativity, Wisdom, and Beauty

1

Publisher: *Mmap*
Mwanaka Media and Publishing Pvt Ltd
24 Svosve Road, Zengeza 1
Chitungwiza, Zimbabwe
mwanaka@yahoo.com
mwanaka13@gmail.com
https://www.mmapublishing.org
www.africanbookscollective.com/publishers/mwanaka-media-
and-publishing
https://facebook.com/MwanakaMediaAndPublishing/

Distributed in and outside N. America by African Books
Collective
orders@africanbookscollective.com
www.africanbookscollective.com

ISBN: 978-1-77933-152-6
EAN: 9781779331526

DISCLAIMER
All views expressed in this publication are those of the author
and do not necessarily reflect the views of *Mmap*.

Table of Contents

Introduction

I have never been a beggar and never will be one. Especially not one that begs to be changed to be accepted, or to be given what I know I deserve having. But, if there is one thing that I would not shy away from begging from the intellectuals and nation-builders of this continent, it is this. Please, let us stop giving these people (our detractors) reasons to think that they are justified in considering us immature. Africa, if you correctly and four-eyesismatically read into history, has more mature people than any other continent. Do I need to spoon-feed anyone here? (Fossungu, 2015c: 118-19).

This educative narrative cuts across two continents (Africa and North America) though being heavily set in Ambazonia and Cameroun, yet, with far-flung consequences for and in Canada. Its whole essence is pitched on how children's lives and future are seriously affected by the way love, family, and marriage would be viewed and defined, especially by parents and other relations. I write the book solely because of my concern for the future of children (who Dr Cho Ayaba says "can walk in and feel at home" - cited in Fossungu, 2023: 202) and social work departments that have enormous powers over the making or ruining of the future of children (whatever the definition attached). I talk of Africa and North America, but I think the message applies around the globe. I write from the perspective of a child that has been through it and seen it all and would not want other children (especially in Ambazonia) to have to "walk in and not feel at home" through going through what I have had to go through. It is my view that no child should have to go through all what I went through simply because of some particular individual's selective definition of family or of child. A designation, moreover, that is exclusively geared toward making readily available resources for educating children unavailable to some children. A child must not be considered a child by the parents only insofar as the child's services are concerned, but regarded not as a child when it comes to the education and other needs of that child. I was able to surmount some of the ill-conceived definitions and other road-blocking devices largely because of some inborn powers, which can also be very easily perceived in Ambazonia's ordained liberator, Dr Cho Ayaba. Not every child has those Ayabacholization powers. Even in regard of the survival strategies that I learnt or quickly developed, that capacity to learn and adapt too can never be the same with all children: this being amply evidenced in the numerous cases in the book.

Figure #1: Momany in Yaoundé in August 1991 – only a month to first arrival to North America for graduate studies
Source: Momany Fossungu's Album

I also write from the viewpoint of a parent who is concerned about the way some parents are using children as mere means of acquiring revenue from, or tools of punishing, the other parent. And they persist in doing so to the total disregard of the future of said children who, paradoxically, do not even

5

feature in their un-African and un-Canadian definition of family. Social work (and other governmental) departments, particularly in Ambazonia, are also enjoined to ensure that, in addition to having the academic qualifications, people working for them do satisfy some basic minimum attributes incidental to what their job is all about. In the final analysis, I truly think "Africa is in dire need of dedicated and visionary torch-bearers [like Captain Traoré & Dr Ayaba] to help reverse the moneyintriguist or selfish un-African trend that is indeed behind the continent's governance and development problems" (Fossungu, 2023: 205).

The book's lessons are many but I think the main lesson (from where many others radiate in all directions) that you should take home, whatever your academic discipline or professional career, is that when you are destined for great accomplishments, there is nothing that can stop you except you. If this book teaches parents generally but divorcing or divorced ones specifically that the future and interest of the children, whatever the cause of their going apart (or calculations for the non-divorcing others), should always be the prime mover for whatever arrangement (or decision) they do or should make (see Fossungu, 2023: 320), then it would have achieved one of its purposes. In short, I think the world would be a better place if people are generally zoomedeyedists. That is those looking at the larger picture of things. Hisofeans (or zoomedeyedists) are usually not only pioneers of big projects. They are also better suited to give children, without definitional distinctions, a brighter future than what they themselves have, irrespective of their societies. Ayabacholization and Traorélization, don't I hear you well? The book's "principles" are of general application although the story is personal and true, revolving around me and my "family" and "lovers". The story is worth the telling because of its potentials for, inter alia, motivating and helping many people who might learn from my intriguing experiences. It is not so much about the story, captivating (with some parts of it perhaps unbelievable to Canadians) as it is; but so much about the rare strategies that have aided me in surmounting obstacles (some being really life-

6

threatening) and moving on in life. Most of these stumbling blocks are clearly and simply the result of the inconsiderate way some parents, partners, and other relations schemingly define family and children (and marriage) and love.

With all the focus on the meanings of love and understanding, family, marriage, as they impinge on the future of children and social work, Chapter 1 surveys Ayabacholization and justifies Ambazonia's torch-bearing role for Africa, while also sternly addressing the ethnic political entrepreneurs and banishing confusioncracy for the sake of building a a community were every child can walk in and feel at home. Chapters 2 and 3 examine some strategies for overcoming hurdles and progressing, especially within the intricacies of the African family, and particularly one in which defining a child took more than a single connotation from both parents for different purposes. These two Chapters acquaint you with the foundational bases of my successes and failures from the angle of my unique family setting and upbringing, as well as from the direction of some important early family relations studied in Chapter 3, a Chapter which hinges on the household's farming creed. These two Chapters, therefore, furnish good background and springboard that greatly aid in the comprehension of the theories in the rest of the book.

Chapters 4 and 5 study the brilliant short cutting of the African family money and other complications to obtain university education and secure an ideal family. Analogize them to the largely unanticipated 'Ambazonia Rising'! Chapter 6 protractedly shows how the short-cut was elongated by the bombshell of African family hurdles and other backstabbing acts that are rooted in biology and 99-Sensism. This blow-up then initiated my roaming days that also occasioned the ideal-spouse flop, leading up to the eventual spouse's wholly new 'un-African' and 'un-Canadian' outrageous definition of family in Canada. Analogize it to the social media chaos and the traitors prolonging the Ambazonia War of Liberation (AWOL).

Also put it and the entire book alongside legitimacy and genuineness in the AWOL: Who is actually fighting for Ambazonia and who is just using the AWOL for something else, such as money-making and political relevance? There is a conclusion that harps on the importance of openmindedness and giveantakism in relationships.

Chapter 1

Ayabacholization and Ambazonia's Torch-Bearing Role for Africa: Addressing Ethnic Political Entrepreneurs and Banishing Confusioncracy

Congratulations Ambazonians. You employed logic and not sentiment. You listened to Freedom, not Slavery. You sacrificed for Ambazonia, not Cameroun. Your action today, your sacrifices today, your defiance today registered once more your rejection of occupation, tyranny, and dispossession. You embraced resistance and Freedom of our country (Dr Lucas Cho Ayaba on Christmas 2023).

Ambazonians were being felicitated by the AWOL Leader for their wise refusal to allow Christmas to be employed as a tool to undermine *Kuntri Sunday* – the Monday Ghost Town. Biafrans style it Sit-at-Home. A very useful lesson drawn from the Ayabacholization Classrom in My Life. Knowing that it is not my story *per se* that is important here, but the lessons learnt and drawn from it, I will like to go with the story behind the lessons rather than the lessons behind the story. A literary friend once told me in Nigeria that a good story is one that leaves the experts from all angles speculating on the characters' motives, calculations, etc (see Fossungu, 2015b: ix). I do not know how far that is true, but I would prefer to largely leave the experts do their job while I stick to the lessons. Not claiming professionalism in the domain(s) covered, the lessons are many but one of the main lessons I want you to take home is that when you are destined for greatness, there is nothing that can stop you except you. I am even tempted to think that there is no professional anything as such. I, for one, would not say that I am a *professional writer* but here is a book hinging on

9

love, family and academics intended for your consumption that may become your best companion. Not because it is written by a professional in those domains, but simply because its expibasketical message(s) may be clearer and more useful than professionals would have made it (them) with too much professionalism and/or pretentiousness. In other words, the lesson (learned also from many of my female friends and family relations) that I am trying to get through here, is that there is nothing like being a professional before doing anything. Ambazonians have just proven it on Christmas 2023, *no bi sooh*? Thus, if you have anything to do or say, just do or say it and let others worry later about how you have done or said it. Therefore, don't be afraid of breaking virgin grounds!

The MISSG Picturing the Power of Nginyamanyism

Here, therefore, is a *Momanynizing Imaginary Inaugural Speech of the First Secretary-General of Ambazonia* (styled MISSG) which is just a tip of the iceberg of what great, brave and innovative Ambazonians should be expecting both from their patriotic governors at all levels as well as from themselves:

Fellow Ambazonians: I shed these tears not for you and me. I shed them for those patriots who have not been able to be here with us today to mark the end of the regime that crucified them in our Homeland and the new beginning that we are all here today to imprint on history. I shed these tears for them, knowing fully well though that they are happy still to realize that they did not die for this Nation in vain.

......

People are telling me to get many advisers in several domains. Yes, I surely need numerous advisers, I have told them. But these counsellors don't need to be foreigners and here advising me because the only advisers I need I already have – the Good of our People. So all the advisers I now need ought to be those who can competently advise our great and brave people on their rights and freedoms and obligations. Therefore, consider yourself my competent adviser if, for example:

As the big title holder that I have been, you let the titles shine only from under;

As the school teacher I have been, you correctly teach our People;

As the intellectual that I have been, you dutifully enlighten our People on the good of the General Weal;

As the farmer that I have been, you selflessly feed our People;

As the taxi driver that I have been, you correctly transport our People;

As the labourer that I have been, you counsel our People by example;

As the university lecturer that I have been, you teach our People to know and assume and defend their rights and obligations;

As the writer that I have been, you write to teach our People to know and assume and defend their rights and obligations;

As the Diasporean that I have been, you come back home to guide our People to better understand the ways of the world;

As the lawyer that I have been, you use the law to fairly distribute justice and defend our People's freedoms;

As the civil servant that I have not yet been, you diligently serve our People rather than requiring our People to serve you before being grudgingly served;

As the man or woman in uniform that I have not yet been, you protect our People rather than brutalize them;

As the law-maker that I have not been, you make and promulgate laws that protect our People from abuse and further their development; and

As the Patriots that we all must be, you promote the love of country and Fossungupalogy among our People.

Like my late father once said to me, I wouldn't like the next set of Ambazonian Administrators to be like me and those with whom I will be working in the next ten or eight years. I would want them to be better than us because they will be coming in when Ambazonia would not only be more mature in self-reliant governance and development but our institutions too would have become stronger than they were at inception.

Celebration is over. It is time then we all begin working seriously to make our posterity proud of the Ambazonia we will be bequeathing to it. A Constitutional Committee of experts would be convened in ….months to start reworking on what we now have in order to bring forth a permanent and robust Constitution of Ambazonia. Long Live Free Ambazonia!

That brings me to the background of this narrative. My main goal in life has always been and still remains that of ameliorating the life of the greatest number of persons possible. As a child growing up, I always wanted to become, first, a pilot; second, a medical doctor; and, third, a judge/lawyer. Why I ended up with or close to the third rather than the others could also explain this book's whole essence. As a young child, aeroplanes always fascinated me and I wanted to fly one myself one day. That is why I took my science lessons (especially mathematics and physics) in secondary school very seriously, becoming one of the few students selected on merits to do additional maths in St. Joseph's College, Sasse, Buea, Ambazonia (Sasse College). If there could be any doubt about that in your mind (since I am not now Einsteinistically killing you with formula and laboratory experiments), then doubting would not even be the case with a picture (like the one in Figure #2 that one of my classmates posted on our class forum on 25 November 2011 and which is duly) attached to the statement (see Fossungu, 2016: 90-91).

Figure #2: The Sasse 1975-batch mathematicians
Source: Titus Fofung

The Power of Nginyamanyism: Nginyamanyism defines the philosophy that is captured in the Momany-Ngi-Nyam communications. The invaluable importance of pictures like the few 'story-telling ones' encountered in this book has been duly brought home to you by the 'Lion of Judah'. As the *Lion of Judah* (as Lucas Esambe Lobwede Ngi-Nyam likes to be called) reiterated in the first paragraph of his famous 2006 letter to me,

Beloved Doctor, often enough, memories fade fast but as every picture tells a story, I had been able to locate you with one of the pictures you sent to me from Alberta while I was still in Yaoundé a couple of years ago. How did it all happen? Early this year, while looking at the pictures in my Album, I caught sight of one of the three pictures you had kindly sent to me and then asked myself, where the hell is this man now? As a

13

matter of interest, I removed one of the pictures and sent to my son-in-law, Solomon Tatah currently in Boston with his family, being that it has been through him in Yaoundé that we got to know ourselves. It has been through his recent letter of March 2, 2006 received here in my village on April 9, 2006 that, apart from enclosing the picture, gave me the vital information about your whereabouts. He indicated that he had gotten in touch with you and that you were eagerly expecting to read from me. This I now do with confidence and sincere love (Fossungu, 2016 : 157).

That is very correct, Ngi-Nyam. Pictures speak volumes that the alphabet is yet to accurately grasp. Thus, "pictures are extensively used in this book because of their universal non-lielistical characteristics, in addition to their being able to tell the cultural tale (in certain circumstances) even more accurately than any voluminous amount of words can" (Fossungu, 2023: 7). It is not to ignore Abongwa Fozo's (2015) warnings regarding the pictures of the notorious Biya-Dead Soldiers honouring farce though.

I always dream (even until date) and find myself actually flying without wings; and most often flying to escape from some sort of danger below. The pilot profession literally had nothing to do with what I considered even then as my objective in life – bringing more happiness to the greatest number of persons possible – that greatly influenced the other two choices. I would not be talking much about those choices as I would about defining myself with my objective. I think a life objective such as mine would surely be worthless until you know exactly who you are and what you are up against in becoming what you want to become. The following are a few of the strong messages of this book. You cannot know yourself until you can confront the truth about yourself and also about those you deal with. If you are not afraid of your own truth, you will hardly be

14

scared of someone else's truth. Those who tell the truth about themselves do not do so to get pity and/or praise; only those who tell lies do. You do not hurt by telling the truth. It is the truth (that you have learnt to embrace) that hurts. If you learn to embrace the truth, you will seldom be hurt by it. This book, for example, could still have been written as a fictional story. But I think that would be a big lie since I would be telling you my story without actually letting you know it is my story. There are certainly many other facts of my life that cannot all be brought in here and must be left out, not with the intention of hiding them. There is no part of my complex life that I am ashamed of. On the contrary, I take a lot of pride in my multi-dimensional life, an invaluable source of strength for me. If much has not been brought in here, it is simply because of the well-known fact from Basil Davidson (as cited in Fossungu, 2013a: 5) that the writing of history (moreover one as multifaceted as mine) would in any case become a hopeless venture if it involved explaining everything. I cannot even begin to tell you just how hard it has been to sift through it all to come out with just what you now have in front of you.

Most people who know me just do not know me at all. And this includes the woman I eventually ended up with as wife. Most of them do not have an idea of what I have been through to be where I am. That is why many people around me just cannot figure out how I am able to carry on, bitter-free, after all what they know as having happened in my life, including insults and disillusioning comportment from those I dearly love. That is one of the many reasons I tell this story so as to share some of my ingredients of and strategies for surviving adversity. Some of them are inborn, others are learnt and acquired. This is certainly not the first book written with such a goal in mind (see, for instance, For-Mukwai, 2010); but I think the most important thing to the matter is to know exactly who you are. Knowing so, and having objectives with which you define yourself, would make things a lot easier since your worth is then also known to you.

Twocubesosugarism: Calamity in Not Knowing the Two-Cubes-of-Sugar

If I have to reiterate, the only secret I can say there is to the matter is to know exactly who you are, including the problems facing you. When you know what you are up against, you will often correctly anticipate problems before they actually come. (Don't I hear our brave Boyses in the Bushes well?) There is thus nothing as easy as solving a problem that pops up when you are ready for it. What makes a problem really bad and daunting is when it takes you by surprise. You are caught off guard. La République du Cameroun (LRC) obviously didn't know the 'Two Cubes of Sugar' it had been toying with for sixty-something years: YES or OUI? Of course, Ayabacholization chooses both because its architect always diligently Confronts the Truth about Ambazonia and feverishly Understands the Problem Confronting Ambazonia. I strongly believe, like Dr Cho Ayaba, that an independent Ambazonia is the hope of an independent and united Africa – the UDA whose suggested states abbreviations are in Table 1.

Table 1: Suggested State Abbreviations of 55 of the Present Countries Coming into United Democratic Africa (UDA)		
Current Country Name	*Capital City*	*Abbreviation in the UDA*
Algeria	Algiers	AGR
Ambazonia	Buea	AMB
Angola	Luanda	ANG

16

Benin	Porto-Novo	BNN
Botswana	Gaborone	BWN
Burkina Faso	Ouagadougou	BKF
Burundi	Gitega	BRD
Cabo Verde	Praia	CVD
Cameroun	Yaoundé	CMR
Central African Republic (CAR)	Bangui	CAF
Chad	N'Djamena	CHA
Comoros	Moroni	COM
Congo, Democratic Republic of the	Kinshasa	COK
Congo, Republic of the	Brazzaville	COB
Cote d'Ivoire	Yamoussoukro	CDI
Djibouti	Djibouti (city)	DBT
Egypt	Cairo	EGT
Equatorial Guinea	Malabo (de jure) Oyala (seat of government)	EQG
Eritrea	Asmara	ERT
Eswatini (formerly Swaziland)	Mbabane (administrative) Lobamba (legislative,	EWT

	royal)	
Ethiopia	Addis Ababa	ETP
Gabon	Libreville	GAB
Gambia	Banjul	GAM
Ghana	Accra	GHA
Guinea	Conakry	GUC
Guinea-Bissau	Bissau	GUB
Kenya	Nairobi	KNY
Lesotho	Maseru	LST
Liberia	Monrovia	LBR
Libya	Tripoli	LBY
Madagascar	Antananarivo	MDG
Malawi	Lilongwe	MLW
Mali	Bamako	MAL
Mauritania	Nouakchott	MTN
Mauritius	Port Louis	MRT
Morocco	Rabat	MRC
Mozambique	Maputo	MZB
Namibia	Windhoek	NMB
Niger	Niamey	NIG
Nigeria	Abuja	NGR
Rwanda	Kigali	RWA

Sao Tome and Principe	Sao Tomé	STP
Senegal	Dakar	SNG
Seychelles	Victoria	SYC
Sierra Leone	Freetown	SRL
Somalia	Mogadishu	SML
South Africa	Pretoria (administrativ) Cape Town (legislative) Bloemfontein (judicial)	SAF
South Sudan	Juba	SSD
Sudan	Khartoum	SUD
Tanzania	Dodma	TZN
Togo	Lomé	TOG
Tunisia	Tunis	TNS
Uganda	Kampala	UGD
Zambia	Lusaka	ZAM
Zimbabwe	Harare	ZBB

My aim of having to update, expand, and republish this book (and others that will follow) is to aid visionary and dedicated African leaders like Dr Cho Ayaba and his enviable team (of the Ambazonia Governing Council (AGovC) and the Ambazonia Defense Forces (ADF)) in the construction of the new society being envisaged in (the Gulf of Guinea of) Africa that appropriately "ensures respect for fundamental human rights and certain basic shared values that were dolefully mistreated by the [illegitimate] Foumban arrangement and [so-called] Federal Constitution" (Fossungu, 2013a: 2). For close to a century Cameroon had shown that it was incapable, as a neocolony, to live up to the task and Ambazonia would seem to have risen/be rising to fulfil Africa's God-ordained destiny. Yes. You heard me right. I said Cameroon failed colossally to lead Africa out of the dungeon, despite all the invaluable aid some visionary and creatively audacious Ambazonians put at its disposal, and the torch got passed to Ambazonia.

My informed use of *Camerounese* (rather than Camerounian) most of the times in this book, of course, is because Ambazonia is no longer babysitting even 'the European Cameroun' which it valiantly dropped out of the Unity-Daycare from when the French-Biya genocidal war was officially declared in 2017. My argument on Southern Cameroonsian as against Southern Cameroonian (see Fossungu, 2013a: 40-45) should also be read in here. *Togolais* in English is Togolese (not Togolian); so too are Gabonais, Senegalais, etc. It was Ambazonia's illegitimate marriage with LRC that offered and legitimized the *nian* to *Camerounais* in English. No more comfort in there, it's gone forever. Ambazonia is clearly gone because of the gross failure to heed to the counsel and caveat of *Understanding Confusion in Africa* (Fossungu, 2013a) which are now in the past! The malfunction is now Ambazonia's vital history that it cannot afford to ignore in any meaningful development endeavour. In other words, Ambazonia must master the journey so far made to be able to properly chart its course to the destination envisaged in its uniquely creative Anthem, an inspirational hymn which you can readily find in Fossungu (2023: 164-65).

As I have said, Cameroon ignominiously failed to lead Africa out of the dungeon and the imperative role passed on to Ambazonia, an entity reputed for being the first to have had democratic transfer of power in Africa (while even still a colony). You can also get testimony from the motivating and sane Message of the leader of the AWOL, Dr Cho Ayaba, to Chadians and to All Africans, delivered on 21 April 2021. He 'hisofely' brings out Ambazonia's leadership role and the imperative need for authentic unity in the opening paragraph:

My fellow Ambazonians, this is Dr Cho Ayaba. We have been observing what is happening in Chad, and this is what I would like to let our people know. Our struggle for independence is at the epicentre of a dramatic change that may be necessary in the continent of Africa. Building original states, instituting political systems, value systems that reflect the reality of the people living within those states; instituting languages that are the very essence of our communication strategy; and ensuring that sovereignty is actually vested in the people and that the peoples within the continent can alter their government and put into place new governments that are accountable to them. Governments that exploit resources to, first and foremost, focus on the personal development of their people and their countries; institute political systems that are accountable to the people. I want to congratulate the people of Chad for taking out the old tyrant, and I call on France to allow the people of Chad to decide who leads them and to engage in bilateral relations that are mutually beneficial to both countries. The era of instituting political systems and putting into place autocrats whose sole responsibility is to the colonial master has not benefited France or those countries. Autocracy, corruption are at the heart of massive poverty, the displacement of thousands of people most of who would end up on the shores of France and other countries. Poverty in Chad has an impact on the development of France, on the creation of opportunities for the French people. The very reason why Ghislain and others worked together to ensure peace, collaboration and free trade mechanism, democratic pluralism within the continent of Europe was because of their understanding that what affects one European country negatively is going to trickle into the other countries. We watched the economic crisis in Greece and the impact it would have had in other countries in Europe, how Europe pulled together to ensure that Greece was afloat (Ayaba, 2021a).

Figure #3: Dr Lucas Cho Ayaba, President of AGovC & CIC of the ADF
Source: AGovC

Of course, no one must doubt that other Africans (notably in BKF, MAL, & NIG – see Table 1) are/have been keenly listening and planning well. The Sahel-Axis! The Ambazonia-Biafra Alliance! Also important to the imperative issue is Dr Cho Ayaba's "Address to the People of Biafra on 17 October 2021" in which he also harped on the Pan-Africanism concept being redefined through self-determination, stressing the fact that 'before the colonial creation of Nigeria, there was Biafra'. Anything that comes out of this guy's mouth makes a lot of sense for the welbeing of Africans. He had elaborated on the concept in the must-read 5th and final paragraph of his 21 April 2021 message:

The notion of Pan-Africanism begins with the concept of self-determination where peoples can decide the kind of political systems they want and these people and political systems can in turn collaborate, trade, with other countries for mutual benefit in terms of prosperity and security. The continent has been hijacked, poverty has been induced deliberately; it is being recolonized by foreign political powers that dish loans at low interest rates, indebting the continent at a speed that a hundred years from today the next generation will never be able to pay. Colonialism is no longer the marching of tanks across borders, seizing of political systems and resources. Financial colonialism is taking place through deliberate indebtedness. African resources are being mortgaged and there is no accountability, there is no replication in terms of development and the creation of opportunities (Ayaba, 2021a).

That is certainly an incontrovertible Hisofean talking. The remainder of this crucial eye-opening paragraph of the AWOL Leader is found in Fossungu (2023: 228 & 161-62). But all these progressive things cannot happen in the midst of confusion. I am sure I hear AGovC Spokesman Lucas Asu well in his theorizing that "We as Ambazonians want to be part of a stable, structured world for peace, security and transparent democracy" (Fossungu, 2023: 214)? In that light, let me take this occasion to also sparingly address the shortsighted and unhelpful so-called Ambazonian thirteen states that are fully empty of viability for the federalism they are claiming (in 'Federal Republic of Ambazonia' (FRA)). It is nothing but clear vectors for tribalism promotion, which can hardly furnish the locomotion for being any 'part of a stable, structured world for peace, security and transparent democracy'. Don't forget that these so-called 13 states are mere tribal divisions (and subdivisions) that were created by LRC solely for purposes of divide-and-rule: just as the splitting of Ambazonia into the so-called NW/SW Divide. My informed view is that Ambazonia has to be governed as an effectively *decentralized* parliamentary polity with three main zones (provinces, if you prefer) as I have humbly suggested in 'Lexicon of Ambazonia Governance' (see Fossungu, 2023: 5-6). My detailed arguments that sustain these suggested models had already been thoroughly made in two of my 2013 books on Confusion and Manipulation: *Understanding Confusion in Africa* (2013a) and *Democracy and Human Rights in Africa* (2013b). Reading into the future, oh yeah! Applied HISOFE, for sure!

Dr Piet Konings of African Studies Centre Leiden, The Netherlands, has said the following on both books. Regarding *Understanding Confusion in Africa*, he pointed out that "The book critically examines the multi-cultural nation-building experience in Africa, with a detailed case-study of Cameroon. While there is already a relatively large body of literature on this subject, this is one of the few studies carried out by a legal specialist, albeit often transcending his own discipline.... His suggestions for change are based on an admirably wide comparative perspective. This is a well-argued and readable book" (Fossungu, 2013a: back cover). Relating to the other, *Democracy and Human Rights in Africa*, the doctor tells readers that "This book is a provocative but masterful study of federalism in Africa. With a detailed case-study of Cameroon, the author convincingly demonstrates the 'confusioncracy' and 'manipulation' existing in this country around the issue of federalism, clearly reflected in the so-called 'Anglophone problem'. I find the author's comparative perspective particularly attractive. The book provides us with many constructive building stones for the creation of truly federal states in Africa" (Fossungu, 2013b: back cover). Ambazonia's nation-builders desiring success and valuable aid in their job MUST have to pay keen attention to both books which, I must emphasize, duly took authentic history and objectivity into account.

For example, my 3-Province proposal is informed by authentic Amba history as well as by an objective, innovative and sane desire of banishing the so-called LRC-created NW-SW Divide that seems to be so entrenched now in the psyche of Ambazonians and requires smart critical thinking to efface. Historically, Ambazonia (as British Southern Cameroons – BSC) was administered as three provinces which almost approximate what I have put forward – namely Victoria Province, Mamfe Province, and Bamenda Province. Directional names have LRC as architect. My argument has been dictated by the understanding (as experts like Professor Miecyslaw Maneli of City University of New York have told us) that resurrecting old wisdom from oblivion and presenting it in light of new conflicts and antagonisms usually constitutes an innovation and a significant step forward. According to Daisaku Ikeda's *Lasting Peace* also, two Chinese proverbs ('to study the old to understand the new' and 'to know from antiquity to explain the present') have also been advanced to "amply testify to the traditional belief that history is a mirror reflecting the present, a source of light serving as a guide to the present age" (Fossungu, 2021b: 25). Basil Davidson also comes in to confirm that this is precisely why the tradition of Malawi unity in ancient times was lately called in aid by modern Malawian nationalists as a powerful emotive influence for the building of a modern state (Fossungu, 2021b: 25). Was Africa not different from what it is today before the 1884 Berlin Conference that indiscriminately parcelled it out without our input or consultation? Why wouldn't that history also be called in aid now as a commanding emotional pressure for the building of the United Democratic Afrika (UDA)? (Fossungu, 2021b: 25)

Does the theorization on positive employment of history not also tie in with Ayabacholization's thesis that before the colonial creation of Nigeria there was Biafra? Before LRC's annexation and occupation there was BSC, aka Ambazonia, governed as three viable near-autonomous provinces, each with an international airport – Tiko, Mamfe, Bali. These points resonate very well in the visionary and patriotic AWOL leader's talk during the Ambazonia-Biafra Alliance press briefing of 9 April 2021. Dr Cho Ayaba made it very pellucid on that date when, after taking the podium, he fearlessly stated:

Thank you very much. Thanks to my brother, Mazi Nnamdi Kanu, the leader of the Indigenous Peoples of Biafra (IPOB). We have assembled here today in front of our two peoples to declare our intentions to work together to ensure our collective survival from the brutal annexations that have occurred in our both nations. We understand the difficulties that both peoples, the peoples of Biafra and Ambazonia, have faced in the past sixty years. But we have been discussing in the past few months to ensure that our collective strength be brought together to be more impactful to ensuring that we do not bequeath to the next generation a more oppressed homeland than we inherited. The Ambazonia-Biafra Alliance is critical in an era where Nigeria and Cameroun have established two autocracies that have used violence as a political tool to suppress our both peoples. Within Nigeria itself, you have in the North the Hausas and Fulanis who have cross-border relationships in Niger. In the West you have the Yorubas who have cross-border relationships with Benin. The people of Biafra have been denied access to Ambazonia. We must recall that during the Biafran war of independence, while countries like France that is the highest investor today in Nigeria provided support, countries like Ivory Coast, Norway and others, the one country being ruled by a Fulani man that refused Biafra the opportunity to receive support and prevent genocide was Cameroun. This is because Ahidjo, a Fulani man, preferred the domination that was exercised by Fulanis from within Nigeria and Cameroun over the Biafran people. Ambazonia is the only access you have. And within Cameroun itself, while the other people have relationships with the Central African Republic and other countries, Biafra is our only closest neighbour with massive investments within Ambazonia. Biafra is also the place where thousands of our prople have sought refuge, and they have been treated with great hospitality. For this I want to thank the people of Biafra who have taken care of our refugees and I ask you to continuously support them. Going forward, we are going to work together in different areas to ensure that our both nations emerge from these exclusive servitudes imposed by both Cameroun and Nigeria. In coming to this Joint Press Conference, I have taken time to brief other leaders to make sure that I allied the worries and fears of our people. These worries and fears are rooted in history. We were part of the Eastern House of Assembly in Enugu. One great difference is that when our leaders walked out of that House there were no helicopter gunships that mauled our people. Our people were not massacred because we chose to establish a capital in Buea. But in the last four years we have observed with great dismay the repressive policy of Cameroun, the tyranny of a system that is intended on

26

governing Ambazonia without consent. If I would be given a choice to make Biafra my friend or Nigeria my friend, I wouldn't stand a state that kidnapped and rendered hundreds of our people who were then locked up incommunicado, subjected to torture, brutality, and sentenced to life in jail. I would prefer the people providing sanctuary to our people. If I would be given a choice between Nigeria and Biadra, I would recall the thousands and thousands of Biafrans who are part of our economy. I would recall history, that when we had a wonderful trade with Biafra, the port of Tiko was vibrant; the port of Victoria was vibrant. So too was the port of Port Harcourt and of Calabar. But the Fulanis that had been governing Cameroun at that time dismantled our economic infrastructure, making it impossible for bilateral trade between our country and Biafra to take place; subjecting our population to impunity; making it impossible for any cross-border relationships.

As you said, we are one people, inter-culturally linked. I also want to remind Ambazonians that I take your concerns seriously. That is why this Alliance is split into three phases. Firsrt, to ensure that both people are liberated from the tyranny imposed on them. And to establish within a transitional period methods of collaboration and cooperation to dismantling the economic blockades that have impoverished our two nations. And within this period there will be massive consultations with Ambazonians to ensure that any treaty that would be binding between the two nations is approved by the Ambazonian people. This relationship in the Alliance is critical. Across the globe nations and countries are coming together to ensure the liberation of their people. The Biafrans have been subjugated to genocide, ecological hazards, by a few greedy people who have hijacked an entire nation and made sure that they treated the Biafran people with impunity. For the past sixty years Cameroun rolled its tanks into Ambazonia, subjugated our people to economic deprivation, political asphyxiation, cultural intoxication. Those who spoke were murdered, those who escaped were haunted like games, renditioned and incarcerated incommunicado in the jails of the

27

occupier. For us the Ambazonian people, we have resolved in the past four years to match Cameroun method for method, ideal for ideal, to make sure we arm ourselves to the teeth, to ensure that the brutality that our people have been subjected to during the past sixty years comes to an end. So that we can establish within our own borders economic and political systems that are indigenous to our own cultural and political realities, that our leaders are accountable to our people. That our bounties should be exploited for the development of our people and those who believe in our own values; that our nations would never again, the nations of Biafra and Ambazonia, be taken hostage by few greedy men, our women raped, our children subjected to misery, and our men turned into boys. The era of domination that benefited a few who are within our continent and beyond its shores, leaving millions in destitute, forcing millions moving across the Atlantic and dying in the ocean must come to an end. We must redefine the contours of the continent. The notion of Pan-Africanism must be redefined to ensure that self-determination of nations that have been caught under political systems that do not represent their interests becomes the norm. Before there was Nigeria, there was Biafra. You cannot allow yourseves to be taken hostage by a few men who have decided to rape your soil for their own interest. So too are Ambazonians. We don't seek this Alliance as an aggression against others. We seek this Alliance as a means of self-preservation against tyrannies that have curtailed for both peoples our right to survive in our own shores. We mean no evil to others. Everyone has the right to self-determination. And we are determined to exercise this for ourselves and for our people to ensure we bequeath to the next generation a better country than we inherited. God bless Biafra. God bless Ambazonia.

I just cannot stop listening to anything that comes out of Ayabacholization, Traorélization from BKF being synonym. That is surely patriotism, which has been defined by J.A. Simpson and E.S.C. Weiner as "The character or passion of a patriot; love of or zealous devotion to one's country." A patriot, if the first sense of the definition has to be adopted, they say, means "One who disinterestedly or self-sacrificingly exerts himself [or herself] to promote the well-being of his [or her] country; 'one whose ruling passion is the love of his [or her] country' (J); one who maintains and defends his [or her] country's freedom or rights" (cited in Fossungu, 2013b: 54). It is good time still to hear the truth again for yourself in the visionary AWOL leader's celebrated Message to Chadians and All Africans on 21 April 2021:

We have also been observing the political wrangling within Nigeria. It is important that African countries and leadership understand that the concept of statehood instituted and forced within the continent and sustained by violence, the deliberate institution of poverty, environmental degradation, massive exploitation of resources to build large army and police forces that in turn destroy and molest civil society activism cannot be sustained. The basis of the Charter of the United Nations was on the concept of self-determination. That every people have the right to self-determination; and to establish within their own nations political systems that reflect their own contextual realities, and works primarily for their own benefit. The concept of statehood within the continent is unsustainable, having been built on violence, oppression, corruption, and the institution of governments that are not accountable to the people. That is why Nigeria must understand that the agitation within Biafra must be factored in any policy development formulation and to engage with the Biafrans to ensure that the Biafrans themselves can determine the kind of political system that they want for themselves (Ayaba, 2021a, 3rd paragraph).

I have already said over and over and over that regression is the word that properly describes any nation-building that is carried out without authentic history. To properly understand the points, do hear Dr Ayaba's directives to France in the 2nd paragraph of his 21 April 2021 Message to Chadians and all Africans:

We observed the Syrian crisis thousands and thousands of miles away. How millions of refugees, millions of people ended up within Central Europe, gradually changing the demorgraphic balance, having an impact on the welfare stage; and posing a security challenge. The guarantee of real independence for Chad and other countries is beneficial for those countries and for France. Economic prosperity in these countries is beneficial in terms of economic development and security for France. If the Chadians are able to institute systems that reflect their own reality, governments that are accountable to them, it is a win-win situation for everyone, whether within the continent or beyond its own shores (Ayaba, 2021a: 2nd paragraph).

Is Ambazonia not thus trying to effectively break away from dependent and colonial LRC to properly assume the leadership role in uniting Africans through meaningful federalization rather than further splitting them into incapable min-states on the challenging world stage? Can anything in the nature of an accurate response be gleaned from both my imagination and these Ayabacholization messages to Africans generally? It looks like only 'The Bangwa As Federalists' (Fossungu, 2013b: 119-25) in Lebialemzone of Ambazonia "can capably answer this query, since they are those well noted for competently 'Knowing and Announcing the Unknown in Africa' just as the Cameroonian POR who can so easily double the unknown size of the Cameroon Supreme Court without much ado" (Fossungu, 2019: 140). Get it right then from this other Bangwa with a ʒoomedeyed or largeyedist approach that whatever the answer you put forward, just know that in Cameroon the regression from 'uniting one history' (at France's behest) is euphemistically called "advanced development" whose handmaids are 'balanced development plans', a tortoise-walk development that is paradoxically not balanced on history and/or the country's cultural diversity (Fossungu, 2013a: 208).

Talking of nation-building without authentic history also in the 13-states of the 'FRA', I have thus shown that in 1961 the concept of federalism was similarly largely used by some individuals only as a bargaining medium for personal favours from the President of the 'Federal' *République du Cameroun* who, on his part, employed the concept solely as a tool, first, for the annexation of Ambazonia and, second, for the ruthless crushing of the 'stormy and heady' opposition in LRC (Fossungu, 2013b: 48). This stance I firmly take despite the contrary portrait presented by most of the intellectuals and scholars. I think I have already also shown that the relationship between the status of a country's government and its constitutional scholarship is not a very difficult one to establish. And that any academician worth the name cannot but be very critical of the manner in which most of the scholars in Africa generally but particularly pre-2017 Cameroon twist plain facts. The facts-twisting is especially accentuated in regard of the 1961 Foumban Federation or Constitution about which there are numerous confusing theses on separation of powers, human rights guarantees, full citizen participation, etc. It is even doubtful if one should continue referring to the facts-twisters as intellectuals since, by definition, intellectuals are supposed to be shedding light on the issues, not emasculating them (Fossungu, 2013b: xvii).

For example, some of these 'intellectuals in politics' have tried to cover up incompetence in leadership and governance by arguing that Ambazonia was handicapped in Foumban because of its dependent status. But I have instead elaborately argued that "the dependent status of Southern Cameroons at Foumban could not have been exclusively decisive in the achievement of what was there attained" (Fossungu, 2013b: 68-69). Some of the experts have instead stressed 'previous separate existence'. And here goes my counteraction to that: Didn't their walking out of the Nigerian Eastern House of

Assembly in Enugu in 1954 duly affirm and emphasize this 'previous separate existence' that then even required their choosing between *Nigeria* and Cameroun in the plebiscite? If Ayabacholization has not sunk it deep into the brains above, then let a straight-talking 'Man of God' strengthen the outing-point for us as he discusses 'the truth of self-determination which can never be killed by bullets'. This thesis and the carnage going on in Ambazonia (with the complicity of the international community) is brought out with the aid of Reverend Gerald Jumbam's thought-provoking Open-Letter to the head of the National Episcopal Conference of Cameroon (NECC), in the person of Archbishop Samuel Kleda of Douala:

Your Grace, I wish to conclude here by saying that the capacity for self-determination is Christian. No one can conquer the British Cameroons. You can't extinguish the fire that led our forebears out of Nigeria. That fire burns! If our effort is not enough to win the battle, our children will win it with better effort. But it shall not be postponed this time around. And yet, the cry of the agonizing British Cameroon[s]ians has fallen on deaf ears around the globe. For them, the pogrom in the British Cameroons is only some localized problem. The abductions and butchery of humans are hidden, ill-reported. Along with the nonstop infiltration of our land with armed killer squads and military bastards criminally excused from any probe, query or answerability, we are witnessing an experiment with "ethnic cleansing" authorized and sustained by the French Cameroon psychopath, Paul Biya. Strange that those that obtain the just publicity of terror in our land are only the French Cameroons controlled media. A military selected for the assignment of absolute "pacification" of the British Cameroons is doing its work unopposed. Where is Britain's assuagement in this matter? It is impossible to believe these things are happening under the nose of international human right bodies and the silence of Great Britain in this carnage in its trusteeship territory it sacrificed its independence in the altar of De Gaullism (Jumbam, 2017).

'Previous separate existence', I have submitted therefore, is not the synonym of 'previous separate *independence*'; otherwise, the 'separately existing' but dependent Canadian provinces (as well as the Australian states) would never have been properly federating. Their argument here on Foumban is thus reminiscent of the forest shitting narrative (see Fossungu, 2015c: 109-111). Hypocrisy and confusioncracy! The demeanours of some Organization of African Unity (OAU) leaders would also aptly make the point (see Fossungu, 2013b: 93). To further sufficiently master the point I am trying to make, just see Dr Arikana Chihombori-Quao being sacked as African Union Ambassador to Washington, D.C, (by the French 'nchinda' from Chad, Moussa Faki Mahamat, being called the African Union Commission Chairman) just because of her fearlessly highlighting French never-ending massive exploitation of Africa! And the international community is not exempted from the hypocrisy classroom. See the hypocrites all out there condemning and actually fighting against Putin's Russia for invading to annex Ukraine. But not only annexation but also genocide have been visited on the Ambazonian people for close to eight years now by France/LRC: without any coughing from the same so-called international community. Spokesman Asu is quite right that they are now (in mid-December 2023) talking/calling for negotiations simply because *two-cube* Ambazonia has not only defeated LRC in battle but also destroyed it, with its crumbling signs being now so visible for hiding. Hypocrisy! Reverend Jumban, please, do lecture them a bit for me.

Darkness has descended on the British Cameroons in the killings, imprisonments, abductions, rapes, graves of mass burials and maim. Bamenda/Buea is facing viral alteration of psychic conditioning. In this state of affairs, silence is criminal. The sense of urgency has lagged so much that a month ago I lost my anger on a letter to a compatriot invading media space with the banner, screaming: Homecoming or Home-going – the Southern Cameroons! It is a wakeup call no more on failed internal religious and political bodies, but on Britain and International Human rights institutions and activists, not to delay, because what happened in Rwanda is at our doors. AU and UNO look up and act! UK look up and speak! The urgency of speaking for despoiled peoples is so felt that I don't really care if this anger breaks the bounds of office. How could it be when a priest is first and foremost a citizen? He owes his community a contribution to its wellbeing for his upbringing. He serves God and recognizes that the cry of the powerless and the voice of the voiceless are the cry and the voice of God (Jumban, 2017).

Defining Being Amba to the Confusionists/Confusioncrats: Meritocracy or Ethnocracy?

Ambazonia is defined by its international borders, and not by the colonial language of expression. Just being "Anglophone" does not make someone Ambazonian. That must be made very pellucid. I think briefly discussing some of my girlfriends or ex-lovers would help your easy understanding of the point. I think the appropriate category for most of my lovers is 'Anglophones' and not 'Ambazonians' since English-speaking Anna, being Bassa like the infamous Tiko parliamentarian (below), is Camerounese. Similarly, my French-speaking common-law partner, Flavie, is Bassa and Camerounese while my Bangwa ex-wife (Scholastica) is Ambazonian. In the same way, English-speaking Jane, being Dschang like French-speaking Chantal, is Camerounese (like Elizabeth, Bamileke) although like English-speaking Odilia who is Bangwa and Ambazonian (like Scholastica). To reiterate, Ambazonia is defined more by its internationally recognized territorial boundaries than by the colonial language of expression. More on this particular nerve-tacking issue (to nosifeans) can be pursued in Fossungu (2013a: chapter 2). But you can also easily pick it up from our famous Toronto advocate's reaction to the publication of my *Royal Burial and Enthronement in Ambazonia* on 20 May 2023. On 24 June 2023 Maitre Tesi had problems with "Ambazonia" in the title and I responded with: "A lot of you still don't believe Ambazonia is real, right?" His response: "Wayo. Some woman was saying to me and insulting my family that we are Bamilekes. That we brought problems. Now she is begging me to intervene to renew her Cameroon passport. A shame. Cameroon is one and undivided country. To hell with Ambazonia. To the pit with Ambazonia." I replied: "Thats your opinion, which you are entitled to hold. To the pit with one undivided Cameroun. What about that?" The 'charge and bail' Camerounese Canadian lawyer then dived into the Canadian citizenship denunciation nonsense of the easy-way thinkers.

Following this up with the "blood-thicker-than-water" reaction of the Tiko Bassa parliamentarian to a journalist's questioning (see Fossungu, 2013a: 85), I certainly take firm side with some AGovC's officials that these *tontou* people must not be allowed to hold certain positions in Ambazonia if granted citizenship through permanent residence. Just like in the USA where the presidency (for instance) is legally and completely out of the reach of Americans not born in the USA. Just imagine that Ambazonians refuse to learn from their sad history and again allow the emergence of another LRC's John Ngu Foncha as head of the government of Ambazonia! Their blood would always be thicker than water; and the attitude of most of these people in the liberation struggle (the gang in South Africa that Dr Cho Ayaba has referred to as not being able to stand him in the same room) is telling enough not to be properly recognized. But also get it from some fossungupalogists in America, such as Dr H. Bate Agbor-Baiyee of Akron, Ohio, USA talking of the evil of silence before evil (as cited in Fossungu, 2019: 153-56),

Now, squarely on the useless Thirteen-States, let me very quickly re-discuss a few of the numerous relevant portions of Fossungu (2013b: 77-80) by saying that you will also find this tribalistic nonsense being "stirred up from time to time by ethnic political entrepreneurs" (Konings, 1999: 305) such as the authors of the All *Anglophone* Conference (AAC) draft federal constitution which Dr Konings (1999: 311-316) has outlined and discussed. To begin with, I emphasize *Anglophone* before giving the authors of that tribalism document the necessary credit for the effort of even tendering something we could start working with. Which is why I am even consuming precious time talking about the attempt. Two of the members of the august drafting committee (namely, Professor Carlson Anyangwe and Dr Simon Munzu) are among the few of my University of Yaoundé (UNIYAO) lecturers that I use to hold in high esteem for their academic integrity and honesty (until January 2017, of course, after which they *completely* lost it). What I really find obnoxious with their draft (which is also a very good pointer to their attitude relating to the AWOL) is its putting of people's ethnic affiliations before their competence in a supposed democracy. It seems to me that over sixty years of dictatorship would have had such debilitating effects that most of us (the nosifeans really) can simply not be able to move on without letting the divide-and-rule devices of the dictatorship to continue influencing everything we do. I am here also then to pointedly address the *13-staters* of Ambazonia too. If what the committee proposed is really intended to be a constitutionalism-based democracy and federalism, rather than an 'ethnic-based-rotationary federalism', I do not see any reason for the too much stress on the ethnicity of who

36

succeeds who; as well as their lengthy arguments "that such a detailed constitution was absolutely necessary in the specific Cameroonian context characterised by 'the Anglophone-Francophone divide', inter-ethnic suspicions and rivalries, bad governance, unequal distribution of the 'national cake' and arbitrary and despotic government since independence and reunification" (Konings, 1999: 311).

My criticisms of the Biya-Ahidjo stance on federalism and democracy (see Fossungu, 2013b: chapter 3) apply here as well. In addition, I think the drafters clearly seem to have all their eyes on the "national cake" rather than on the National Interest that requires the fashioning of clear-cut rules for getting to or eating the cake. My critiques on the a priori personification of public debates (especially in Fossungu, 2013b: Chapter 4 & 2013a: chapter 1) also come in here. But Professor Emmanuel Anyefru seems to have grasped the matter well when he posits that "its [Anglophone Problem's] intensification following the wave of democratisation in Africa since the early 1990s has seen an increased rather than decreased extent of ethnic politics and conflicts in that it has reshaped the struggle among elites seeking to defend or challenge the distribution of state power and resources....The introduction of some degree of political liberalisation triggered renewed claims to rights in Anglophone Cameroon" (Fossungu, 2013b: 78). If liberalism can only lead to this, I really want to know, what is the need for condemning the dictatorship then? What else is their justification that "The governor could not be then succeeded by a member of the same ethnic group or municipality" (Konings, 1999: 315)? The same applying to the prime minister, I simply do not see why Oben should be barred from showing his own skills as governor of Midlandzone (MDZ) simply because the out-going governor happens to be an Orock from Manyuzone (MYZ) or Victoria (his municipality of choice).

As intellectuals (lawyers and jurists or not) we simply cannot escape from the issues, if we must retain those descriptions given us since, by definition (according to Professor Egon C. Guba), "the task of any intellectual inquiry is to raise people (the oppressed) to a level of 'true consciousness' because only when they truly appreciate how oppressed they are, can they act to transform the world" (cited in Fossungu, 2013b: 6). The AGovC Team (aka Ayabacholization), don't the experts hear you well? Sure! The contrary is what largely holds true for then Cameroon with the rampant confusioncracy, thus making it almost impossible for the oppressed to 'act to transform the world' since they cannot 'truly appreciate how oppressed they are'. The consequence of this inverted and curious intellectualism in Maitre Tesi's one undivided Cameroon is that "a lot of the issues in Cameroon have simply left several people, who are normally supposed to show the way, bewildered. Why wouldn't they be so until they are well schooled in Four-Eyesism or HISOFE?" (Fossungu, 2019: 140) Fon DF Fossungu of Nwangong Fondom (in Ambazonia), don't I hear you so well?

My Bangwalangwalistic take is that the constitution, for instance, does not need to spell out every toilet-going rule in it if the system is one clothed with an independent judiciary (which the AAC drafters have interestingly made room for) whose role it will be to interpret and uphold the *general* principles therein embedded. Principles can clearly not be of general application when people's ethnic groups have been put ahead of their competence and other abilities. Ambazonia is supposed to be a Meritocracy, *no bi sooh*? What then is the difference with the Biya-ethnically-based appointive system? Indeed, you will appreciate what I am saying here about an independent and competent arbiter if you consider, for instance, that the constitutional distribution of powers and responsibilities in the Australian federation has proved to be exceptionally flexible despite clear indication from the experts like John M. Williams and Clement Macintyre that it was originally "conceived as a decentralized federation with the bulk of powers remaining in the hands of the states, in fact there has been a steady accretion of power to the Commonwealth government since shortly after federation in 1901" (Fossungu, 2013b: 79). All that has been able to happen without any of the states or citizens crying for secession because the judiciary, to which anyone/state feeling aggrieved turns to, is independent and has upheld or dismissed complaints based on the court's interpretation of the founders' briefly stated intent. Here then is my advice. Just give us an independent and culturally-balanced judiciary that is jammed with persons of integrity (even if they are all from the same ethnic group or family!) and even LRC's 1996 unitary centralized constitution will become a formidable 'Federal' Constitution in their hands. True, since, according to a Canadian professor, "Some see the [1996] document as centralizing, others as decentralizing. [But] The reality is that both tendencies can be found" (Fossungu, 2023: 23). Joseph R.A. Ayee would also think that the independent judicial organ's inevitable presence is exactly what goes into "The Measurement of Decentralization". Don't ever forget that federalism is just another form of decentralization.

In addition, I wonder if we are looking for competent people for effective national leadership or mere tribal rotation? Let me use a very banal but real illustration here before you also can go on to further read this absurd ethnic requirement in the context of 'the mathematics of representation' (Fossungu, 2013b; chapter 4). Granted even that there should be constitutional provision for rotation between the two cultural groups of then Cameroon, why does the candidates' ethnic group have to come into play here? If the outgoing president, for instance, was a competent English-speaking Bamileke person like Maitre Tesi, that means all competent French-speaking Bamileke people are automatically excluded from vying for the position. Yet, this is supposed to be a federal democracy? I would rather we make the candidate's bilingualism (or tri-lingualism: English, French, & Njangawatok/Ambatok – see Fossungu, 2013a: chapter 4) an important factor rather than mere rotation between Anglophones and Francophones. This requirement would seem to have been more promotional of national unity and multiculturalism than the 'rotation stuff'. Also, any political party that has only competent Bamileke candidates for the position is therefore also excluded from fielding any candidates; etc. Let us get this clear and simple message: In a true federation (such as the viable Belgian-style 3-province one I have proposed in the Lexicon) those who cannot think anything but ethnic would still be entitled to limit themselves to the 'ethnic level' (zonal administration) while those who think above 'ethnic', 'provincial', 'regional' lines would be entitled to vie for federal or national leadership positions. That is the main reason why a federal system is adopted in the first place: not to kill but to give forceful expression to those peculiarities without letting the same threaten the national entity, as they often do when we want to forcefully eliminate them through Biya's NEG or New Ethnic Group (see Fossungu, 2013a: chapter 3). Is the Ambazonia-Cameroun genocidal war not all about the brutal response to persistent peaceful demands for federalism?

Of course, Ambazonians demanding fundamental redress to their disheartening situation represented an 'obstacle' to their one undivided Cameroon that bullets must be swiftly used to eliminate. This forceful eradication or genocide is capped by the ceaseless killings and burnings of homes and assets, sparingly exemplified here by (1) the *Ngarbuh Massacre* of 14 February 2021 regarding which, according to Human Rights Watch, government forces, including members of the Rapid

Intervention Battalion (BIR), the Israeli-trained elite unit of the Camerounese army, and armed ethnic Fulani militia killed 21 civilians in Ngarbuh (close to Ndu), including 13 children and a pregnant woman, burned five homes, looted scores of other properties, and beat residents. And (2) the *Mautu Massacre* of 10 January 2021, wherein Cameroun soldiers from the 21st Motorized Infantry Battalion (BIM) raided the village and killed 9 civilians, including a woman and a child, injuring 4 civilians, looting scores of homes and threatening residents. All that is the result of the 'advanced democratic' stance, which is normal to the genocidal regime because, even the churches that these targeted people are so devoted to would stay mute even when some of the genocidal killings have taken place right inside their places of worship. All because the hierarchy of the church has been bought over, I guess. Reverend Gerald Jumban would help me here again (see Fossungu, 2019: 156 n.8):

The brutality is freely carried out by the terrorist regime because the ethnic political entrepreneurs simply could not grasp even simple and straightforward (ten-state) federalism that would have saved Cameroon from obvious disintegration. They instead compounded matters with their NW-SW-Divide-inspired SDF four-state federation, which sadly "does not at all try to meet these [requisite federalism] conditions but merely assumed that there are more important things (regarding governance and development especially) that do bind an English-speaking [Ambaz]onian from Savannazone to a French-speaking [Camerou]nian in Bamboutouszone than to a fellow English-speaking [Ambaz]onian from Debundschazone and/or vice versa. Should that be the case, would there be any reason for the general bitterness from the English-speaking people in Biya's 'Republic of Cameroon'?" (Fossungu, 2013b: 76). They had better not even venture near what I am advocating for, which Professor Arktar Majeed sees as "Belgium's double symmetry, which involves two different kinds of federating units that cut across, and overlap, each other" (cited in Fossungu, 2013b: 80) because they just cannot handle it. They should give way then or simply "pass on" disgracefully like traitor Ni John Fru Ndi and let competent

41

and savvy nationalists patriotically take care of national/continental business, with Traorélization also vehemently confirming.

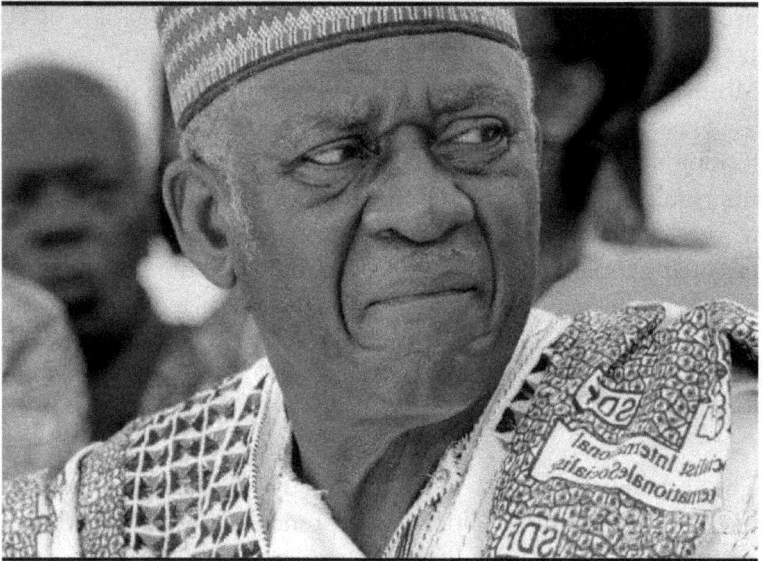

Figure #4: Ni John Fru Ndi of the SDF
Source: found on Google from www.baretanews

What all this means is that the three Provinces of ATZ, MDZ, aand SVZ would be in double symmetry with the thirteen zones (BYZ, BUZ, DMZ, FKZ, KMZ, LBZ, MYZ, MMZ, MCZ, MZZ, MOZ, NDZ, & NKZ). In effect, just as the Ambazonia Nation would be playing the Federal Game with the Three Provinces, each of them would also be engaging in Federalism with the Zonal entities; as well as the provinces and zones inter se. Very simple to the innovative, but very complicated and incomprehensible to ethnic nosifeans. Thank God that, because of Ayabacholization, Ambazonia is now brimatized with Hisofeans. As Hugues Dumont and colleagues would agree with me, "It is not easy to use simple [ethnic] language to describe something that is not simple, and Belgian federalism is far from simple [because,] Built without preconceived ideas or an overarching doctrine [like the North West/South West Divide], it accumulates original – sometimes labyrinthine – solutions as it goes along" (Fossungu, 2013b: 80). Amba Hisofeans, I am very confident, would be more than able to embrace and handle the stimulating complexities since they do not usually build liberation and national policies and programmes with any preconceived regressive doctrines like the one in square brackets, which also promotes other stupidities such as 'County-by-County'. Charming, brave and motivational Mama Wally OGC, thank you so very much for clearly bringing out their ridicule in reducing the whole of Mezamzone (MZZ), for instance, to a county! In short, I would simply dub the 65-member *Anglophone* Standing (but actually 'sitting down there' like John Ngu Foncha in 1961) Committee's proposed document as the anti-federalism "Ethnic Federal Draft Constitution" and place it alongside the infamous "Confusioncracy Passing for Balanced Development" (Fossungu, 2013a: 206-235).

The Federal-Parliamentary Mixture

My proposal of *The Federal-Parliamentary Mixture* for Ambazonia also brilliantly exposes the confusion thesis with regard to the AAC Draft Federal Constitution that is still endlessly under fire. The choice for a presidential system by the 65-member *Anglophone* Standing Committee, according to Konings (1999: 314), seems to have been made for two reasons: "In the specific Cameroonian context marked by great ethnic and regional diversities, a presidential system, according to the authors, was more likely to forestall administrative chaos and political instability than any other form of government." Confusioncracy, isn't it? Then why are they also proposing the parliamentary system for the states to be headed by a prime minster? The nation is presidential with a president who is both head of government and head of state; the two states (why two?) are parliamentary with a prime minister as head of government (and who is 'head of state' of the states? Still the P.M. or the federal president?); and the provinces are what, with a governor? Are they actually Belgianizing here or merely confusioncratizing? You just cannot separate the different (vertical) levels with different governmental systems without both confusing powers; as well as greatly compromising the ability of a person to "rise", say, from district or zonal head to president of the federation called Federal Republic of Ambazonia. "One can even see this from the fact that most American presidents have been state governors prior to becoming Number one American" (Fossungu, 2013b: 211). It is thus either all one or the other, not the confusioncratic mixture of theirs. The problem with these people, I think, is one of trying to eat their national cake and still having it. Another name for it is foolerrandism. They find, for instance, that the so-called North West and South West exhibit "great ethnic and regional diversities" but they just would not countenance the two regions developing separately within a ten-state union but try to twist the facts by lumping them up in a small-one-state against the rest of the eight-province-Mighty State. Here lies the source of *twocubesosugarism*, for sure. Let us get real here. If we recognize a Divide, the best way to deal with it is to let the Divide be and deal with it as such, rather than pretending over it because such pretence is what would actually result in "administrative chaos and political instability". By the way, if we still need two and eight provinces within the two culturally-based states, why not just have those provinces as the ten states with each competently managing itself while electing the required number of their representatives to the federal parliament? And we should not forget that the "great ethnic and regional diversities" are not limited only to the 'inter-state' or 'inter-provincial' level but would apply as well within the same state or province, for instance. I have fossungupalogistically confronted the issues in my 'Lexicon of Ambazonia Governance' which I have since been elaborating on till now.

Parliamentary democracy is not the best form of government according to some experts (like Humphry Berkeley, and R.H.S. Crossman) although being to yet others (like Boris Mirkine-Guetzévitch and Marcel Prélot) "the most perfect modern form of government that is without doubt also the one that has been largely adopted by other nations" (my translation). When combined with federalism and with other new elements grafted onto it, as it is done in Canada and Germany, I think the parliamentary system provides a better system of protecting both the rights of individual citizens and groups as well as those of state institutions, and in particular the judiciary and its independence. This protection results from what I have termed the system's "rights-protecting combination". I am by that alluding to (1) its practice within the federal structure, (2) genuine multiparty politics, including strong third parties, (3) bicephalism, (4) bicameralism, and (5) parliamentary procedure. The rights-protecting character of the parliamentary system results from its potential to fragment power and authority and diversify their centres. The parliamentary system is able to furnish this because of its *bicephal* executive (i.e., head of state and head of government are vested in two different people, with each having particular competence) and its *bicameral* legislature: which means, the existence of Upper and Lower Houses of Parliament. For Ambazonia that must not just follow or copy blindly, the suggested head of state is the *Governor-General* (GG) and the head of government is the *Secretary-General* (SG), whereas the upper house is the *Chamber of Reviewers* (CORE) and the lower is *House of Representatives* (HORE). That was at the national level. At the provincial/state level of the proposed three (Atlanticzone (ATZ), Midlandzone (MDZ), & Savannahzone (SVZ)), the head of state is the *Regent-General* (RG) and the head of government is the *Prime Administrator* (PA) while the upper house is the *House of Chiefs* (HOC) and the lower is the *Legislative Assembly* (LAS). These diverse independent organs, *inter alia,* further ensure judicial activism and inde-pendence: an inevitable consequence of the existence of several potential disputants, none of whom will afford to see the arbiter's impartiality jeopardized. This applies equally to the executive heads in situations of effective bicephalism, with its effectiveness being heavily tied to real multipartism. This is just a rapid snapshot, a perfect grasp of the issues requires a keen and complete perusal of my two 2013 books in question, including also the 2019 one that uses "one of the contunent's supposed legendary pathfinder [called] Cameroon... to interrogate[] judiciary in Africa in three domains. First, as the third branch of government, second, as the acknowledged umpire of federalism, and finally, as an exquisite means of reversing the institutionalization of inhuman rights and injustice administration in Africa" (Fossungu, 2019: back cover).. With these features effectively in place, coupled with proper public enlightenment that Ayabacholization has been very efficient at furnishing so far, we could be entering an era of active citizen participation and, therefore, human rights respect in Ambazonia particularly and Africa in general.

Anglo-Eat- Anglo Journeying into the Dark Sixties

The AAC drafters' proposals are thus very akin to the lielisticalism in the mosquito narrative (see Fossungu, 2015c: 112-17) and the numerous confusing theses of the dark sixties. I think it is by properly comprehending what indeed happened (authentic history) that the youths have been properly educated to avoid repeating or committing the same errors, especially in the new political society that Ambazonians and Africans generally are clamouring for. It is in this vein that some of my previous studies (Fossungu: 2013a & 2013b & 2019) undertook the task of throwing some unquenchable light on the darkness created in this continent by some of the "intellectuals in politics". It is comforting to know that Spokesman Lucas Asu

(Oh these Lucas people! Over positive sense people!) in his *Freedom Now* and ex-DDC Capo Daniel (in his *Daily Podcast* – before he was 'ngongly' and 'woman-wrapperly' bought over by the enemy, LRC) have been doing a fantastic job to educate our people out of the ignorance promoted by some of the previous Ambazonian leaders in Figure #5 below. It is not for nothing that Spokesman Asu is properly credited with being 'the most dangerous educator of the Ambazonian people' (Fossungu, 2023: 47). The proof is even in the astronomical sums of money that the LRC gangsters have used in attempts to buy him over to no avail. The man is truly committed to freedom, a keen believer in Benjamin Franklin's popular saying that those who will give up essential liberty and constant vigilance, to purchase a little temporary safety, clearly deserve neither liberty nor safety (Fossungu, 2013a: 27). John Mbah Akuroh of the Consortium has regularly been singing the same song on his Youtube Channel (*JMA Connections*), emphasizing that those who settle for less than they deserve would always end up with less than they settled for. Is this not the lesson Mr. Biya has always believed the bulk of Ambazonians never comprehended? It looks very much like it despite politickerizing arguments to the contrary.

Figure #5: Ambazonian Prime Ministers until 1972: Dr EML Endeley, John Ngu Foncha, Augustine Ngum Jua, & Solomon Tandeng Muna
Source: Cameroon

As you can see, the bulk of Ambazonians would seem to be very good only at fighting themselves over belly-issues rather

47

than scrutinizing and fighting against thugtatorship and some of the numerous anomalies in defunct Cameroon generally but particularly those that endanger their dignity and cultural and other group rights that the AWOL is out to secure and protect in an independent unoccupied Homeland. This attitude was greatly encouraged by both the Ahidjo-Biya administration and the SDF opposition led by the traitor called Ni John Fru Ndi (see Fossungu, 2013b: 69-81). My well-considered view is that federalism has a better future in Ambazonia under the Three-*State* federal model than under the thirteen-state one, with the thirteen zones constituting a second tier of *provinces* (or vice versa) within the three *states* – resembling the Belgian intriguing formula. Federalism traditionally has been adopted to solve the kind of ethnic, cultural and political problems that Ambazonia and many other African states face. But this solution is being "proposed" by many not because they actually understand and believe in it; but solely as a political expedient of *cloning Cameroun* in Ambazonia – confusioncracy. Otherwise, why the stubborn clinging onto LRC divisive creations in independent Ambazonia?

Figure #6: Amadou Ahidjo (1st President of Cameroon: 1960-1982) & Paul Barthelemy Mvondo Biya (2nd President of Cameroon)
Source: Republic of Cameroon

Talking of historical confusion in LRC, for example, Professor Richard Bjornson has put it very well, charging that "From schoolbooks and the official propaganda, the younger generation imbibed a misleading picture of what had actually taken place during the colonial periods, [spiced with the fabrication of] the villainy of the UPC" (Fossungu, 2013a: 20). The UPC is *Union des Populations du Cameroun*. It is a political party that demanded outright independence for and unification of the two Cameroons and was banned in 1955 before the farce of independence was staged in 1960, with French-appointed *'chef d'état'* (like Ahidjo & Biya in Figure #6) put in the place of the patriots to camouflage independence. Sékou Touré's Guinea also tells the story well. As I have explained, the French-appointed *chefs d'état* then needed to distort history in order to stay in power, knowing fully well that as soon as the masses are aware of the truth, they would no longer be able to stay in power. Knowledge is power, it is said (Fossungu, 2013a: 20-21). Do you not see the direct link between Ambazonians' rising consciousness of their authentic history and their steadfastness in the Revolution for Freedom, and especially its *Kuntri Sunday* that even Christmas 2023 could not displace? It is thus scarcely surprising that Norbert Tchuiam has opined that 'these Camerounese youths who are supposed to be leaders of tomorrow are completely lost because they do not even know what this Youth Day feasting is about' ("*cette jeunesse qui devrait être sur les rangs demain…est perdue. Malheureusement, de cette fête [même] elle ne sait rien*") (cited in Fossungu, 2013a: 21).

Figure #7: Reuben Um Nyobe, the legendary UPC leader
Source: found on Google from face2faceafrica.com

Figure #8: Ernest Ouandie, Roland Felix Moumie, & Albert
Kingue (some of the top murdered UPC members)
Source: found on Google from face2faceafrica.com

The politickerization or disturbing noise-making involved in
the dark sixties has also eaten so profoundly in the
Ambazonian liberation war that Dr Cho Ayaba has seen only
the plunging of a pacifier or a 'baby-shut-up' into the mouths
of the social media crying babies so that he and his team could
have some tranquillity in prosecuting the liberation war to
bring independence and justice to Ambazonia (see Fossungu,
2023: 147). Is there anyone who is still in doubt that, in a
scenario such as the Anglo-Eat-Anglo one (see Fossungu,
2013a: 20-33), there is bound to be many facts twisting and the
equation of personal for general interest? It is often when these
narrow interests (egoism or self-centeredness) become the only
and overriding concern in public affairs that something else
(bellytics) is usually mistaken for politics. People like ngong-
dog Capo Daniel thus have to invent facts to emasculate the
case (Fossungu, 2013a: 32). Pastor Dr Samuel Sako Ikome and
Sisiku Julius Ayuk Tabe, do keen observers also hear you both
well with your fake and obstructionist Interim Governments?
All that being because they just do not know themselves nor
the Cameroun they are/were purportedly working for.

51

Once you know who you are, it becomes very easy to know who or what you are dealing with. For instance, if I already know myself like Ayabacholization does, there is no need to get angry or become bitter if someone describes me exactly as I am. Concretely, if I have a big clock-ticking head, and you tell me that I have that, there is no need for me to be angry about that. But if I did not know that, then I would be really annoyed. If I know exactly the type of head I have, and you tell me (like I am here also telling Ayabacholization): "You are really making good use of that your big clock-ticking head," then I will be happy that I am not wasting God's gift to me. Conversely, if you describe me as what I know I am not, there is no need for me to get annoyed, because your description can never change me from what I know to be me to your description. Thus, describing my head that I very well know as "small, empty and oblong" does not need to make me angry because your saying so can never change the shape and content of my head as I know it to be. With an outlook like this on life, you will hardly have problems facing the truth and with others because you will know as well that telling them that they are what they are not, will never make them what they are not. Furthermore, a good knowledge of yourself and situation reduces your reliance on a lot of professionals. I am by no means saying that you should never go and see a therapist, for example. All I am saying is that your therapy (if not the cure itself) begins with you understanding yourself and situation. This is great wisdom that I have gained over the years; and would further be sharing with you through my large extended royal family generally but particularly my two sets of parents in the next Chapters.

Chapter 2

The Secret to Progressing Against Numerous Obstacles: Confronting the Truth about Yourself and Understanding the Problem Confronting You

Africa thus lacks just dedicated and visionary pioneering culturally-well-seated leaders and intellectuals for Africans to easily and quickly return to their Paradise Lost – Get Africa back into Africa that is. Independence Means Independence, as the Ambazonian Nationalists, sapiently led by this rarity called Lucas Cho Ayaba, have steadfastly said. Are other Africans keenly listening and planning well? (Fossungu, 2023: 73).

No one doubts "that the study of families is an important avenue for the study of society" (Beaujot, 1992: 283). Family, considered to be "the basic unit for raising children," is defined variously by some experts as (1) a basic social unit consisting of parents and their children, considered as a group, whether dwelling together or not: *the traditional family;* or a social unit consisting of one or more adults together with the children they care for: *a single-parent family;* (2) the children of one person or one couple collectively: *We want a large family;* (3) the spouse and children of one person: *We're taking the family on vacation next week;* (4) any group of persons closely related by blood, as parents, children, uncles, aunts, and cousins: *to marry into a socially prominent family;* and (5) all those persons considered as descendants of a common progenitor. In human context, a *family* (from Latin: *familia*) is a group of people affiliated by consanguinity, affinity, or co-residence. In most societies it is the principal institution for the socialization of children. Anthropologists most generally classify family organization as matrilocal (a mother and her children); conjugal (a husband, his wife, and children; also called nuclear family); and consanguineal (also called an extended family) in which parents and children co-reside with other members of one parent's family. According to some sociologists and linguists, the social unit that lives in a house is known as a *household*. Most commonly, a household is a family unit of some kind, though households may be other social groups, organizations, or individuals. This book uses household throughout to signify a family unit such as ours. Two types of family units dominate in this book, namely, the nuclear that is predominant in Canada and other Western societies and the extended that is most prominent in Africa.

There is already much out there on Nwangong (see Fossungu, 2023), which comprises the following six quarters or districts: Emollah, Lekeng, Letia, Ndenkop, Njilap, & Nwancheng. In the Nwangong Royal Family a few people have adopted the 'Fosungu' version of the family name but the majority goes with the 'Fossungu' option (Fossungu, 2016: 12 n.9). It is important to also note, first, that all my uncles and aunts in this book bearing Fossungu are in reality my father's half-siblings, as the Fon had so many wives, with some of them like papa's mother bearing only one child for him. Second, that we usually referred to those of them that came to live with us in the household as "Brother" or "Sister" X although I will here be using the appropriate "Uncle" or "Aunty" X. And, third, that some of them like Uncle Vincent Temenu Fossungu later became Chief Fonenge and switched from the regular royal family name to their own. Because his first name seems to be the most favourite name within my family circles, I would prefer using only the nobility name of those of them who have one, such as Chief Foletia (meaning Chief of Letia quarter in Nwangong) who, otherwise, is Uncle Vincent Aghegndia Sixtus Fossungu.

54

This naming innovation is informed by the incisive comments of Dr Piet Konings who reviewed the original script (which was then titled 'The Definition of Family and the Future of Children and Social Work in Africa and Canada: Blending Canadian and African Lifestyles?') that "Generally speaking, it has become a captivating story. However, there is a risk that the reader feels almost overwhelmed and even confused by the flood of names and the number of the author's propagated survival strategies and learning moments. On the other hand, the book provides the reader with a number of useful insights in the complicated African family relations, which s/he could hardly have acquired in the standard scientific, and more specifically anthropological, literature." It was then in quick response to *the flood of names* confusion that the original manuscript was hastily broken into two books. Being (1) *Africans in Canada: Blending Canadian and African Lifestyles?* (Bamenda: Langaa RPCIG, 2013) and (2) *Africa's Anthropological Dictionary on Love and Understanding: Marriage and the Tensions of Belonging in Cameroon* (Bamenda: Langaa RPCIG, 2014). It is the first book that largely constitutes the base or skeleton of the present script that is pivoted on the 'Man of Many'.

I think the only bad idea is one that has not been expressed. I say this because you will also discover that I personally often find things positive even in things that most others will consider negative. You easily cultivate this habit when you are a Hisofean or someone who is farsighted or looks at things with zoomed eyes. Put differently, I am saying that, instead of letting your worrisome past or troubles (for instance) haunt you, always strive to put it/them to positive use, whether you are a professional or not. For instance, most people traditionally have just one father and one mother; I have more than that; not to mention the complex web of brothers and sisters, uncles and aunts, nieces and nephews, cousins, and friends. A 'Man of Many' indeed! Most people live all their life

55

in one city and country, but I can scarcely give an accurate number of cities I have dwelled in, in four different countries (Ambazonia, Cameroun, Canada, and Nigeria) and in two continents. Most also go through primary school attending just one school but I attended at least three; also passing through three different secondary and high schools. It seems to me that anyone who has had the privilege of living the type of life I have and had the kind of relationships I have would naturally not define father, mother, brother, sister, and child (family, in short) in the very restricted way most people and academic disciplines do. Some people would consider it a negative. But Hisofeans often find things positive in things that a lot of people will consider negative, such as effectively having two fathers and two mothers. Four parents and eight grandparents, that is. My *ncheng* upbringing was precisely in three different towns in Fakozone and Memezone of Ambazonia: Victoria, Muyuka, and Kumba. The two parents of this upbringing are known in this book as my mother and father (or papa) – the other two obviously carrying birth or biological before them.

Two Sets of Parents: The De Facto Family and Ninety-Nine Sensism

I was born on 15 August 1960 in Nwangong Fondom to a couple but brought up (from the age of about six) by another couple in the coast, what is known as *ncheng* in Bangwa. The Bangwa used to be in Debundschazone of Cameroon (see Fossungu, 2013a: 4), but now in Lebialemzone of Ambazonia's Midlandzone. I am one of those who think that the federalist tradition of the Bangwa also mainly explains their numerous palaces; wondering though why then Cameroon's administrators appear to have been infected only by the love of these palaces but not also by the federalism that is behind the palaces (Fossungu, 2013b: 119). Nwangong Fondom is often referred to as Fossungu, the name of its Fon; being one of nine

Fondoms that constitute the Bangwa ethnic group. These Fondoms are known today under these names (which are actually mostly titles of their Fons – to distinguish from the many other Chiefs): Fonjumetaw, Fontem, Foreke Cha Cha, Fossungu, Fotabong, Fotabong II, Foto, Fozimombin, and Fozimondi (Fossungu, 2013b: 121-22). The Fondom of Fossungu is also known as Nwangong. More education on these Bangwa fondoms is provided by Brain (1972) who is unable though to teach you anything relating to the Bangwa's (in)famous epithet.

A Globavillagist Glance at the 99-Sense Theory and the CEEP

The 99-Sense Theory (with its two ugly arms) is shortened to 99-Sensism and deals with the Bangwa people's popular epithet in (Cameroun and) Ambazonia (see Fossungu, 2021b: 52). An epithet is: (1) any <u>word</u> or phrase applied to a person or thing to describe an actual or attributed quality: *"Father of Ambazonian Self-Defense" is an epithet of Dr Cho Ayaba;* (2) a characterizing word or phrase firmly associated with a person or thing and often used in place of an actual <u>name</u>, title, or the like, as "Ambazonia's best friend in the diplomatic world" for Ambassador Tibo Nagy; (3) a word, phrase, or <u>expression</u> used invectively as a term of abuse or contempt, to express hostility, etc. I will be returning later on to the concept but, for now, know that the third connotation is particularly useful to one of this book's main research questions which, intricately tied to Cameroonian Ethnic Epithetization Politics (CEEP) as it is, would demand the attention of anthropologists, among other social and/or behavioural scientists. Behavioural scientists must not be confused with, and limited to, those of them using or adhering to the behavioural approach or method and who are popularly known as behaviouralists.

Ethnic Epithetization was just as popular in pre-2017 Cameroon as was soccer, a sport which competed for supremacy only with beer-drinking. Like most ethnic groups in then Cameroon, the epithet of the Bangwa was 99-Sense. The explanatory attachment to it is that these Bangwa are so craftily clever that they would not sell you a hen (but only a cock) for fear that it would produce chicken for you, thus preventing your coming back to buy from them (Fossungu, 2021b: 52). I do not know how far or correct the Bangwa epithetical thesis (as all the others) could expound the attitude of most of the Bangwa people (including me and my family members, of course) that you will be meeting in this book especially and others. You will be the judge as I smoothly pilot you to and around Bangwaland (aka Lebialemzone) and the world.

I would begin with this globavillagist or 'all-encompassing' stance from my prompt reaction to the following 99-sensical question, posed to me by someone in late 2007 in Montréal (Canada). "Why do you not attend Bangwa meetings?" I took a close look at the questioner and asked back: "Does that diminish the fact that I am a Bangwa-99-Senser?" You shall be educated on nose-pokers or useless 'nosers for information' in subsequent Chapters, but I was not yet done with my nose-poking questioner. "By the way," I further cross-examined the interrogator, "what am I to benefit from always flocking around with people who have ninety-nine [per cent] senses like me?" My questioner was obviously stunned and perplexed; so, I hisofely helped him out by indicating that I thought I could be a better Bangwa by not narrowing myself to Bangwa but rather associating with all in a grand-perspective setting like the Cameroon Goodwill Association of Montreal (CGAM). Because "in that way I can easily pick up that one percent sense that the Bangwa is missing and become a 100% human being while also sharing the ninety-nine percent I have with the 1% people. Just imagine a world with a lot of 100% or near 100%

human beings!" (see Fossungu, 2014: xi-xii) Yes, indeed; I am inviting people to clearly view the world globavillagistically like this village boy from Nwangong Fondom now lecturing you all. Nwangong is ruled by the Fon. Limitng to those I personslly know, HRM Fon Sunday Tendongmo Fossungu (Fon ST Fossungu) was succeeded in 1979 by HRM Fon David Foncha Fossungu (Fon DF Fossungu) who was also succeeded in December 2007 by HRM Fon Nicasius Nguazong Fossungu (Fon NN Fossungu).

Figure #9: L-R – Chief Peter Ateafac Fonwancheng, Fon Sunday Tendongmo Fossungu, and Chief Fomellah
Source: Richard Ngufor Fossungu

I have a lot of parents, grandparents, sisters, brothers, aunts and uncles (some of them you will meet later). Many of them never went too far in, or at all to, the Whiteman's school. But I cannot help marvelling when some of them open their mouths to talk. Take, for instance, Fon ST Fossungu (in Figure #9) who many in the family and out of it have described in terms that would fit those of King Solomon in the bible. As young as

I then was, I still remember a lot of things the Fon used to do or say while I was growing up in and around the Emollah Palace. But take for now an example out of the palace when the Fon was visiting my father for the first time, since my departure from Nwangong and arrival in Victoria (Ambazonia). Grandpa said that people who *always* conform to what others say or think have no idea of who they really are. As a young lad listening to him from a distance talking to other elders, I tried to make sense of what he had said but was not sure I got it. So when the crowd had thinned out a little bit, I approached and requested to ask the Fon something. Everyone in his entourage was sort of furious at "this child without manners and fear of elders" and beckoning me off.

But the Fon, to their astonishment, hushed all of them down and asked me what I wanted to know. Not wanting the others to hear, I approached and whispered in his ear my question as to what the Fon meant by what I have outlined above. The Fon was himself so surprised that, at my age (I was then about nine or ten), I had been listening to, and following, their conversation. My grandfather stared at me hard and then laughingly said: "Because every individual must have something that sets them apart from the rest of us," observing that he had always known I was going to be like my father. "Which of my two fathers," I asked aloud. At this point a deafening silence fell into the living room and I then realized not only grandpa (but also some uncles in his entourage that I knew very well but had pretended not to know) heard the question. I quickly ran out to continue with the dishes I had been washing, knowing well that what I had just said must be hurting some of them in the same way as this book may affect some others, including my parents and siblings of *The De Facto Family* particularly.

Thecla Anangafac Fosungu (Née Njumo): The Prime Mover and My Likeability

Known in this book as my mother or Mamie Thecla, she studied in one of the most prestigious girls-only Catholic Mission secondary schools – Queen of Rosary Secondary School, Okoyong in Mamfe, Manyuzone of Midlandzone of Ambazonia. Going as far as form four, she dropped out due to pregnancy. Mamie Thecla occupies a very important place in my life, not just because she is the mother who brought me up. Of especial importance is the fact that she provoked my very first "defining moment" as a very special kid destined for great accomplishments. You are obviously anxious to know how, I know. Hold your patience. Don't we often say the patient dog eats the fattest bone? Would the impatient dogs actually agree here that the other would have any bone at all, let alone the fattest?

Whatever the case with the arguing dogs, unfortunately, I have not been able to lay hands on any of Mamie Thecla's photos. None of my siblings of the household that was contacted by email or phone for the purpose of acquiring a photo of Mamie Thecla (their biological mother) ever responded at all. For instance, in my email of 28 February 2013 titled "I Need Few Good Photos", I had written to Bernard, Maurine, Justine, and Marie-Claire, addressing:

Hi Chiefs, Hi Mafor, Hi Sis. Maurine, I believe members of your families are all doing well as well as yourselves. On my part, I cannot complain. I would like to have a recent nice photo of each of you to include in my book (*The Ingredients of Success: Lessons from the Life of a Man of Many Professions and Relations*). I also like to have nice photos of the following (if any of you can provide them): Dad, Mum, Joe, Beatrice, Annastasia, Gladys, and Quinta. Including your photo is optional and anyone who does not want their photo included can let me know. Meanwhile, you can check out these two books of mine that are already published: ......Thanks for your time and may God bless you all. PAF (altered paragraphing)

I got no response at all. It is kind of strange, but not so to anyone who understands what Mamiteelization signifies. That

61

is, the idea put into their heads by their birth mother (Mamie Thecla) that I was "an outsider" who should not be trusted and associated with whatsoever. The Nwangong Royal Family is made of a lot of people who think in similar lines and thus give Mamiteelization the boost that should have been lacking. Nevertheless, just looking at two of Mamie Thecla's daughters – Josephine Forzi Fosungu and Annastasia Chamo Fosungu (in their pictures I have provided in other books, notably Fossungu, 2021) – would not be far from according you a good representation of her facial image. While you are getting her physiognomy as directed, I will continue discussing her importance

Mamie Thecla was known in the Emollah Palace and Nwangong Fondom as Mamie *Ncheng* (Mum from the coast). She was respected and held in high esteem, if not for her own sake, then because of her *massa* or husband. When she often arrived in the Emollah Palace, the number of fowls, pigs, and goats that went about crying and begging for their lives to be spared was equalled to none. It was always feasting in the Palace from when she landed till when she took off. Her *massa* rarely came as he was working and she, therefore, did almost all of the coming and going. But even her *massa*'s own rare arrival did not bring as much joy to the children as hers. It is often said that mothers usually know better what children like and want – justifying in a way celebrated African musician Prince Nico Mbarga's *Sweet Mother*. That is not only because of the candies and cookies and other such goodies. I brightly remember how Mamie Thecla would usually not eat much of the sumptuous and assorted food from the numerous wives of the Fon and those of the Fon's sons. But she also often made sure the rest of the food was out of the reach of the hawk-like adults; only the children were served with it. How could she be anything but dear to these children?

Imagine then how special and blessed you will feel when one of Mamie Thecla's trips to Nwangong Fondom is solely for the purpose of taking just you (among all the so many children) to *ncheng* where you will thereafter be living. Not just a temporary visit. This is the 1960s I am talking about here. Not the village of today where cars even come to every hour and minute. And it is not like Mamie Thecla arrives today and makes the announcement and the next day you are on the way. She spends a whole week or so before departure. During which time, you are the centre of attention, of admiration, of adoration, of advice given left and right, and of special association with Mamie Thecla. Truly a defining moment, it was for me. My goal in life noted above was thus born out of my innate gratitude and recognition that I was the one chosen out of so many disadvantageously-placed village children whose chances of ever seeing a school classroom were very close to naught. The *naughtiness* not being because we were intellectually incapable, but solely because of the handicap called financial means.

Realization of my objective in life almost came to a stop in high school because of financial or money issues. Yes, there is no doubt about the fact that the availability of financial means has always been an obstacle to my speedy realisation of goals in and out of the household. Not really because those means were not there. But largely because of the selective and inconsistent meaning parents attached to 'family' and 'child'. I hardly fell within that meaning, notwithstanding that I have never myself felt like I was not a child of the household, by deeds or thoughts. My "outsider" status coupled so well with my likeability to spell a lot of unnecessary money issues for me. But Ambazonia's *lingua franca* (what some very much like to denigrate as Pidgin but I do prefer to call *Ambatok*) has to help us out here. It is thus popularly said in said national-unity language that *cow weh noh get tail na God di drivam fly*. You can simply liken this *Ambatokish* expression to what I described in 1998 by stating that "It is common for people born with infirmity... to make up for it by [highly] developing in another

63

less suitable area" (Fossungu, 1998: 5). That thesis comes a few steps further to defining and exposing 'The Power in Me' or, better still, 'The Ayabacholization Classroom in My Life'. Because of the money issue, as I have said, the advance in my objective almost came to a stop in Cameroon College of Arts and Sciences (CCAS) Kumba: but for the fact that I knew myself well and what I was up to and up against in the household that Mamie Thecla was then bringing me into.

Whenever Mamie Thecla came to Nwangong, she stayed at the house of Cecilia Asongu Fossungu (Mamie Cecilia). Mamie Cecilia's only son, Uncle David Ntimah Fossungu (Uncle Ntimah), was then living with her in *ncheng*. This time was not different. I remember spending three straight days at Mamie Cecilia's at Mamie Thecla's demand. Any village child would have paid a lot to be there in that manner, but not this clock-ticking-headed boy. For, I kept wondering what the reason for the three-day house change was, despite the boost it gave to my being special in the eyes of the others. Did Mamie Thecla want to find out for herself just how obedient or foolish or intelligent I was? Whatever it was she was finding out, I am sure my inborn powers worked well for me and I passed the test, since she had let me return home with indication that we were leaving in two days.

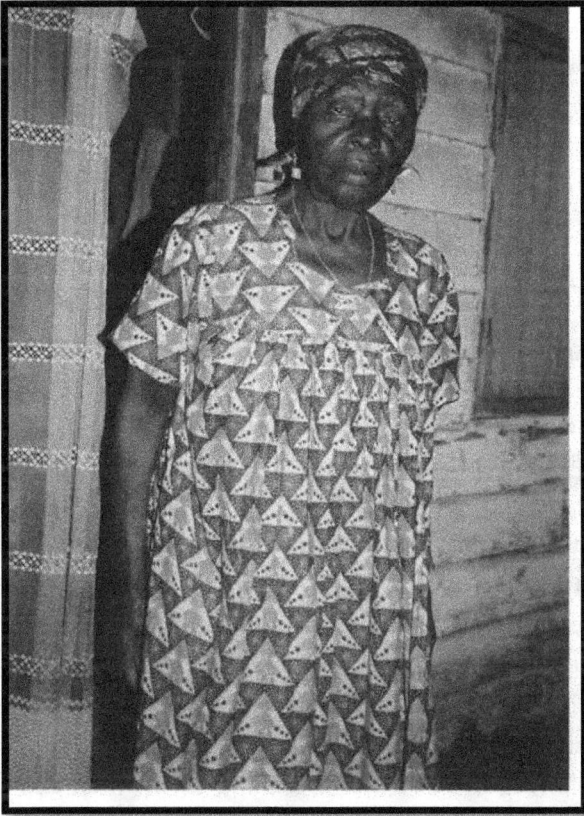

Figure #10: Mamie Cecilia Asongu Fossungu in Yoke in June
2004
Source: Photo taken by Momany Fossungu

Mamie Thecla is special to me, in addition, because she is the
one to whom my birth mother personally handed me over.
Taking her significance to higher grounds is also the fact that
she is the prime mover behind most of the events that have
altered (for good or for bad) the course of the lives of so many
people. All this is hinged on her definition of family and of
children. The affected people also include not only the children
of the household and those that spent time in it. It englobes as
well the entire Fossungu Royal Family, many members of
which would obviously see Mamie Thecla as unloving, egoistic,

scheming, and uncaring. I, for one, cannot say Mamie Thecla did not like or love me. There are two especial reasons.

First, she would not have been the one who (still breastfeeding her little baby boy called Bernard Mbancho Fosungu) came to get me from the village. I think Mamie Thecla could be summed up as the one woman that has greatly impacted on my life by not comprehending and appreciating me for who I really am. For example, as a child who never saw her in any other terms than a mother. This misunderstanding has had across-the-board consequences on most of my junior brothers and sisters of the household whom I raised and babysat. Coming behind Joseph Njumo Fosungu (Joseph) is Bernard (that you have just met) who is followed, in order, by Beatrice Ngwikem Fosungu; Annastasia; Maurine Nkengafac Fosungu; Gladys Mazanue Fosungu; Quinta Lonche Fosungu; and Justine Mamefat Fosungu. Justine was born almost at the same time with Delphine Fosungu from papa's other younger wife, Julie Fosungu. Marie-Claire Efuelancha Fossungu, a cousin, adds to the list, having lived in the household from when she entered secondary school in the early 1980s to graduation at the university in the early 1990s. The few older children in the household at the time I arrived there were: Therese Nkengafac Fosungu; Josephine; Vincent Akana Fonwancheng, the son of papa's friend (and the man from whom I got all my names, except the family one); Uncle Ntimah (Mamie Cecilia's son you have already met); and Michael Njumo, Mamie Thecla's younger brother. The last two were not there for long after my arrival, most probably because they had soon completed primary school and left the household.

Mamie Thecla, moreover, could not have hated me because I am a very affable person. I do not know anyone that has had the chance to be with me even for a short time and did not like me. My amiability, I know, is simply infectious. It has often put

66

me into lots of trouble, including the definitional one unfolding here. I think Mamie Thecla's main problem (stemming from the likeability?) was her fear that I was a threat to her *own* birth children. It seems to be a protective motherly trait, as you can see in many other moms (including my own birth mother). Exceptionally intelligent and generous, Uncle Richard Ngufor Fossungu (Uncle Ngufor) could not go beyond primary school simply because of similar home conditions in his senior brother's (Chief Fonenge Vincent's) home in Fontem. He was not the birth child of the madam of the house who must have had similar fears and distrust of him as did my mother (see Fossungu, 2021: 138-50). It seems to be most mothers' characteristic (as said earlier), judging also from the way my own birth mother must have treated my half-siblings who are to be encountered later. I was not there in Nwangong with them. But I could gather this from the way my birth mother, first, never even mentioned them to me. And, second, she categorically refused to stay with them in Ekona, as I had arranged in 2004 when I visited Cameroun/Ambazonia. The whole idea behind the arrangement was to regroup the family and make it easier for my guidance and help in catching up with the lost years of scattered living. But Mamie Regina would be willing to stay with my girlfriend's family in Bafut in Mezamzone of Midlandzone in 2007, and also with the family of young Uncle Calistus Tenangmock Fossungu (Nkemanang) in Douala from 2008 to her death in 2014. As you can see, it is not just Mamie Thecla who is in this *not-my-birth-children* pot.

But if you are wondering a lot why mothers generally behave that way, then wait until you meet a Black-Canadian 'mother' (in later Chapters) who does not even see children (birth or not) as being part of her own definition of family. I cannot exactly explain why most mothers behave that way, but I can explain why I say Mamie Thecla's fear seemed to have dominated all her dealings with or concerning me. Because of her failure to manage this fear (founded or unfounded) she was unable to see that I (like Uncle Ngufor) was rather a searing guide, than an obstacle, to her birth children's progress and future. These are children that she also appears to have intoxicated in my regard. I, therefore, became the greatest 'sinner' when my father (her *massa*) sang my praises, particularly as I not only did just the right things papa wanted but also (since I did not share in their fear of papa or anyone else) quickly understood him more than my brothers and sisters. These siblings would be quick to describe papa as difficult: which is quite true if you do not understand Emmanuel Nguajong Fosungu or Chief Formbuehndia

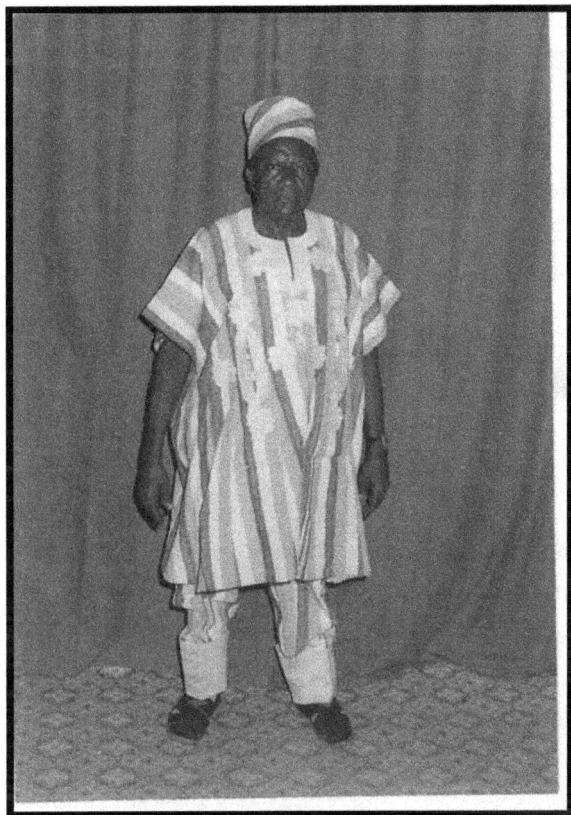

Figure #11: Chief Formbuehndia (aka Emmanuel Nguajong
Fosungu)
Source: Chief Formbuehndia

*Emmanuel Nguajong Fosungu (Chief Formbuehndia) Fortifying My Life
Objective and Tumekongilogy*

Chief Formbuehndia in Bangwa means 'chief who is the
support or foundation of the family or house', 'the one who
sustains the family or community from downsliding into ruins
or disrepute' (Fossungu, 2016: 112). The only father I know,
Chief Formbuehndia was born in 1931 (like my birth mother)
and died on 11 October 2002. Studying in the then British
Southern Cameroons (now Ambazonia) and in Biafra (Nigeria)

to become a statistician, he returned home to then West Cameroon and began working with the West Cameroon electricity corporation, Powercam (later destroyed by LRC and replaced with Sonel: *Société nationale de l'élétricité*), until his retirement in the early 1990s.

I have had so many defining and un-defining moments in my life. But my most memorable defining moment (that also concretely cemented my main objective in life) is this conversation I had with my father in Kumba, Memezome in Atlanticzone of Ambazonia. This dialogue also makes the important point about papa's financial means. It relates to his always letting his tenants (and he had a lot of them in Yoke, Kumba, and Victoria) who had not paid their rents for so long to go scot-free. Don't you think, papa, I thought aloud to him, that doing so would encourage other tenants not to also pay and at the end go free? Papa had a particular look and smile that always lid his face whenever I asked him one of those Momanynized hooky questions and this time was no exception. Papa then said son (or better, Pee) those who have no intention of paying their rents would still not pay – whether or not they know I let one tenant off the hook. In this life people are not the same (I was wondering here if it was not my grandpa speaking). By the way, papa pursued, you see Mr. Lucas has not paid all his rents for the past six or so months. The good thing though is that all his children are still in school and doing very well too, like you, my son. If their father has any small amount of brains, my father went on, he will be thankful. He is not giving me my rents which I clearly deserve to have. But I myself am happy that he is not using it unproductively. Therefore, Pee, papa concluded, I am not only sending you and your other siblings to school. I am also doing so in a way to the children of Mr. Lucas.

Wow! What a true Hisofean! A real Globavillagist! Largeyedist! What about an Ayabacholizalist? A Traorélizalist? I could not help but see an angel talking to me right then in the image of my dad. I said simply: "Thank you, papa, for opening my eyes. In fact, I would like to be like you when I grow up." Papa replied: "You don't need to grow up to be like me. And you don't need to be like me but to be better than me. That is the way you could ever thank me," he concluded, quickly leaving the scene before I could ask any more questions. I was transfixed for a while reflecting on all what had just transpired. Some of the things that immediately struck me were the way papa looked at the larger picture of things, not the narrow. Not judging B from A's action, and not restricting the net of help to just his own family and relatives. All of these and more have greatly impacted on my outlook as would be evidenced by some instances of defining and un-defining moments and by some of the battles I have fought in view of becoming better than papa. If I could then describe Chief Formbuehndia in just one sentence, I would simply say this. He is/was a far-sighted and scrupulous man, with a second religion called farming, who indeed liked helping people without limitation as to family ties – attributes that obviously did not sit well with his somewhat narrow-minded partner and her own extended family.

Indeed, Aunty Constance Tumekong Fossungu (Aunty Tumekong), who lived for a while in the household in Yoke, is even known to have mused as follows. That it was as if, since papa could not say NO to anyone that arrived his home, conditions in the household had been fashioned to make 'they' themselves say NO to staying there. This aunty seems to have observed well and she brilliantly captures the astonishment as well of many in the Royal Family and Fondom as to how I have been able to academically achieve as much as I have, living and growing up in the household. As you will see throughout this book, the two young boys *of* the household especially were socialized to promoting Katerina K. Frantzi's "Us-Them" dichotomy. That demeanour conveniently created the 'invisible hand' decision of many of the 'them' to 'quit the

71

household by themselves'. Many of the 'them' that would have gained from this unique man's desire to indiscriminately help people were thus barred by papa's partner who did not seem to share his perspectives and who instead made the household very intolerable to those that her definition of family clearly labels as "outsiders" and parasitic "children with dead fathers". This Tumekongilized Theory (Tumekongilogy) is quickly seen right away in the case of Marie-Claire.

Another "outsider", Marie-Claire almost left the household in Victoria like many others before and after her: but for my timely intervention and *her willingness* to listen and learn. I found Marie-Claire one day weeping so much and on the verge of packing her small bag and leaving. I asked her why she was in that state of mind and she sobbed even more, explaining how the boys *of* the household (Joseph and Bernard) had insultingly labelled us as "children whose fathers have all died and they are here eating our father's money." She was astonished when I demanded if that was just what was making her cry that much and about to go away, almost pitting me on the other side, not hers. "My dear junior sister," I said to her, "stop your crying and let's go to the nearby store and get some candies." Away from the house and making sure that no one was eavesdropping, I asked again what we were called that made Marie-Claire cry and she repeated it. "Is it not true that your father and mine are dead and that *their* father is bringing us up?" Marie-Claire began weeping again and I sternly told her to go and pack and leave if she did not want to learn anything at all. I do think that sometimes you need those you consider your friends to fling the truth into your face for you to see truth, and not insult. That is what real friends are for. I had, therefore, emphasized to Marie-Claire: "By the way, before you go, know that I would be without any tears today if I had to weep over everything like you are now doing. Remember also that I will always be here 'eating' that money, no matter what, until papa himself tells me to leave. If you think your late father was very foolish in personally bringing you here when he did, I don't think papa was stupid in sending for me after my own [biological] father died." I then told Marie-Claire to go and pack if that was what she wanted to do with her life. But she had already made up her mind to stay, knowing that success was hers "as long as I have you as my brilliant and courageous guide." I told her she had a deal and that I was proud of her. And anyone sensible should truly be proud of Marie-Claire for being the first to listen and learn. Because she could listen and learn (unlike many others similarly counselled before and after her), today she is the only other "outsider" that made it to university graduation in the household despite all the stream of insults about dead fathers like Karlemon Tale'eh Fossungu, one of my birth parents of *The Biological Connexion*.

The Biological Connexion: Karlemon Mbugnyi Tale'eh Fossungu and Regina Akiefac Fossungu (née Fonge)

Tale'eh is my dead birth or biological father. I have already talked briefly about the father who cared for and nurtured me. Now is the time to say something about my biological parents, with a father who I do not quite know. That is in the sense of not having his image in my mind. My lack of physionomical knowledge of him is not because I was too young to know him when, after his death, I left Nwangong for the city of Victoria – contentiously called Limbe in Biya's 'Republic of Cameroon'. My biological father was almost never there at home since, being the first son of Fon ST Fossungu (and, therefore, the heir apparent to the throne), he was always journeying to represent his father or do some errands for him. Although I am currently the first of his children (see, however, Fossungu, 2023: chapter 6), I understand that I was actually about the eighth or tenth (from my biological mother's side). The story even goes that I might have been (or be) this troublesome baby – an *obanje* in one of Chinua Achebe's novels – going and coming and going just to upset the parents. This tale is explained with some marks that were put on me at birth so that I would be recognized if I returned (again). Could it really be that I am an *obanje* that refused to go only because of the marks on one of my ears and neck? How come I *have four eyes*? That is, easily see what others don't see – a characteristic traditionally

73

attributed to *obanjes?* Is it not all about witchcraft which I prefer to more elegantly style africanscience?

Four-Eyesism and the Two Arms of Africanscience (Witchcraft)

Most Africans believe in witchcraft and/or sorcery to the extent that even very rudimentary things like farsightedness are attributed to it (see Fossungu, 2023: chapter 2). Dr Akoh Asa'na had lots of people agreeing with his thesis on witchcraft because on the same day in March 2015, Kevin Njabo wrote in response, concluding by hoping "we'll carefully read the mail from Asa'na again and ask why" (Fossungu, 2015: 76). Yes, most. Africans don't ask why and how. One of the popular ways to describe someone that is able to visualize what they often fail to see is to say that the person in question "has four eyes". Which leads some of us to wonder whether or not they are including the two normal eyes and the other extra two from africanscience? I do not quite know why they think this way but those who are interested in the witchcraft subject could consult Fossungu (2023) while I continue *four-eyesing*. I have posed the queries because every scientist, the experts theorize, is interested in finding out about something, understanding it. Whatever a scientist wants to find out about, there are four basic goals that can contribute to that understanding; namely, (1) description, (2) prediction, (3) explanation, and (4) control (Reaves, 1992: 20-24). Does four-eyesism or africanscience also involve all of these basic goals? And which branch of four-eyesism, are we talking about by the way? As can be seen, four-eyesism (like 99-Sensism) also has two arms or connotations (farsightedness and witchcraft) in this book and there is much talk of the apparent influences of both arms in this narrative on love and understanding, family, and academics (see Fossungu, 2023: 95). Better watch out then, especially as my birth mother has answered the *obanje* query with a different story. In Mamie Regina's words, while "I was 'shitting' the children, *they* were picking them up and eating like a hawk does to a hen's chickens." Who '*they*' is referring to, I have never gotten anyone who has been willing to explain, notwithstanding all efforts. Not even from my birth mother herself over whom my biological father is said to have fought such a ferocious battle.

Figure #12: Mafor Regina Akiefac Fossungu in June 2004
Source: Photo taken by Momany Fossungu

Regina Akiefac Fossungu is referred to in this book as my birth mother or Mamie Regina. She was born in 1931, giving birth to me at the age of twenty-nine. Although I have not grown up with her, she is the first influence in my life; with her influences having greatly aided my shaping of the other later influences in unimaginable ways. Furthermore, Mamie Regina and I do not often feel like we never grew up together physically, notwithstanding that being the case. Although papa was not used to letting me know, I was aware of the "messages" (helping financially) she often sent to him through visiting uncles. These uncles also always passed on my own small private "messages" from her. Mamie Regina regularly came down to Yoke to help with farm work. On such occasions, I got to know certain things about her from our casual conversations; still remembering a lot also from the time I spent with her before my departure for the household in Victoria.

Very hardworking and full of unimaginable energy, Mamie Regina is highly intelligent. I remember her once telling me in Yoke that she always knew I was going to stick to the pieces of advice she had given to me. Mamie Regina and I understand each other so well, even without talking, that I often wonder if we communicate by telepathy. I never told her anything concerning the tribulations in the household. She never behaved as if she was concerned that there could be trouble. But I remember her asking me one day in Yoke how I was doing (*Allekoh*, in Bangwa). I simply said "I am very grateful for the pieces of advice you gave me in the village. They have been very helpful." She too merely said "I know." I did not ask how she knew. I am sure that most mothers who do not understand their son the way she does would have wanted to know how helpful, as well as the son wishing to know how the knowledge came about.

Mamie Regina has this uniquely strange way of seeming to know what I am thinking and usually stops the questioning before I even start asking. It seems to me she has been intelligently protecting me from something by hiding something from and about me. Most often, as soon as I say 'Mamie', she cuts in with "Ateh-Afac will one day kill me with his questions." I usually then kept off my query, most probably because both of us knew somehow that something was not okay. But at the same time we both also understood (*sans aucune discussion*) the need not to know, at least for the time being. It seems that my father and several others in the Royal Family were astutely part of this conspiracy to keep me ignorant of whatever it is. I know very well that Mamie Regina trusted me a lot and knew that I am not a trouble maker. But sometimes I got this feeling when I always looked at her that she was very concerned about losing me to what or over what, I cannot tell. This often happened when I looked her straight into the eyes and she would ask with much concern: "What, Ateh-Afac?" I loved looking at her like that for no other reason than to enjoy her innate beauty and charm that even old age and hard times were not able to dry out.

My biological mum is said to have loved being the centre of attention and her prettiness and other rare qualities duly gave her that position. Popularly known as Mama Regie, she would perfectly fit what Americans would separately call a singing, dancing, and beauty, queen. I still fondly remember her singing while she would be bulldozing on the farm around Letia, to which she usually took her two little boys. I guess I took after her too in those domains. In her youthful days she was a real hot cake, with the competition for her being so fierce – my birth father, of course, being in that ferocious struggle. Chief Fonenge Vincent has been of some little aid here. As he once explained to me in a brief interview on the Fossungu family, in order to outwit the other competitors, my birth father had "carried" Mamie Regina. This Bangwa idiom means that he had 'forcefully eloped' with her before coming after alone to formally ask for her hand in marriage from her parents – another royal family. Women naturally find it easier talking about some of these things to their daughters-in-law than to their own sons. This was the case with my ex-wife, Scholastica Achankeng Asahchop (Scholastica). Scholastica once told me that Mamie Regina had explained to her that my birth father was not really her first choice but that "the way he had acted certainly won my heart and earned him the place." Who were or could be the other competitors for Mamie Regina that my birth father outwitted?

Figure #13: Scholastica Achankeng Asahchop in 1997
Source: Scholastica Achankeng Asahchop

The question is important to ask because, first, most of my uncles have evaded responding to it. Also, because the circumstances surrounding my birth father's death have never been clear or explained to me (see Fossungu, 2023: chapter 6). No one has bothered to let me know. Uncle Ngufor who even talked about it, on being asked, merely stated to me that he fell from a palm tree and sustained some injuries that later killed him. But I cannot remember ever seeing my birth father lying sick at home at any time. I can still remember the day my birth father died. I had a premonition that something wrong had happened. Although we (children) were then not allowed to come close to where there was a corpse, things were happening so fast that day. For example, the way we were rounded up and taken to a compound out of the Emollah Palace; and the general commotion and near confusion provoked by the extraordinary Night Society or *Etough,* the feared arm of the law, the secret weapon of the Fon who carries out fearful punishment on witches, adulterers, and murderers (see Fossungu, 2013b: 114). All the commotion told me that it was not normal. Of course, said abnormality could all have been due to the fact of my biological dad being the first son of then Fon. Nevertheless, the suspicious manner through which my birth father must have died dawns on me whenever I look back at some facts, four of which suffice here.

First Factor – The Beating Ups: Hardly had Tale'eh Fossungu been gone when some of his brothers (my uncles) started coming home every night and "beating up" his wife. 'Beating up' is the way that a young innocent child would describe 'having sex with' because of the mother's crying or groaning he often hears at night whenever any of those uncles comes around. I remember once supposedly going to my birth mother's rescue only to be sent off with the uncle's painful slap and angry rebuke for even daring to come there. I would imagine that Dieudonné Asongu Fossungu (Dieudonné) must have seen a whole lot of the 'beating ups' of mother and other such traumatizing acts that, until his death in June 2011, he could hardly hold on to any of the two wives that successively came into his life. Dieudonné is the only sibling with whom I supposedly share both biological parents. But he is not the only blood sibling I have (see Fossungu, 2023: 376-84).

Both Esther Asongkeng Fossungu (Esther) and Vincent Awandem Fossungu (Awandem) also have the same biological father with me. Their own mother was his second wife. I never had the chance to know my birth mother's *mbanya* – appellation for the other woman/women that have the same *massa* with you. Quite apart from my not being a nose-poker, I did not know my birth father had a second wife and the wife herself also, most probably because both co-spouses were not living together or in the same household. Of course, I knew "Awandem" well in the Emollah Palace as one other favourite grandchild to the King Solomon of Nwangong (the others including "Ateh-Afac" – me). But I only knew that the second wife's two surviving children were my half-siblings in 1994. This was after Esther's tearful trip to Douala where I was then based. Just imagine meeting a blood sister you never knew you had at Uncle Ngufor's home in Douala. You casually greet her like anyone else and take off; only to learn later how much she had cried before returning to Ekona in Ambazonia. The sole purpose of Esther's trip to Douala in Cameroun having been to see her senior brother just back from Canada whom she thought knew exactly who she was to him. "Why didn't anybody present her to me," I had asked Uncle Ngufor. His response was that they thought I knew her. I was truly overwhelmed and only God knows how I was able to drive to Ekona that day, as unplanned as the journey was. I will simply leave the rest of what happened in Ekona (where my sister is the second wife of a man with a large family) to your imagination.

Figure #14: Pa Asah Ndem William & wife (Esther) in 2004 in Ekona
Source: Photo taken by Momany Fossungu

Second Factor – Helpful Virtuous Ignorance: I can remember too well my very first return to the village in the early 1980s, after high school. I am here talking about Uncle William Asongu Fossungu (is my younger brother, Dieudonné, named after him and why?). This uncle had long chased my mother and brother away and *owned* my birth father's compound in the village. Also the one who was the first to start the 'beating up', Uncle Asongu spent all the time trying to discover if I knew this or that. All through his sneaky interviews I feigned ignorance and saw how contented he was that I did not know anything about the village when I had left it. Ignorance is at times a very powerful tool and a virtue.

Like Josephine's case, Julie Fossungu is also one of the clearest cases of helpful ignorance on my part. I never really understood why Joseph and Bernard were often grossly maltreating this little girl the way they did. Because of *their* lost battle with me (that is studied in the next Chapter), I was able to defend Julie from time to time, not actually realizing exactly what I was doing and inviting upon myself. To me, defending the underdog was just the natural thing to do, especially so when it was a small girl being unnecessarily beaten up by two bigger boys. When Julie had arrived in the household at about ten to twelve (at the most), it is like everyone except me was aware of who she in fact was. To me, she was just another Fossungu 'outsider' that had come, as usual. After so many years growing up in the household, with the constant maltreatment as just described, she "carried belly" in primary school, as the school pupils put it. Only her pregnancy brought the message home to me that Julie Fosungu was the wife of papa, the author of the "belly carrying". It was only then that I fully comprehended why Joseph and Bernard had been doing all what they had been doing to her; and that, in their eyes, I must have been regarded as having taken the wrong side in their fuss with papa's new and very young wife. Whatever the case, I do think my ignorance here was very useful because, had I been aware of the facts, perhaps I would not have been valiantly standing between the helpless little girl and her

81

multiple aggressors as I did, for fear of the implications. Who knows what would have become of little Julie in their unrestrained hands? Is this not among some of the positive things that resulted from my own 'negative' *Leaky-Leaky Neck* nickname? More on nicknames is in Chapter 3.

Third Factor – The Mysterious 'They': In the late 1980s I was then teaching in the UNIYAO. While in the village one day as a grown-up man and without prefacing it with 'Mamie', I confronted my birth mother with the question: "What happened to my dad?" We were just two of us in the house that evening. But she became so frightened, looking around as if there were more people in the room than just the two of us, shaking and saying the following almost to herself: "Please, God, help me. With this kind of questioning, *they* would also take his head!" I do not know who this *they* would actually stand for. I really wanted to know but, seeing how shaken Mamie Regina was, knowing that I was right there in the village, and recalling all the village witchcraft stories that had led papa not to be taking his children (including me) to the village for so long, I wisely desisted from pursuing the topic further.

Fourth Factor – Seeing the Nwangong Angry Lion: My suspicion on Tale'eh's apprehensive death would seem to be confirmed also through the children he left behind. I am sure that my ignorance of their blood relations to me for so long could be some sort of helpful ignorance or an ingredient of my progress. In November 2002, after the burial of Chief Formbuehndia in October, I gathered the other three siblings and we headed to Nwangong for a cleansing ritual. It was said that we, and especially Awandem, were wandering a lot due to the fact that our birth father had not been replaced or succeeded. That was the general belief and talk going around and Esther particularly pleaded with me that this should be done as I was then around – with it not being possible without me. So we were in the village for that purpose. My initial idea had been to let Awandem be the successor since I am not based in Africa. But thank God that I have this hunch that I often follow almost religiously. As you will further see below, it has proven to be an indispensable component of success to me in a lot of domains. At the last minute when Fon DF Fossungu wanted to know who was to be the new Tale'eh, I indicated it was me. God alone knows why this happened. My three blood siblings (but Awandem especially) had, unknown to me, teamed up with other elders involved with the ceremony, insisting that our father's succession could not have any sense until the preliminary question of his place of abode had first been settled.

Frankly, I had never till then seen a lion except in books and on television (though I would not say that in the village as the belief there is that saying NO to anyone that asks if you have seen a certain animal invites his or her showing you one: being himself or herself transformed). But I saw one in Uncle Asongu sitting right there. Up to this day I do not know if others saw what I saw. But I am sure I am right in what I saw – an excessively angry lion ready to devour whoever stood in his way. Uncle Asongu's anger must have been on two fronts, should my siblings' insistence or suggestion be followed: (1) public knowledge of what had happened that he was then on our birth father's land and property and (2) my not buying adjacent land from him (as per a previous plan with my uncle) to increase the one I already had in Letia quarter. I am very sure none of Tale'eh's four children would have left the village alive if I had also joined the chorus or let Awandem be the successor of our biological father.

I had, therefore, told everyone present that I did not come all the way from Canada to fight over any land or property left behind by whosoever. I made it clear that I was capable of acquiring same for my siblings and myself. Therefore, I had concluded, let Uncle Asongu get the witnesses for the Letia land sale so that we could quickly close that up and go on with the main ceremony that had brought us all there that day. You could actually feel the dangerous tension that had already built up in the air then rapidly loosening up and falling apart and the lion reassuming its human form, happy at the turn of events.

83

When Awandem and the others (perhaps because they know much more than I do – virtuous ignorance) continued privately to complain to me that our father's property could not just have been surrendered in that way, I dryly inquired: "What is this property that you guys value more than your lives?"

Thus, from that day in November 2002 Nkemtale'eh became my nobility name; deriving from when I formally succeeded my birth father, becoming Tale'eh. During the sucession ceremony, Fon DF Fossungu (perhaps in appreciating the manner I had wisely and far-sightedly handled every catastrophe that was just waiting to unfold) also surprisingly bestowed on me the title of *nkem* or notable of the Fondom and adviser to the Fon. I say surprisingly because people usually lobby a lot to have some of these titles, but I had done none of those things. I was completely unaware of the Fon's intention prior to the surprise. In Nwangong, therefore, you will hardly hear anyone addressing me with any other name other than Dr Nkemtale'eh (which is now Chief Dr Fotale'eh, since July 2014); this being that same little village boy whose future Mamie Thecla greatly helped to chart and define, wittingly or otherwise, within the framework of a household with a second religion called farming as exposed in the next Chapter.

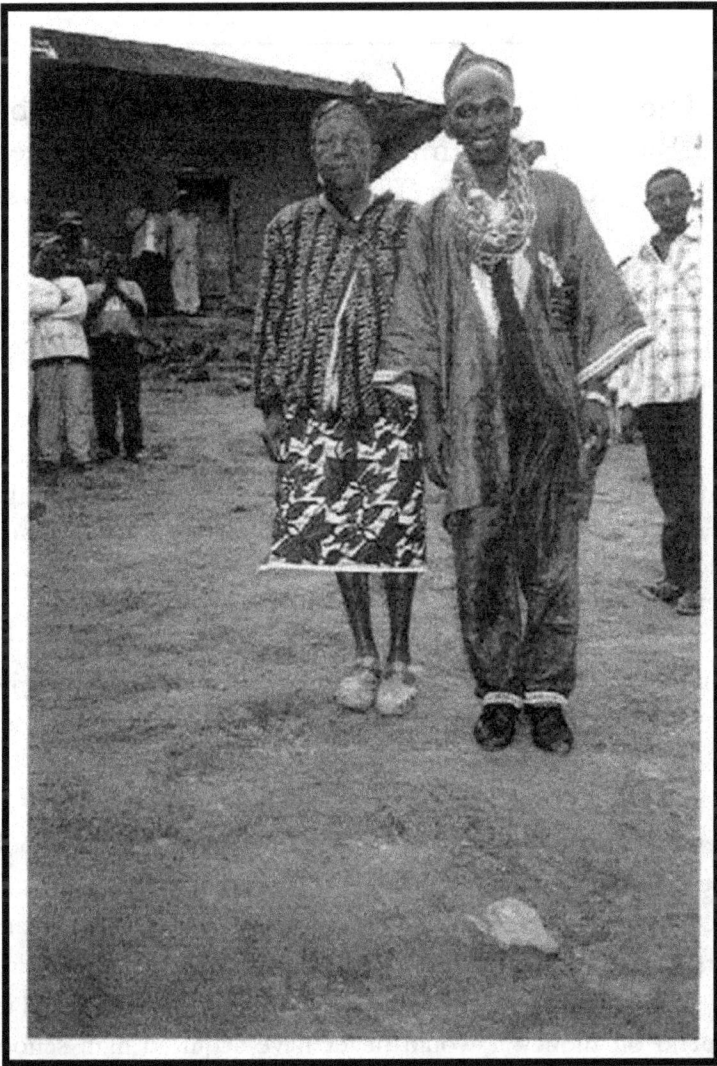

Figure #15: Mafor Tendongmo posing with (formerly 'Asoba
Tendongmo' now crowned) Nkemtale'eh
Source: Photo Dave, Yaoundé

Chapter 3

The Magnificence Of Self-Help And Foresight: Backing Academics With The Farming Creed And Surviving With Papa's Religion Across Continents

Can you now see why Ayaba, with all the power at his beck and call from being the CIC of the ADF, still refused to 'go it alone' and instead brought the other 'leaders' into the fold for the Canada Pre-Negotiation Talks? Is Ambazonia not truly blessed to have people of such calibre leading the most consequential organization in its AWOL? Isn't Ayaba steadfastly 'standing between Ambazonians and their colonizers' to 'make sure you get your freedom' as he promised them in 2017 in South Africa? (Fossungu, 2023: 229-30).

A lot of people seem to believe or think that money is the singular ingredient of success in life. Many often talk about money in terms that would make you think happiness in life completely depends on the quantity of it that you have or spend. While not denying the importance of money, this book questions its primacy to success in certain fields such as becoming educated; showing that there are far more important personal attributes to success and happiness than just having the money on-hand. You will discover that if everything had to depend on money, I would never have acquired high school education, let alone set foot in a university amphitheatre. The AGovC would similarly not have sustained the Revolution up to now that the full effects of its ground-breaking Liberation Strategy and Roadmap are dawning on LRC and its nosifeanistic citizens. Of course, money has been one of the major obstacles to my smooth progress to acquiring university education as well as having a normal family and marriage, but it has not been the only hindrance; nor have the multiple negative forces completely succeeded in barring me from the attainment of some of my goals. Why? A very good question indeed! Extensive answers are proffered in this book.

As I have indicated earlier, a lot of people who think they know me don't actually understand me. Some of these people have not been able to hide their amazement. They have sometimes even wondered aloud: "How come he is having so *many* academic degrees and certificates and yet would not only do odd jobs but also does so with much pride?" When this particular question has come to my attention, I think as follows. If this query was specifically posed to one of the elders in Nwangong Fondom in Ambazonia, the sure short Ambatokish response would be *Na condition e make njanga e back e bend* (It is tough times that bent the shrimp's back). But then I quickly realize that this does not quite explicate things. Because that short elderly bangwalangwalistic reply can also mean that the shrimp had been doing nothing and, consequently, tough times caused its back to bend. That is quite a very different thing from saying that the shrimp itself bent its back in order to counter or weather those menacing conditions. Just like Chinua Achebe's little bird, *nza*, justifying that it has learnt to fly without perching because men have learnt to shoot without missing. This book, as you must already have realized, finds a home more in the second than in the first category, especially in view of the double-sided matchet called *99-sensism*. Could this realization perhaps explain why I seem to have a destiny with *many*, including professions and academic qualifications? The *njanga*'s reasoning that would be behind all these numerous professions would obviously be unacceptable to anyone who finds his or her worth only in the type of job he or she does.

Papa was clearly not a farmer of circumstances but indeed a farmer at heart. Upcoming Ambazonia Administrators have to pay very close attention here. Ayabacholization has amply demonstrated in the Messages that Agriculture alone is capable of sustaining Ambazonia if properly handled, so that what is plentifully in our *basement* might not even have to be touched now, being cautiously preserved for future generations. Farming was simply a religion in the household, and my ability to practise it well has been an invaluable ingredient of success, most often almost overshadowing my non-inclusion within the meaning of 'child' or 'family'. Farming did not just back up my academic progress but actually charted the chequered course of my education, both positively and negatively. On the positive side, I was able to subdue the negative forces most probably because (unlike many others that spent time in it) I already had lucid objectives with which I defined myself on arriving in the household – thanks enormously to the Just Lecturer's imparted wisdom. My abilities regarding the household's religion thus quickly extended to also include an enhanced understanding of how to employ the farming-religion not only as a survival instrument, but also of how to easily use it sometimes to get even papa over when no one foresaw its being possible. That singular understanding may demonstrate how I could succeed not only in the household but also in situations where many people similarly placed just would not be able to figure a way out, like surviving as a moneyless foreign student in North America, Canada precisely.

Prayerful Thankyouology and Useful Lessons from Heaven's Njanga: Saluting Ambazonian 'Boyses in the Bushes'

Not waiting until things actually go wrong before turning around to blame heaven for not helping, is a virtue worth cultivating. And you also clearly see it (reflecting the *njanga* philosophy too) at work in my self-help initiatives communicated to my father in November 1995 (see Fossungu, 2015: 83-85). Mr Njanga, do the Hisofeans not hear you well enough? Deaths have at times seemed to almost overwhelm

Goodwillers. At the same time these sad events have not failed to engender and solidify the communal solidarity that Africans are well noted for. A visionary CGAM President aptly described all these things in his '*When It Rains, It Pours*' message (see Fossungu, 2015: 81). I think the most important reasons for such astounding coping capacity have to do with a couple of things, two of which are prayers and thankyouology. We all know the well-known idiom that *heaven helps those who help themselves*. Some people do not quite grasp the proper meaning of the slogan. Let's take a quick example relating to Ambazonia's Freedom that would also Properly Salute Ambazonian 'Boyses in the Bushes'. As 'the son of God' Anyefru has clearly made known, "The aim of the [numerous Ambazonian] petitions against the new state [of Cameroon] has been to draw the attention of the UN and the international community to the injustices inflicted upon minority English-speaking Cameroonians by the ruling government. The Anglophone elites believe that by making their plight known to the international community, the latter might intervene to restore the statehood of Southern Cameroon" (cited in Fossungu, 2013b: viii). Daydreamers these Force-of-Argumenters were! That is obviously coming from the AGovC and ADF, true believers of Heaven Helps Those Who Help Themselves! The Argument-of-Forcers! Yes, Multiples Of Twnty-One Gun-Salutes To You, Ambazonian 'Bosyses in the Bushes'! All that coming from Dishonourable Mbile with his confusioncratic Size-and-Numbers Independence Theory (see Fossungu, 2013b: 82)! Thank You Bushes' Boyses Endlessly For Shattering The Elitist Enslaving Myth!

As I said earlier, the self-help thesis is hardly grasped correctly by many nosifeans. But Bendrix Tabu broke the maxim down quite well on 25 March 2015 (see Fossungu, 2015: 81-82), indicating "that Jesus taught the people to give to Cesar what belongs to Cesar, so should we not obey the Canadian and

USA laws?" Yes Brother, even Campbell and Putnam (2012) would agree and confirm that "God and Caesar [are] in America", and delineating "Why Mixing Religion and Politics Is Bad for Both." This little exposition validates the well-known idioms of self-help and of foresight; with Papa (who embraces both) practising another religion called farming or handwork. I intensely remember him telling us on several occasions that schooling is good. But that it is best when backed by handwork. Yes, indeed, many of us might not have seen the validity of this thesis then. But I can easily vouch for papa's farsighted and zoomedeyed view. If you could profess this religion well, you were always welcome to the household. It was so much a religion that papa would certainly have refused his transfer and probably resigned if he were sent to a city like Tokyo or New York, where he could not find a farm to buy and cultivate. This Chapter harps on the importance of this 'religion' to staying and progressing in the household in particular but in life generally. I will first do so (1) through papa's transfers and my own forest and farm experience, before cementing with (2) three uncles that I would call *nyanga* man, yard boy, and driver, and (3) the market day revolution and learning opportunities in the household.

The Job Transfers and Farming/Forest Experience of the Multidimensional International Man

Papa's job transfers and farming could exquisitely account for why I seem to have a fortune with *many* (of almost everything). For instance, as I said earlier, most people go through primary school attending just one school. I attended at least three; also passing through three different secondary and high schools. Most others live all their life in one city and country. I can hardly give an accurate number of cities I have dwelled in, in four different countries and in two continents. These job-related transfers and farming could also partially account for

90

my somewhat 'unstable' love life in the early stages of my primary schooling. But they would here illustrate how firmly implanted the farming 'religion' had become. So, too, would be my own forest and farm experience, including my unique understanding of how to easily get even papa on my side using the religion (discussed later under the Market Day Revolution).

My father was being constantly transferred to different towns; and he always had farms in every city he lived in. But Yoke was actually the Farm Capital. On the second day of school in Catholic School, New Town (Victoria, Fakozone) we were rushed out of school because papa had been transferred to Yoke. I, therefore, spent less than two days in that school. Attending Presbyterian School Yoke until class three (second term unfinished), papa was again transferred to Kumba in Memezone. I was enrolled into Sacred Heart School (SHS) Fiango, Kumba, where I went until class six before papa was sent back to Victoria where I completed my primary education in the same school I had started it in. The transfers just kept coming.

Papa was even transferred to Douala (LRC) but he refused, hiding behind his not speaking French (or what Ambazonian Nationalists now deride as *Egyptian*). But I think the real reason might have been the belief that he might not find farmland in Douala, if we go by the usual 'over pepper and salt' stories of the "been to" people. We did not also move to Bamenda (aka 'The City of the Braves') in Mezamzone of Midlandzone. As there was no *Egyptian* cover, papa went alone: most probably because he found the cost of moving the entire family (with close to fourteen children then) from Bamenda to the Farm Capital for two weeks' work not worthwhile. Realizing he did not move his family to Bamenda as expected, Sonel quickly re-transferred him to Victoria, where we had still been officially based while papa was gone alone, though practically but in

Yoke during all holidays. Most people in the various other cities where we have lived (such as Victoria and Kumba) never really considered us as residents of those towns. As soon as holiday began, we were heading for Yoke in Muyuka the very next day and only came back 'home' about two or three days to resuming school.

If I say that I began working in the forest only in Canada (precisely with Aménagement MYR Inc. (MYR) in Dolbeau-Mistassini, Québec), then I would not only be undermining said religion but also not being truthful about the essential survival training my father gave me. In the forest in Canada, when you arrive for the first time, old or experienced workers (the *ancients*) have this tendency to frighten you with bear stories (see Fossungu, 2015a: chapter 2). These stories did not frighten me at all, thanks to papa's handwork. For one thing, our farms were mostly forests when papa bought them. This fact can be seen in the names given to some of the farms. One in Muyuka was called Black Bush and another Monkey Bush (in Yoke). Black Bush got its name because while in it you could hardly see the sky. It was almost as if it was night time in that farm by the time we started clearing and cultivating it. Monkey Bush was due to the great number of monkeys and others of the same 'family' that would be playing noisily from treetop to treetop while we are tilling the farm. Big Bush (in Yoke) was the largest of the farms; being also noted for the huge number of reptiles, rat-moles, and tarantulas that inhabited it. And what is more, we worked in those farms that were highly infested with more dangerous forest animals without much personal protective equipment like safety boots, helmets, gloves, etc.; and with cutlasses and hoes, not fast-cutting engine saws like the ones we use in the forest in Canada.

Some of the *ancients* thus came up to me with their bear tales and were amazed when I cut them short with my own probing. "Would you *ancients* be working in the same forest as *nouveaux* like us?" They said 'of course'. "Can these bears clearly distinguish an *ancient* from a *nouveau*?" They were stunned that I was not falling into their trap and so I continued: "What makes you think then that those bears would only come after me?" They left me alone, but I did not let them get away with it. The next morning in the bus that was taking us to the patches I reassured my fellow *nouveaux* with this free lecture (in French, since it is a French-speaking company in Québec that is infested with Africans from Burwanda, my preferred way of referring to those two mini-states that should normally be one):

Listen to me very carefully, guys. Those who see bears or other animals in the forest are those who want to see them. If you get into your patch and just bear in mind that you are there to do your work, the bear will obviously see you since you are actually visiting its place of abode. But it will be happy that you are there cleaning it and will just pass by unseen while you are busy with the cleaning. But if you get there and instead of doing your work you go nosing around for a bear, you will certainly see one. Because it will come to you, wondering why you are there and not working; and, with the sighting of a bear, it will be practically hard for you to work on that same patch, at least, not on that same day.

The Colourless Colour in MJ's Classroom with Paradoxical Self-Made Victim Idiotickerizing Africa

You would be told sometimes by Funnyman to go figure out what to come out as, being a Black who entered a Montreal-based company like Encore Automotive which is in town. But you are here in Quebec's vast forests where you may not even come out, whatever the colour of your skin that went in.

93

Remember that just as bears don't distinguish *nouveaux* from *anciens*, they wouldn't also make that difference between black and white. This Forest must certainly be where Michael Jackson (MJ) did his university programme! Thus, you hear him in one of his moving tracks singing that it doesn't matter whether you are black or white. 'Nice try, M. J., but really?' That is O. J. Simpson asking, not me. I remember the day the O. J. decision was handed down in 1995. I was at McGill University. This McGill expibasketism all over the place! I was really amused by the reaction of the large LLM class that had just three Blacks (a Kenyan gentleman called Hannigton Ukomu, a Nigerian lady in the person of Annastasia Gbem, and myself from Ambazonia, then under Cameroun occupation). The white students were all in complete shock that O. J. was found 'not guilty' as charged. Asked about what I thought of the verdict, I made it clear that I was rather surprised at their surprise because it clearly told me that, to them, there is justice only when a Blackman like me is unjustly condemned (George Floyd, is the knee not still on your neck?), not when he is justly discharged. One of them, a very pompous American, asked what I meant and I stated: "It seems to me that because O. J. has been found 'not guilty' you no longer have trust or faith in your justice system that is considered the world over as the most robust. Or am I wrong?" He merely walked away without another word. Hypocritical white people, you would say? Don't jump-start the group stereotyping thing or anything like it.

Figure #16: McGill University LLM class 1995/96
Source: Institute of Air & Space Law (IASL)

But what is this colourless colour thing all about? Who then is even this coloured person? I am wondering here because we hear so much talk about "the rights of people of color" (Crehan, 2013: 67) and "an elderly man in a wheel-chair with someone who appears to be his son and a woman of color with her two small children" (Crehan, 2013: 67). Colour down, without colour up! What is going on? Is white not a colour? Are there even white people? This question may seem extraordinary but I must ask it because the only time many of us see white people is when they are in their Ku Klux Klan attire. But then it is the outfit that is white, not the one putting it on. Have you ever thought of that? Do most homosexuals not emulate this *Ku Klux* Kla*n*-*Dubious Logic (KKK-DL)*? That is, homosexual in hiding and heterosexual in public. Leave McGill's classroom now to the MYR forest programme.

There was a day during the 2011 season that a Zairian insisted on breaking the law by travelling in the baggage compartment of the pick-up truck, boldly and happily justifying that "In Africa we travel in parts of vehicles worse than this." Wow!!! Funnyman was completely flabbergasted when he immediately retorted that "*Ton Afrique là n'est pas l'Afrique que je connais!*" ('That Africa of yours is not the Africa I am used to!' See also Chapter 6 below: exposing my wonders in Nigeria.) Nevertheless, the inhabitants of the 'different Africa' were all scrambling for a hang-on position in the passenger-prohibited section of the vehicle that is solely meant for the machines and flammable fuel, etc. Why? First, they want to start working early to make the money, according to them. Come to think about how much they are even paid for the dangerous job! Second, now that Zaire has short-sightedly made the dangerous rule, even those who do not care so much about early start (or the many *tankés*) still have to climb on. If you don't, just know that no one is then coming back for you as was the case before. It is now also habitual for the machines and fuel to be transported in the Forest School Bus because there is no 'camion' available. It is the Africans themselves justifying here too. What they do not see is how they are, for example, putting both (a) their safety on the line (see Fossungu (2015a: 143-47) and (b) more money into the pocket of the MYR owner, thus reinforcing the *Whites Getting Richer and Richer while Blacks Poorer and Poorer* situation. I have largely used this issue to illustrate how we Africans are really 'Paradoxical Self-Made Victims. Let me exemplify it briefly here with the hang-on rule. Before the Zairian Hang-on Rule, the pick-up had to make about four 'to-and-fro' trips which have now been reduced to one one-way trip. Leaving out wear-and-tear, etc., the cost of fuel (or *gas* as it is known in North America) alone for the other three abolished round trips would stay in the white owner's pocket (see Fossungu (2015a: 147-48).

I very quickly realized, on first encounter, that fighting for general and collective rights in MYR was not worth my time and effort. Is there any need for any general to lead a war knowing full well that the supposed soldiers are the ones to shoot him/her from behind? That is exactly what happened to Bertrand-Raymond Mabo, a Camerounese and accounting student at the Université de Montréal at the time; with another Camerounese who calls him 'my brother' all over the place taking the lead (see Fossungu, 2015a: 149). Camerounese and backstabbing! Make it AFRICANS, please! Say *The Drinking Water Tale and the Nouveaux Theses* (see Fossungu, 2015a: 148-52). During the first meeting with the MYR management in 2010, I complained seriously about our drinking water. It was really what Ambazonians would call *wata-rain* (running water in gutters from rainfall). Before the MYR proprietor could respond, the bear-audacious *grand coupeur* from Guinea advised him not to worry about these *nouveaux* who complain too much, adding that "This water is a lot safer than the one we have in Africa and some of us [the *ancients*, that is] have been drinking this water for over six years and it has not killed us." Diallo means in effect that if I and others like me cannot drink the mess in the forest, we should take off to town. Until that particular day, I often held Guineans in very high esteem from the mere fact that Ahmed Sékou Touré (like Captain Ibrahim Traoré of BKF) was a well-known '*qui-a-osé*' defender of human dignity. I have since learnt to evaluate every Guinean on their particular merit since it is now too apparent that Touré fought in vain. His legacy in Guinea is a sham, judging from comportment as (its current president's – Colonel Mamady Doumbouya's – and) Diallo's here. How can any group succeed without unity or cohesion? Bravo therefore to the Sahel Axis (BKF-MAL-NIG) for the cohesion and for Ambazonianly kicking the asses of the western bullies and their ECOWAS puppets.

Guineans are not the only problem in MYR because Bami-X, another conspicuous *ancient* from LRC, seconded Diallo's water-theory by asking to know when *nouveaux* like me even had the right to talk in a meeting. Yeah! Francophone Africa and this over belief in *ancienité* or longevity of *unservice* in public service! Sure reason/explanation why 92-year-old senile Paul Biya must continue being their president even in his grave! In short, empty titles! So, where would the pioneers ever come from? They even make it look as if an *ancient* was never a *nouveau* in all of his/her useless life!

Hear the same Diallu again in the matter of dangerous patches pricing. In 2011 we were assigned to a sector with patches that were very tough to do. The $500.00/hectare price was not good enough and another brave Camerounese called Jules-Raymond led the fight for a better price of $700.00/hectare. The ensuing sit-in was something the MYR management could not easily play off. The owner (through his father who was permanently in the Camp) accepted the new price. Guys were back into working and working with joy. But that success of the group as a whole was not something Diallo could live with. Like Pastors Chris Anu and Samuel Ikome Sako in their CDC Deals with LRC (see Fossungu, 2023), Diallo therefore secretly contacted the owner's father and gave the management ideas on how to play down the $700.00 price on the basis that the father had no authority from the son when he asked us to do the job at that price, with the original price of $500.00 being what Mario Richard ended up paying! "Since I am not writing a law textbook here, I will simply leave the legal and other experts to wonder if the parties here even know of binding oral contracts and the rules of agency and of vicarious liability" (Fossungu, 2023: 184). It was only after another malaise that took hold of the Camp that the secret patch-selling plot was divulged like Pastor Anu himself did to Mimimefo. During the argument that arose, with fingers being pointed at the old man,

Mario's father publicly made known how it was Diallo who had engineered the reneging of the $700.00 agreement because paying the $700.00/hectare would not have facilitated his selling of many patches to *nouveaux* especially.

Africans and egoism, Pastors Sako Ikome and Christopher Anu in the CDC Deals, when are we ever going to stop this? Yet, we go around singing white exploitation of the black! Who was actually exploiting who here? Ayabacholize them a bit, please. You find the same manipulative trend with the traitors of now that have been heavily responsible for Ambazonian liberators having had to lose a lot of momentum and lives in their bold and innovative struggle to be free and free and unite Africa. At the very heart of it all is the IG-Care of Sisiko Julius Ayuk Tabe that Dr Ayaba calls "one of the most stupid organizations I have ever seen in the world". His reasons for saying so go to the very essence of traitor studies, being embedded in his eight-minute "rare message to our friends of the IG-Care" that was delivered on Wednesday, 20 December 2021:

Now, let the IG-Care know the following. Dr Samuel Sako is their creation. The divisiveness in this struggle is not that of the Sakos. The Sakos are a beneficiary of the divisiveness created by the IG-Care. The solemn desire to hijack a multiparty platform and use foreign troops to throw out participants and install yourself as president of our country and go on a rampage on everyone else who opposed it, is the foundation of the division that we have today. So many were hurt, disenfranchised. You see Pa Nfor? You see Tasang? They are victims of an entitlement-leadership. They don't love Sako. The Sakos are a fallback to them. Their vote for Sako is not really for the Sakos. It is a vote against the leadership of the IG-Care. You see all those morons who have fallen into the hands of La République du Cameroun? They have been pushed into the arms of the enemy by the entitlement politics of the IG-Care and leadership (Ayaba: 2021c, paragraph 7).

Figure #17: Sisiko Julius Ayuk Tabe, President of IG-Care
Source: IG-Care

Figure #18: Dr Samuel Sako Ikome, President of PIG (Pastors'
Interim Government)
Source: PIG

My first season with MYR would also speak volumes not only in regard of the farming experience but also in connection with knowing what I was up to and up against. After about a week or two cutting trees, I was at the centre of the talk of the Camp. There were, of course, other newcomers that equally excelled but my case was outstanding for some reasons. Knowing that I was not only a university graduate with a doctorate degree but also a university lecturer, many had given me just the first day before they were to see me packing and leaving. Even the guy (Alain Tchato) who had taken me along explained later that he did not just know how to refuse bringing me along (like many had done before him). This is especially as I had been very helpful to him when he had arrived in Canada, not knowing what was in store for him in the country. That he was not at all sure I was going to cope with the task. But he would still have done his part by taking me along as I wanted.

My first patch of almost three hectares was between those of two *grands coupeurs* from Cameroun who had patches of almost the same dimension. They had been talking among themselves in Bamileke that they did not know I somewhat understood. To them, I was to spend not less than two weeks there after they would have been long gone. As these *grands coupeurs* advanced, they kept looking back to see how far behind they must have left me. But they realized I was always on their heels. Unbelievable for a newcomer, they later told other West African *grands coupeurs* from Guinea and Mali who were not present to "*chop* Christmas with their own eyes." The one on my left (the guy that had brought me along) finished on the sixth day and I completed on the seventh day, about an hour before the one on my right whom I aided for those sixty minutes. The news spread around like wildfire in the MYR Camp. Like in the academic world, anything I enter into doing has to be excellently done.

101

Because of the frightening bear stories from the *ancients*, a lot of the *nouveaux* are forced to take to working in pairs. This is usually also a big distraction as most of the day is spent talking to, or checking on, each other. The bulk of those who have actually encountered bears have done so while they were not busy working, or had brought along some foodstuff that attracted their attention. The truth is that most of these stories are narrated by the *ancients* for obvious reasons. The most important is that you will spend most of your time being afraid of bears. Consequently, by the end of the season (about four to five months) you will badly need to "buy" a lot of patches from them so as to be able to meet the minimum amount required for full unemployment benefits (insurance) for the non-season months. It is thus a business strategy for the *ancients*. A lecture like the one I gave in the bus does not sit well with these *ancients* since it lets their potential clients know what they are up against – very unlike many of my nose-poking neighbours of the patches I have had to work on.

Some of these nose-pokers were clearly not able to comprehend how I go about it with so many stops of the machine and concomitant "schooling" in the forest. That is, doing two jobs in one and yet I did not: first, have accidents and, second, end up at the end of the season "buying patches". It all boils down to knowing yourself and not unrewardingly trying to be someone else. There are many known cases of workers who would not even stop their machines in order to eat a sandwich or an apple simply because they continuously hear the neighbour's machine going almost all-day. They thus behave as if they are in some sort of Tree-Cutting Olympic Game. Or, as if the neighbour would have cut all the vast forest before they could complete their particular patch, if they took a break. And, most often, they end up taking more than just a few minutes break, and not in the forest's forest but in the town forest called hospital.

Several people do not have more than one "career" in their life but I have had so *many* that I find it hard to sometimes describe myself with any one of them: Lecturer-in-law; warehouse clerk; tutor; taxi driver; library clerk; writer, office messenger; student; production line worker; author, *débroussailleur;* research assistant; *préposé aux bénéficiares;* farmer; general hand; night watchman; teacher; construction worker; and independent researcher. None of these 'professions' has provided the most incentive and immediate ingredients for the writing of this book (and others) as that of *débroussailleur.* The advantages associated with this job are many, but a few stand out. First, there is the freedom; second, the time; and third, the reflection potentials of the forest. Freedom entails the fact of being practically your own boss. You decide when and how to work without, for instance, the *yala-yala* yelling from supervisors and other heads associated with factory and other jobs in town. All this derives from the forest remuneration style that is based on piecework rather than timework. By the time benefit I am not just referring to the off-season months. I include the ability as well to create or take time off work and do something else, such as developing an idea that has struck you, or to just relax without having to ask permission from anyone. Time and freedom thus intertwine here to give impetus to the third reason.

As I once told my girlfriend in school in Kumba, I have what a brother would call a magnetic *ekapoulapon* (brain). But I could very vividly remember most of the things that took place many decades ago not only on that score. I have found the forest to be an ideal place for reflection and development of my own proper ideas. And this began since working on the farms in Yoke, the Farm Capital. The sole difference is just that in the

103

Yoke case there is too much room for interruption of thought since we work very close together, very unlike the other forest where (but for the machine noise) you might not even realize that you are not alone there. The first season was solely for focusing on sufficiently grasping the techniques of the job. While working in the forest in Canada for the second and third seasons I was able to relive, in a unique way, the events in my head, grasping all the details of some of the conversations and facts herein included. All these were happening while the tree-cutting was going on – thanks enormously to the Ritaian crisebacology developed long ago in the Kumba primary school. I sometimes stopped the machine just to be able to jot down the details before they could vanish by way of ceding place to more behind them waiting for their turn to resurface. All these occurring, thanks also to my quick grasping and positive employment of papa's "handwork" – very unlike many of papa's relations that flocked to the household but could either not profess its religion (like the *nyanga* man and yard boy) or did it so profusely well (like the driver) and yet could not be 'ordained' as expected.

The Driver, Nyanga Man and Yard Boy: Posteuring Nicknamization Driving the Muhicosy Big Mamie Trouble through the Land Rover Affair

I am sure papa got his farming practice and philosophy from his own father, Fon ST Fossungu. This fact can be picked up from Aunty Tumekong who babysat me. She was very proud of me when I was leaving the village because it is often said there that if the child you babysit is going places you also are going places. She too had come the day before to say goodbye and here is one of her pieces of advice to me: "My junior brother, you are very lucky because your chances of studying without interruption are great. Do not play with that. We here in the village cannot study in that way because of farm work

104

over which the Fon does not joke. He is right though because, without the coffee and cocoa, how could he be able to send so many of us to school? Please, don't forget all what I have been telling you over the years." Aunty Tumekong was right (although quite wrong about farming practice and philosophy in *ncheng*, like most of those rushing to the household?). While still in the Emollah Palace, I used to witness a lot of what Fon ST Fossungu did to any of the farm-going age children he found at home while others were on the coffee farms, such as *nyanga* man and mates.

Figure #19: Momany & Aunty Constance Tumekong
Fossungu in May 2023 in Douala, Cameroun
Source: Photo taken by Mr. Paul Nkengafac

Father Joe, the Nyanga Man

There are usually a lot of children in the palaces that some Fons do not have an idea of the exact number. But that is not true of my grandpa. He not only knew every child by name. He also knew who it was, just from their voices, including grandchildren like me – Ateh-Afac. In the village that is the way one is called, not by the first name like Peter (except to distinguish from another Ateh-Afac) and never by the family name, Fossungu, that usually designates the Fon. I vividly recall this incident when four big boys were at home rather than on the coffe and cocoa farms and heard grandpa coming. Three of them managed to escape, one being badly caught by grandpa's baton. The fourth, Uncle Joseph Efemlefo Fossungu (later Chief Fosanoh), had thought he was very sage by quickly climbing on and hiding in the barn. To his surprise, grandpa stood at the door and yelled: "Efemlefo, come down and get your punishment. I have always known that you have nothing in that coconut of yours that you call head. Otherwise, you will not be acting like the stupid rat that ran into a bottle to escape from the cat. Come down by yourself or I'll bring you down myself, animal!" Before showing himself up, grandpa must have listened for a while to them talking and laughing and thus knew (without even seeing them) who and how many they were.

It is a sure guess that I quickly learnt *posteuring* from this uncle. 'Father Joe' is the way Uncle Efemlefo insisted on being called when he came to live in the household in Yoke. He was clearly not the farm type but more of the showbiz guy. Back from the farm (when he went at all), 'Father Joe' would spend so much time bathing. To scrub off anything that has to do with the farm from his body, he would often justify. The time thereafter in front of the mirror dressing in complete white (did he really want to be a priest or father?) would be about thrice as long. He would take many and different *posteurs* as he went about it, while also self-congratulating the other guy in the mirror at every new positional style taken. When all that would be over, spanning some hours, it would then be time for the sprinting walk around the house in order to select the best moves (or *lancer*) for the evening. (*'Lancer'*, no doubt, is my other nickname that is very popular with Sasse College and Limbe/Muyuka friends.) Where Father Joe used to dress up like that to go to, no one else really knew. In short, it was not long before Father Joe relocated to Douala (Cameroun's Toronto or Hollywood). He was a confirmed *nyanga man* or what the French call *viveur* and, clearly, had no place in a household where the farming that he despised so much was such a religion. Neither could there be a place in it for someone with the 'tree-top' mentality like the yard boy.

Treetopping Nicknamationism
Nicknamationsim is the science of nicknames-giving. Uncle Linus Anamoh Fossungu (Uncle Anamoh) studied in National High School in Kumba and came to live in the household in Yoke. He was so full of himself and evidently lazy, by the household religion's definition. I would say he is in the class of people that put their pride in front of their reasoning. I say this because when you let what you want to accomplish in life define you, and not what you do for a living, you will quickly understand that it is not what you do for a living that gives you your worth. Once you know your worth, you will do whatever you need to do to move on in life and realise your goals. For example, papa secured Uncle Anamoh a job in Powercam as a yard boy. But this uncle saw this as insulting for a secondary school *diplomé* like himself, who should instead be working in an office. He exchanged bitter words with papa and thereafter very angrily left the household. Of course, if papa was like the others, he could have used his position in Powercam to secure the so-called office job that Uncle Anamoh wanted. But I am sure yard boy was the available advertised job, and that papa wanted Uncle Anamoh to get in and earn his exalted position by himself, through climbing through the echelon. You clearly get this impression from papa's description of Uncle Anamoh

107

as someone who "wants to be on the top of the tree without climbing through its trunk." I will illustrate this descriptive prophecy further by recalling the 'Book of Life' event in 1985 that is centred on a lady's life-saving services.

Papa was very upright and endowed with wisdom that sometimes bordered wit and prophetic sarcasm. In 1985 papa had a ghastly (motorcycle/car) accident in Victoria on his way to work. This occurrence almost ended his life. Madam Catherine who was then his *njumba* or mistress (he later married her officially) came from Yoke to take care of him in the Victoria General Hospital where he had been almost abandoned to die. Meanwhile, his wife, Mamie Thecla, was busy mocking and telling Madam Catherine that she was working for nothing. As my mother put it, *monkey dey work bamboo dey chop*, because she (Mamie Thecla) had all the keys to the cupboards and documents and would be the one to access the money and properties when papa will die. Learning of this incident when he had miraculously recovered consciousness, papa wondered if Mamie Thecla had already read *The Book of Life and Death* to have known that he was to die before her. As if he was prophesising (or accurately death-theorizing), my mother died in April 1998, about four years before my father.

Papa could also have been prophetically right about Uncle Anamoh. This uncle later attempted running a university-like institution called CADA (Cameroon Academy of Design and Arts) without capital. I am not very sure I still get the full name of the Academy right. But the acronym was rightly CADA. Uncle Anamoh is the sweetest talker of the entire Fossungu Royal Family. He recruited young college graduates who worked for him round the clock without pay and sleeping on hard floors, always believing in his sweet assurances that money and the good days were just a stone-throw away and coming faster than they could imagine. He almost succeeded, as the story goes, in giving away a lot of the Fossungu clan to *nyongo* or *famla* in his bid to acquire his capital. Capital is the one last thing that was then lacking to have CADA going fully operational. I am sure that Uncle Anamoh (like many others that lived in the household) did not quite know what gives him his worth. If he did, he would have used his natural ability to talk papa into helping him out with the money at that stage. Could this possibility have crossed his mind but his having ruptured links with papa stood stiffly in the way?

Most probably, it is; because papa is that kind of person that would always spring back to help anyone who has proven him wrong or confirmed that he or she can do a thing on his or her own. My whole life would exemplify the point. But a very banal example would make the case right here that papa makes errors like every human being. If you understand him and do not get bitter with him, he will very openly admit his mistake and make amends. No one practically taught me how to ride a bicycle or motorcycle; not even how to drive a car. I did all those by myself, from merely intelligently watching others doing them. Papa had this habit of always attending 'First Mass' on Sunday. While he took his bath and prepared (got dressed, took breakfast), I was charged with getting his Suzuki out and cleaning it, even as it was hardly ever dirty. I usually did so fast enough and went riding for a while and getting back before papa came out to go. One day I miscalculated my ride and by the time I was back papa had waited for quite a while. Evidently crossed, papa stated that he who had bought the motorcycle had not even mastered it as much as I seemed to have. "Now my question to you is: Tell me when you will buy yours! When and how are you going to purchase yours? Is this not how you children of today start thinking of getting into money-getting cults?" But some months later there was a medical emergency requiring rushing to the pharmacy in the main town of Muyuka. Taxis being as irregular as they were in

Yoke, I made speedy use of the Suzuki and saved the day. "Pee," papa immediately admitted when I returned, "I was wrong indeed for scolding you for having learnt how to ride this machine so well. Good Gracious! Just see what would otherwise have happened!"

There are as well other cases in connection with both Uncle Ngufor and myself. After the Land Rover Mess with Uncle Ngufor (discussed below), papa later bought a bus for him while he was in Douala struggling on his own. Having dropped me (as seen in Chapter 6 below), he also came back to supporting my studies in the UNIYAO after I had struggled on my own (going as far as Sokoto state in Nigeria) and informed him in 1984 after my return and stay in Manjo that I was entering the UNIYAO. Both of us never ruptured relationship nor became bitter with him. Uncle Anamoh's problem then could be that his pride ruled his reason rather than the other way round. Thus, we hear of the story of his "mortgaging" people in the family to *nyongo*. In this infamous enterprise, Uncle Ntimah and wife were top of the list as Uncle Anamoh's father and mother, respectively. When Uncle Ngufor was told that he too was part of the list, he merely laughed and retorted: "Since when did wizards and witches begin to eat bitter meat?" He was obviously alluding to the story or belief that *nyongo* does not accept a person you offer them unless you and that person are close enough and see eye to eye. This was clearly the contrary between these two uncles of mine, both of whom lived in the household at different times and towns – Uncle Anamoh first in Yoke before Uncle Ngufor in Kumba (see Fossungu, 2023: 84).

Uncle Anamoh had a huge problem with nicknames, sobriquets that almost everyone in the household had. Joseph was very good at nicknaming people and for creating unique vocabularies and descriptions. I remember him calling

Awandem (who once came to live with us in Yoke) *Dakilo*. This nickname soon became so entrenched that I found myself also using it at times. Awandem is clearly not dark in complexion, being fairer than most of us. This makes it hard to see how he could even come close to a Darky (a nickname usually reserved for very dark-complexioned people). This is very unlike my own *Leaky-Leaky Neck* nickname from Joseph that ties in with some scars on my neck that often send out pus. The two boys usually used this particular nickname chiefly when they wanted to make me really mad. But finding that it often did not produce the intended effect, they once teamed up to beat me up. Recalling my grandpa's famous story about the tiger's hunting tactics of going straight for the prey's immobilizing spot, I successively landed a demoralizing blow on each of them, not giving any opportunity for both of them to attack at the same time. The nickname itself seemed to have died with that lost battle. Decisively making sure that they lost this particular fight was critical because, otherwise, I would have become another Julie to them, and not also being able to defend Julie.

Of course, Joseph was not the only 'nickname giver' in the household. Uncle Anamoh obviously did not like Therese for the nickname she had given him. In Yoke papa was one of two workers that had the company's phones at home, and he had the habit of calling home from work to give some instructions from to time to time. With the multiple arrivals of many uncles and aunts, the status of Bangwa in the household obviously changed (as compared to when I had arrived in the household in Victoria). Most of the newly arrived – although also speaking "good English" – held the mother tongue in high esteem. And since they constituted the majority by then and proudly used Bangwa, those children of the household that did not speak and understand it found themselves at a disadvantage. They earnestly began seeking to at least understand it, in order (as it

111

is often said in Nwangong) "not to be sold in their own presence". One of papa's calls came and it was Uncle Anamoh that picked up the home phone. Papa demanded in Bangwa to know who it was and he said "Me" (*meng*). You who, papa asked, and he again said "Me." Papa was obviously very crossed when he shrieked "You Who?", to which Uncle Anamoh responded: "Me, me, Fo [Chief] Linus." Hence, Therese who was then present gave his nickname in Bangwa, *Meng-Meng Folinus*.

I do not know if Joseph also actually gave Bernard the nickname *Coastman* or Bernard himself adopted it. *Coastman* means someone who was born and bred in the city and has never been to the village. This nickname has often made me to wonder if little babies hear and understand us more than we do to them, a concern deriving from my first journey in life. The trip from Nwangong to Victoria had been so tiring not just because it was my first. It was not straight and, looking back, I have the feeling that we took more than a week to reach destination. We stopped and stayed in several homes in the Dschang area alone (my mother's mother is Dschang); as well as in Kumba and in Muyuka (at my mother's parents' home). Perhaps the journey was that long not just because it was my first. The one up north was not the first (see Chapter 6), but equally long and tiring. It could, therefore, be simply that journeys are often long when they are leading you not only to places you have never been, but also to the unknown. At every home we had arrived my first and sometimes only question had always been "Where is papa *ncheng?*" I guess it had become my way of finding out if we had reached Victoria. There are many other things I would have liked then to also find out, including this strange dream of flying without wings that became so recurrent in one of those Dschang homes that I could almost no longer regard it as a dream. Maybe all the strange things I

112

witnessed in the Dschang homes were just tied to being out of my comfort zone (the village) for the first time?

I particularly remember being left all alone for endless hours with the baby at what must have been a motor park in Dschang. So many wild thoughts had crossed my mind. Have I been brought out of the village to be abandoned here where I know no one? Only the baby's presence reassured me that, come what may, Mamie Thecla was going to come back. But then what was I to do if the baby started to cry? Of course, I had been taking care of Dieudonné and other younger children in the village. But this was a coast (*ncheng*) baby and the caring method could obviously not be identical. For example, could I chew hard food and then transfer to this coast baby's mouth for him to swallow as it was/is usually done in the village? Are these not the kinds of things Mamie Thecla should have been teaching me during the three days at Mamie Cecilia's? Was she just hiding and watching to see what I would do to her baby?

As if hearing my thoughts, little Bernard broke out crying so loud that I had almost dropped him from the startle. This *coast* baby in my hands had cried for a long while, with me not knowing what and how to do in order to calm him. A kind-hearted lady came by and, because I did not quite understand the French language through which she was asking questions, searched through one of the luggage and found his feeding bottle. She then asked for the baby, and I was afraid to give him to her. But did I really have a choice? While she fed the *coast* baby, I was wondering what could have happened and might happen next. I had so many upsetting experiences on that never ending journey to Victoria, but this *coast* baby incident was the least tormenting; making me wonder till date if Bernard had actually comprehended what had taken place in Dschang when he adopted (if he did so himself) the *coastman* nickname. This nickname has often made me wonder if little babies hear and understand us more than we do to them.

Whatever the case, what is obvious is that 'Meng-Meng Folinus' was very unlike the driver who practised the religion of the household extremely well but could still not be anointed as largely expected.

The Straightforward Outspoken Super Intelligent Driver

Arriving in the household (like several others) in search of greener pastures, Uncle Ngufor was very hard-working especially on the farm. His stay was much longer than most others'. As I said earlier, if anyone can practise the religion of the household as well as Uncle Ngufor, his or her staying power is enhanced, notwithstanding the invited *Big Mamie Trouble* (to be explained shortly). In this case the negative forces would concentrate on working against your progress and not your presence. Uncle Ngufor was the only relation that showed insatiable interest in the academic progress of the children of the household as well as in his own self-growth. He was very gifted. I say this for a lot of reasons, a few of which are stated here. First, I remember how he (not having been to secondary school) used to write to me while I was in Sasse College. Whenever I got this uncle's letters I and my friends would have to gather around with our dictionaries to be able to comprehend Uncle Ngufor's language (the style and big terms he used). We marvelled as well at the beauty of his handwriting. Sasse College, it must be noted, is like the Harvard or Oxford of colleges in Ambazonia. Second, I do not know when and where Uncle Ngufor ever took French classes to be able to not only communicate in but also write French perfectly. I guess that must have been the edge he had with easily picking up the driver and do-all job with the Nigerian businessman, owner of Ets. Echo Automobile in Douala and Kumba, after the disillusionment he got from papa.

I am very positive this uncle would have been an ideal mentor to all the children of the household had he been sent to college. He got to the household in the early 1970s while we were in Kumba, with all of us still in primary school. All that this uncle was given was the opportunity to learn driving, which he embraced with an open and grateful mind. I kind of "knew" a lot about the art of driving at that time and age without having formally learned it. Uncle Ngufor is simply the kind that loves to spread his knowledge around through demonstrations and recitations; and this even during my days in the village. Uncle Ngufor excelled in his driving course and graduated as one of the tops in his batch. He was the one nut every taxi owner and other transporters in town were looking for. He preferred nonetheless to stick to papa's promise of buying him a car of his own. Who would want to work for someone else when s/he can be her/his own boss? The materialization of that promise took so long but Uncle Ngufor was patient, working as hard as ever alone in Yoke while we were in school, with the rest of us only joining him during holidays. His friends from the driving school who were then plying the Kumba-Victoria Road (that cuts through Yoke-Muyuka) would sometimes recognize him on the road behind a well loaded truck of farm products. They would stop for a while to ask him why he was wasting his time on the farm in Yoke when he should instead be doing what they were doing. After the wait for several years and numerous missed opportunities out there, the bombshell fell one day. Papa announced to Uncle Ngufor that an old land rover car had been bought for him at an auction by Sonel (papa's employer).

One other thing I admire so much in Uncle Ngufor is his frankness and outspokenness. It is important to know that, in the Fossungu Royal Family, Uncle Ngufor also stands out as one of the few who have actually admitted and explained themselves when they could not stay in contact as expected.

115

Take for example the 2-wives-man's 1996 letter to me (see Fossungu, 2016: 144-45). These qualities of his are evidenced also by what we mockingly referred to as the *Muyuka High Court System (muhicosy)*. When we moved from the Yoke Powercam Camp to Kumba and came back to work on the farms in Yoke and Muyuka during holidays, we used to stay in Muyuka at my mother's parents' home in Strangers Quarter. It became habitual on Friday evenings for my mother, mother's mother, and mother's grandmother (The Prosecution) to put us, one by one, in front of The Judge (papa), demanding for punishment (without defence) for any minute or irrelevant thing that we might have done during the week. It is quite a lengthy tale but just cut it short by saying that it was truly a harrowing exercise to both Accused and the Judge. Imagine papa, for instance, having left work that evening, rode his Suzuki all the way from Kumba (or Victoria) to Muyuka. It is about 50 kilometres. But double or triple it because of the nature of the road and papa's go-it-slowly way of riding. Instead of resting on arrival, papa would sit there for hours on end 'judging' this and that until sometime past midnight. He would then continue his ride to Yoke, where he would barely have slept before it was morning and time to be on the farm all day. All this must have led papa to find a way to put an end to it by redesigning his house in Yoke after the bar that was being operated there closed. We thereafter started staying there instead, when we came for farm work, thus avoiding the *muhicosy* thing.

As one of the notorious accused (Akana and I being the others) in the *muhicosy*, Uncle Ngufor, in always insisting on and actually defending us and himself, might have been inviting more than *Big Mamie Trouble* for himself. I actually coined *Big Mamie Trouble* from the *muhicosy* because of the following factors. When it initially began (before Uncle Ngufor's arrival), Akana and I had tried explaining to the Judge that what the

116

Prosecution was saying was not correct. (And they used to inflate or invent the charges a lot.) Papa's question then was often "Are you Angel Gabriel to think that I would take your word against those of three people?" Stunning, isn't it? My clock-ticking head went to work, turning this over, and applying the arithmetic that I then mastered. I eventually came out with this: If the Judge should one day realize that I am not an angel, let alone Angel Gabriel, and decide to look for the mean of the Prosecution (Mamie +Big Mamie + Big Big Mamie), he would still end up with Big Mamie. This was, of course, still a lot of trouble in the *muhicosy*; hence, *Big Mamie Trouble*. Was Uncle Ngufor conversant with the *Big Mamie Trouble* concept but simply ignored it because of his headiness when it comes to doing things the way they ought to be done? Whatever the case, this uncle also did not mince his words regarding the Land Rover Affair. He told papa there and then that he was going to have nothing to do with that land rover vehicle because it was not an auctioned car papa should have bought in the first place. That the vehicle was surely going to turn him into an evil person and put a strain on their good relationship since it was to be a sure regular patient to the hospital called garage. As later events showed, Uncle Ngufor was right. Papa himself even celebrated when he eventually practically gave that car away for free. Having thus realized his error, papa went into a business deal with Uncle Ngufor some years later, culminating in the purchase of a bus for transportation that you find in Figure #20 in the village, intended for blessings before 'Let Me Try' (as Uncle Ngufor was known on the Douala-Edea highway) could hit the road with it. All this occurred (notwithstanding Uncle Ngufor's tied hands in the business: see Fossungu, 2016: 109-110) because reasoning, not fighting and bitterness, was the tool Uncle Ngufor employed. This is the same strategy I later also used in the market day revolution – an uprising that was badly needed to get a working-day off the household's farming religion.

Figure #20: Fon DF Fossungu & Chief Formbuehndia in front
of the new bus in the village, with Uncle Ngufor at the door
next to Bernard
Source: Photo taken by Momany Fossungu

The Market Day Revolution: Education and Learning from First Nickname in Household

Papa's "handwork" was such a creed in the household that only Sunday (put aside for the other widely known religion) provided the only day off in the week during holidays. Farming was sacred in the household so much so that if there was anything you wanted from papa and you were not sure to get him on your side, it was better to wait until after a good day's work on the farm. He loved hard work not only in school but as well at home and on the farm. I guess my fulfilling all three spheres could be regarded as my "magic portion" for progressing in the household against all the odds. But even the camel needs a drink of water in the waterless desert to be able to get the load on its back across the same. There came a time that I, for one, actually wanted a day off the week. Wednesday is the Yoke Market Day and was the target. The Market Day Revolution had to take place. None of my brothers and sisters thought the day-off thing would ever work with dad (who was so feared by them). I told them to just watch me as I make the 'fight-less' revolution.

As already noted, my father worked in Victoria (also called Limbe) but he always came up to Yoke on Friday evening, riding on his motorcycle, to farm on Saturday before returning on Sunday. One Saturday then, after a hard day's chores on the farm, I explained to him during our 'food break' right there on the farm that we needed to be having the market day off so as to aid our mother with cooking and other market exigencies. Moreover, I added, Wednesday is in the middle of the work week and a perfect day on which to rest and be reinvigorated for the three remaining farming days. Papa did not particularly like the idea. But he could not also see how to condemn it. Especially as it was proposed right there on the farm, with the day's heavy half-day output still very much lightening his heart. He, therefore, put it in the hands of our mother. "Tee" (for that is the way he called his wife, Thecla), "what do you think about Peter's suggestion?" Obviously, papa was hoping that our mother would say she did not need the help. My siblings were amazed that it had even received this reaction, not outright rejection. But I knew it had already won. Evidently, my mother was deeply in love with her drinking and this proposal provided her with more time to be with it. The revolution had been successful especially because reasoning rather than fear was the leader.

Fear inhibits learning and dialogue. If you grew up with papa and, like me, you did not fear him, you would not only learn a lot from him; you also will hardly be afraid of other human beings. I will first talk a bit about not being frightened of others here, and the learning being discussed after. There is a foreman in the forest where I worked that almost everyone says is "racist" and the like. It happens that people are sometimes just afraid of others and have to find a reason to attach to their unfounded fear. Pascal Perron (the foreman or *contremaitre*) is simply strict like papa and many black Africans always see strict people (that they cannot corrupt or bend around at will) as wicked. Because Pascal is white, they rush to equate his strictness with racism. Because of this inhibition in their minds, it is thus hard for them to engage Pascal in any fruitful discourse. For instance, one time we began working in an area where the bus does not reach, and we had to be transported from the bus terminus to the patches by pick-up trucks. The first day I watched Pascal transporting five persons, with the folded sixth place near him unused, and with a lot of the Francophone African workers voluntarily hanging in the baggage compartment of the truck – the Zairian-Hang-On Rule which is even not allowed by regulation. The second day was the same story. On the third day, as Pascal was about going, I called out from inside the bus for him to wait. He stopped and I came out of the bus and reminded him that there was an empty place near him that I wanted to occupy. To everyone's surprise, Pascal smiled so broadly, removed his GPS and other belongings and unfolded the seat for me to occupy. From the fourth day on, that seat was never again empty. And it is not like I was the one always occupying it, even as it had been quickly nicknamed 'Peter's Seat'. It is clear that I could not have gotten papa or Pascal over if I too partook in the fear of him as the others.

First Nickname in Household and the Gay-Thinking Idiots

My first nickname in the household is *Peter-Tekam-Uhm* (shortened to PTU). It is a nickname that taught me a lot about women, learning, and the difference between fear and respect. When I had arrived Victoria, I spoke only the Bangwa language that was widely spoken then in the village; understanding neither English nor French, not even Pidgin or *Kamtok/Mbokotok* (see Ngefac, 2010). Bangwa that I could then speak was not spoken in the household and I was always chastised every time I spoke it. This strongly brought back many thoughts from the village to me. Everyone at home (except Josephine) was always making fun of me by talking in Pidgin (and rarely in English) that I did not comprehend and the only thing I usually would say was *uhm*? (My way of saying "what do you mean"?) Hence, the PTU nickname that only Josephine seemed not to be interested in pestering me with, a fact that quickly gained her my quiet admiration, the more so as we were almost the same age.

The PTU nickname was nothing to me. It was the beatings that traumatized me, and these began almost as soon as I had set feet in the household. Akana (my namesake's son) had especially conferred upon himself the right to hit hard on my head that I almost became dumb to avoid ever uttering a sound in their detested Bangwa language. But I guess several positive things also resulted from that 'negative'. First and foremost, it sent a quick message to my brain that it had better be fast in learning. It paid off as my head began ticking almost round the clock; a fact that could be responsible for explaining most of the other many nicknames that I later bore (such as Mr. English, Mr. First in Class, Pythagoras, Lord Denning, Power, Figaro Cinq, Professor, etc – some of which will be examined later on). It also paid off in the sense that, although I started school on the same day with both Joseph and Akana, Joseph obtained his secondary school diploma the same year I obtained my high school diploma and his high school diploma three years after mine.

The PTU thrashing aided me furthermore – and this is the biggest gain – to establish some sort of *direct-line* with papa whose nickname (that I did not understand) is indicative of the way papa was feared in the household. This fear of papa is clearly seen in the nickname that the older children particularly employed to signal to each other his presence or arrival. Papa's nickname, *EN*, is actually his first and middle names abbreviated. I initially never understood the signal, not speaking 'their' language then and often being 'caught' by the tiger (as they thought); it fortifying the story of my own first nickname. How? Unaware of the *EN* signal that sent the others into hiding, I often was the one papa 'caught'. This 'catching' coupled well with my always remembering my birth mother's last advice to me before I left the village. Mamie Regina had said that no matter how much I was disciplined (beaten) by papa I should always "run and enter only between his legs". The Tufiakwans are obviously thinking otherwise. Take this fastening case from my expibasketism relating to Edmonton, Alberta, to accomplish the requisite U-turn with *the Tufiakwans or Gay-Thinking Idiots* (see Fossungu, 2016: 72-73).

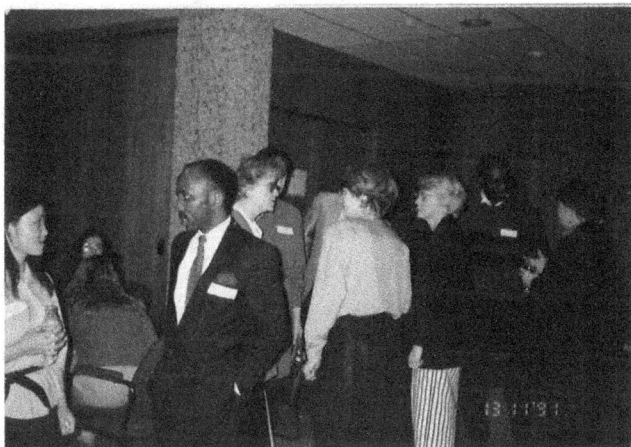

Figure #21: At Welcome-Party at the University of Alberta,
Edmonton, Canada in 1991
Source: Momany Fossungu's Album

The event in question occurred during the first party thrown at the University of Alberta to welcome us, new students (see Figure #21 above). Many of the East African male students were enjoying the party more than any other person or group, freely dancing together and even going *bal-à-terre* and *soukousing*; as well as doing the 'Haitian-dance' or *coller-coller* together. This is 1991, mark you; with most of the white guys not believing what they were witnessing. Openly gay guys at a time when even the likes of Elton John, Rossie O, Ellen D. (name the rest for me, please) had not even thought of leaving the closet! A bunch of them then approached the joyful Africans and demanded if they were 'gay'. The latter sonorously responded "Yeah!" Why not, these Africans must have been wondering how anyone would not even see how gay they were. Coming from the 99-Sense land with a lot of certificateless intellectuals like Mamie Regina, I quickly knew precisely what was happening and had to speedily intervene to calm down the 'gay-thinking idiots', telling both sides how they were ignorantly using the same word but understanding different connotations assigned to the word. That the Africans were just accepting that they were gay (happy) people socializing, and not the gay (homosexual) people that the others were taking them for. The wondering on both sides was huge or *gigantically titanic*, to please lovers of Mpakofrancization.

Mamie Regina's "running and entering only between his legs" is simply literal translation from Bangwa, which means running into his house and never to somewhere else, because "he is the only father you now have". So, I was thinking, if I must only run to papa when he beats me, there is even more reason to go to papa when someone else beats me up the way Akana and the others were doing. Therefore, I usually profited at such times that I was 'caught' to find out from papa (in Bangwa that he enjoyed speaking with me) why the others were treating me the way they were doing. Papa would often reassure me that they meant no harm and were just helping me to learn the English language as fast as I could and be able to go to school. Bingo! Go to school? Me? So, I could one day also demonstrate and sing "One Summer Day I Went By" like Uncle Ngufor used to sing to us in the village whenever he returned from Fontem where he was then living and schooling? Was my ignorance (of the fear-instilling *EN* signal) not being a kind of virtue here? Was Uncle Sam Fonge not visionary in insisting that I should speak only English, not pidgin as the others? The day before departure from the village Uncle Fonge had also been at my birth mother's to say goodbye, leaving me with this advice: "I hear there is some funny way of talking in *ncheng*. I don't want you to come back here talking that way. Speak only English and I would be very proud that my nephew went to *ncheng*. Do you understand me?" My birth mother had corrected him for thinking that he needed to emphasize for me to comprehend. I did not then quite understand both of them because I had been preoccupied with reconciling Uncle Fonge's stress on my speaking only

124

English when I am in *ncheng* with Mamie Thecla's insistence on my English name.

After the three straight days spent at Mamie Cecilia's at Mamie Thecla's request, I had gotten to our compound (that is off the Emollah Palace but a stone-throw from it) without being aware of all the people that had greeted me on the way or those that were behind me. All this was because I had been lost in thought, still puzzling over some of the questions I had been asked by Mamie Thecla during those three days. For example, to what is your name, I had said "Ateh-Afac"; and she had indicated that she was talking about "your English name". I had searched hard because I have so many names various people called me with but was then not sure which of them could be "my English name". For instance, grandpa used only Ateh-Afac; my birth mother called me by two names – 'Ateh-Afac' and 'Fonwancheng'; and Aunty Tumekong who babysat me used 'Fonwancheng' and 'Mbinchang'. Which of these names was English? I was thinking hard. Suddenly I had thought of my namesake Fonwancheng whose names before he became Chief of Nwancheng quarter in Nwangong were Peter Ateafac. I had then shouted: "Peter." All this had taken quite some time, more than anyone who knows his or her name needs. If my questioner had been trying to assure herself that I was not as sharp as she must have heard, then she must have been satisfied to the brim.

Here was I then in *ncheng* and what was I hearing? Is pidgin or Ambatok what Uncle Fonge was referring to as a funny way of talking? What was going on with this only-English thing? And what was I to do to quickly learn the 'school-going' language? I must indicate that I don't exactly know how long I probably lived in Church Street in Victoria before beginning school. All I know for sure then is that Therese's schooling had abruptly ended in Victoria long before mine began. And that I entered primary school the same day in September 1968 with both Joseph and Akana. I don't know for precisely how long Akana had been living there before I arrived; but I know that on the very first day the three of us got to Catholic School New Town, Victoria, he was immediately promoted to the next class because he was just too big and old for a class one pupil. On the second day our schooling was cut short because papa had been transferred to Powercam Yoke where a bully was transformed

A Bully's Transformation and the Pepper Incident

In Presbyterian School Yoke I soon became known as Mr English, thanks to the influences of my first teacher, Miss Mandengue. Sam's Mother openly used this Mr. English reputation as a successful wakeup call to her son. Sam was this boy in the Powercam Camp who liked bullying others, including policing his senior sister. He had been looking for every opportunity to do same to me, but to no avail since I had initially been engrossed by Miss Mandengue at school and almost completely ignored children and their activities in the Camp. Now that I was back in and winning in a big way, I went to their house one day and when Sam was rudely asking why I was there and saying he would beat me, Sam's mother was not amused.

Empty head Sam, just how are you ever going to beat Mr. English with your pidgin? Pocket your petty jealousy and know that if you learn to carry the bag of someone who is more than you, you can gain a lot from him. The only way you can beat Mr. English is not only to be as gentlemanly as him but also to do very well in school, even if you are not exactly Mr. First in Class like him. And don't you ever go about asking him again what he has come here for. I, the only one that should be asking such questions, do not see anything wrong with your

126

senior sister associating with a brilliant gentleman like Mr. English. Do you hear me?

Sam's Mother, I do not quite know if she knew it, was one real icon I had in the Yoke Camp because of the way she always spoke her mind on issues – fossungupalogy. She fossungupalogized no matter how controversial others found these matters and either kept quiet or talked from both sides of their mouths. I think this is one of the major problems (if not the most devastating) facing Africa generally but Francophone Africa in particular. Take the Therese Pepper Incident for instance to demonstrate. Therese was six years older than me and died in 2012. She is papa's first child from a previous marriage. Her mother (as the story goes) had attempted to poison papa at the instigation of her *njumba*, a Nigerian man. I still shiver till date reliving Therese being tied up naked by Akana and Uncle Anamoh in the presence of my mother and papa and most of the children of the Powercam Camp in Yoke. They then introduced ground pepper into her private parts; all this happening simply because of accusations of her having slept with a man.

Apart from Aunty Tumekong from our household, Sam's Mother was the lone outside voice that came out strong and swinging in condemning it. It was very shocking to Aunty Tumekong (who is about same age as Therese) that she left the household almost immediately and settled in Douala. Whatever Therese might have done with a man, she clearly did not merit being treated that way. Doing this to Therese, not even behind papa's back, seemed to indicate that papa had extended his problem with his first wife to the child of that failed union; especially as he thereafter personally took Therese to the village and dumped her there, the idea being for her to stay there permanently and rot. Was papa really someone who treated his children without bias? Therese's "pepper ordeal" indicated two things very clearly to me. The first was Mamie Thecla's make-or-destroy powers in the household. The second relates to the fact that, resulting from the accusation of having sex, it certainly sent an always present forewarning message to my head as to the way I was to go about the boyfriend-girlfriend business. Going to Sam's house that day had nothing to do with her senior sister as he was thinking.

Sam's Mother, having finished with chiding him, welcomed me and offered me something to eat and was back to what she had been doing with her daughter in the kitchen. This time she seemed to have also hammered down the truth nail into Sam's psyche. It is said that truth is bitter and hurts. But that does not mean it must not be thrown at someone's face like she had done to Sam's here. Sam was kind of paralyzed by it because, in addition to "embarrassing" him in front of his Camp rival, his mother had also openly opened the door to his senior sister's heart, ushering me in if that was what I wanted. His sister had momentarily come to say hello and returned to the kitchen. Sam was still saying nothing. But I noticed that he was no longer looking bully-like and started conversation. "Sammy Boy," I began, and he seemed to blush, certainly because of my calling him 'boy', and I added jokingly "Or should I say Mr. Bully?" He now got the message clearly and simply said "Thank you for coming here today." I understood him but wanted him to explain himself further, so I said I did not quite comprehend what he was driving at. At this time both his mother and sister were there, hardly believing that they had heard Sam well.

He turned to his mother and said "Mom, I am sure I would not have seen reason if you were not the one throwing all these things at me. Thank you for making me to see my real self." To the sister, Sam apologized for his past behaviour towards her, a thing that was, according to him, now in the past. Turning back to me, Sam wanted to know if I would be his friend now that he has found himself. I extended my hand, saying "Sammy, you have always been and will always be my friend. But if you are talking about a renewal or reinvigoration of that companionship, I have no problem with that." You could touch and feel the joyful disbelief when Sam turned to the others with "Did you hear English from Mr. English? Mother, you were right, and I wonder why I had not been seeing what I am now seeing in him." Sam and I became real friends and shared a lot of things in attempt to both compete and cooperate with each other. All this happening thanks to Sam's Mother's swift comprehension that Fossungupalogy demands that, bitter as it is, people must be made to confront the truth head on. Only this can help them and thus ameliorate things for more and more people. Just imagine the number of people that no longer suffered from Sam's bullying, and you would have seen how 'ameliorating things for the greatest number of persons possible' works. It works in the same way as strong and powerful arguments (bolargumentalism) – something missed by most of my siblings largely because the infamous definition of family.

Distrust Moving Forward in Peace with Learning Capacity of Householders

My not fearing papa and the PTU beating thus enabled me to quickly learn. In the household I had quickly learnt that most people like papa are not hostile against you as such but against some comportment or trait that you may be exhibiting. Once you can realize this and do your best to take away that mannerism or behaviour, the hostility goes with it. The fear that is consequent on the hostility also vanishes and both of you start relating in a very productive and mutually beneficial way. The advice I would like to give to most parents like my father is that they have to learn to be strict without appearing hostile; because not all children with the ability to learn can go beyond the hostility to do so. Because this elimination of the object of hostility had not been done by most of us in our household (again, most probably because of the exclusionist categorization of family and of children), the fear of papa developed to a point where even my mother was afraid to inform him, for instance, that the monthly or weekly *chop moni* was depleted or nearing exhaustion; always preferring that I be the one to tell him. They thus were seeing me as papa's favourite, with lots of their own trouble for me attached, therefore.

The distrust of me in the household was further enhanced by the fact that I understood papa to the extent of even knowing, for example, when any of us was in for trouble, just from the way he called for that person. And I usually told them they were in trouble before they actually got to him to find out that I had been right. They sometimes even accused me of being the cause of their nuisance: otherwise, how did I know? That is how some would hastily jump to say I "have four eyes" (Four-Eyesism - HISOFE) when it is that simple. My father seldom used our full names unless he was crossed for something you had done. So, when he called out 'Peter!' I knew there was trouble. Otherwise, I would hear 'Pee!' The same goes with Vin, Joe, Ben, Marie, Bea, Anna, Mo, (no trouble); but Vincent, Joseph, Bernard, Marie-Claire, Beatrice, Annastasia, Maureen (big trouble). Ayabacholization, thanks a million for correctly grasping Four-Eyesism which I have dutifully proffered and recommended as an important discipline that all African schools need to institute and make a compulsory discipline: if our vandalized continent must have to be properly awakened to its realities (Fossungu, 2015a: xi). AEB is certainly paying attention, I guess.

It is the foresight I am lecturing on here that obviously drives Ayabacholization to be very selfless and to seek to pacify even those who are accutely suffering from entitlement-mentality, and who would still stupidly squander winning opportunities (do make it 'learning opportunities' for the household). Hear it well from the AWOL Leader:

Now, in my hotel in Lagos, where I met with Sisiko, I offered him the opportunity to be elected as our leader. And I offered him my services to speak to others so that that happens. He failed to take that offer. His advisers told him: Remember what Ahidjo did in 1966 when he obliged all other political parties to self-dissolve and integrate? You can get away with that. You see, it is one thing to sit in Mutengene, sleep overnight and dream you're in bed with Beyoncé. It is quite another thing to get up in the morning and challenge Jay-Z to that. You must build a media empire. You must be successful. You must show hard work. What we are faced today with is the failure of good people to do something. That has given the opportunity for evil to continue to triumph. After my offer to Sisiko, I have still offered in the past year the opportunity for either a joint leadership or alternate leadership. That document was framed by Professor Anyangwe. We have never received a response. This is their strategy, the strategy of the IG-Care. They know Dr Sako is so battered; image wise. They know what they instituted in South Africa against me hasn't battered my image. Their hope, when they always link us, they say the problem in this struggle is the AGovC and the IG of the Sako, their hope is to continuously batter the image of Dr Ayaba and the AGovC to the extent where Ambazonians would have no choice than to fall in their usurpation and entitlement of Zaria after independence. You listen to Bibicic Mancho the other day? I want all of you to read some of the scripts Akwanga wrote while he was in jail. I want some of you to read some of the scripts Mandela wrote while he was in jail. You know why Sisiko is so smart and walks a fine line? It is in preparation for the throne. Now, in the past days we have lost about, I have basically buried a lot of soldiers, so many wounded. When you go through this, and you find people sit quietly; go to SCBC [TV] and talk trash and ask you whether you have legitimacy. You have legitimacy to die, to burry men. You don't have legitimacy to institute policies that can ensure that most men stay alive. The IG-Care is one of the most stupid organizations I have ever seen in the world. How could such an organization lose such a political capital given to them on a platter of gold, when they overthrew the multiparty platform in Zaria and installed themselves! Look at the political capital given to them

131

by most of you! Blank cheque! They lost it! Why? Arrogance! (Ayaba, 2021c, 8th paragraph).

It is the same arrogance that is responsible for the *twocubesosugaric* war and for the decreeing of peace by the thugs in Yaoundé! (see Fossungu, 2013a: 53-59). Tatah Mentan (Theodore Lentz scholar of Peace and Security Studies and Professor of Political Science) has discussed and shamed this "Peace of the Graveyard in Cameroon". According to him,

Merely urging the Cameroonian government to exercise the "utmost restraint" in dealing with the aggrieved Anglophone people, as people-centered governments around the world do, is far too weak a response. The international community, beginning with the United Nations and other international organizations like the African Union, as well as individual countries, should use every means possible to step up pressure on the blood-thirsty Cameroon thugtatorship to:

* allow foreign media, as well as international fact-finding missions, into the country in order to enable objective investigations of what has been happening;
* release all those who only peacefully exercised their internationally guaranteed human rights, and guarantee that no one is subjected to hostage taking, torture, and unfair trials;
* enter into a meaningful dialogue with the representatives of the Anglophone people, not bribed gangsters.
Unless these conditions are fulfilled, the United Nations should seriously reconsider whether restoring the botched independence of the former British Southern Cameroons in a country that includes a peaceful graveyard is not the best idea (Mentan, 2017).

Experts on peace studies tell us plainly that "Peace does not mean to be in a place where there is no noise, trouble, or hard work. Peace means to be in the midst of all those things and still be calm in your heart. That is the real meaning of peace. Peace can mean different things to different people. It is the way freedom struggle and terrorism are used for same types of acts. One can be a freedom fighter for one and a terrorist for another. But we have to distinguish between the two. Same is the case in different parts of the world. For uncouth oppressors, those fighting are terrorists, for people of these areas they are freedom fighters" (Mentan, 2017). Thus, "As I listened to the children of Ngaoubela singing the phrase '*Let's always move forward in peace*', I wondered: What does peace mean to Cameroonians in their everyday lives? And, what does it take to live and move forward in peace? During my fieldwork I discovered that people in the field had many perspectives and concerns of their own about the topic of peace. Not everyone agreed to the state-centered focus of understanding peace as merely the absence of war" (Heum, 2016: 5). Hence, the never-thought-of brave outing of Ambazonia from Cameroon, much thanks to LRC-Biya's senseless and arroganr 'two-cubes-of-sugar' war. Go to Fossungu (2023: 151-52) and also hear from the AWOL Leader how the power-drunk guys of the IG-Care also play the 'if not us in control, then nobody gets freedom' game with Ambazonians' destiny. Do they learn the essential Ayabacholization lessons (as the Doctor himself has asked them to do) at all? What about the householders too to Momany's instruction?

Akana stood the greatest chance to cooperate with and learn from me. But (like the nonsensical IGs) he seemed to have been so contented with being the hangman of the household, totally oblivious of why his father, my namesake, must have sent him there in the first place. Self-esteem was clearly at the centre of Akana's failure to grasp a lot of things. For example, who else but such a person would be ashamed of wearing his uniform and carrying his own school bag or blackboard to school? Furthermore, Akana forgot to bear in mind that I was in a sense his father (like *The Father of Amba Self-Defense*) and, therefore, that a father may know certain things more than the son. Nollywood is always expressing this idea using the old person sitting down and seeing things that the child on the high iroko tree cannot see. When I had explained the logic of the *muhicosy* to Akana, indicating that it was better to go in for *Big Mamie Trouble* without the aggravating circumstances that Uncle Ngufor's insistence on defence was inviting, he had beamed and said "Eh, Mbi?" Mbi here is the short form for Mbinchang. This was the very first time I heard Akana calling me anything out of *Peter-Tekam-Uhm*, *Big Head*, and *Short Thing*. I had then begun thinking that maybe he had finally realized himself (like Sam the bully). But that was only my thinking because (as Sam's Mother would put it) bullies do not think; they just bully.

I recall also telling Akana one day (when he called me *Short Thing*) what I had heard from Sam's Mother. I was telling him this in the hope of making him think and thereby displacing Sam's Mother's thesis. But that only called for more 'shortening' cracks on my head, thus validating the thesis instead. Thinking aloud, Sam's Mother had wondered if "this intelligent boy will ever grow an inch taller with all these cracking from Vincent Akana and the heavy loads he is often made to carry." She was obviously right about the loads, until the advent of the farm truck. But I do not know if her height postulations can find some backing in the fact that all my three blood siblings (Awandem, Esther, and Dieudonné) are quite tall. The experts in the field can occupy themselves with that while I concentrate on the children in the household.

Before I left the village Akana's father (in Figure #9 above) had come to say goodbye and impart advice as was traditional with anyone even remotely connected to me. Conveying several messages to his son, Chief Fonwancheng had specifically implored me "to make sure to take good care of your son, Vincent Akana. Give him the necessary advice so that his stay in *ncheng* is worthwhile. I use to worry somewhat. But now that you are also going there to be with him I am

134

happy and reassured that everything will be fine with him. Don't forget that he is your first son." Imagine then the enthusiasm with which I had first encountered Akana, addressing him as "my son" while passing over his messages from my namesake, his father. It is obvious that my employment of those two words (my son) had completely thrown him overboard, begetting the hostility that he thereafter wantonly exhibited in my regard. This was clearly uncalled for, for anyone who has his or her self-esteem. There are children in the village named after my birth father who, to date, refer to me as their son, and always wanting to know what their child has brought for them, whenever I visit Ambazonia. It is only normal, Gospel according to the *Asahndeming Lecture on African Tradition* (see Fossungu, 2016: 156-59), which also duly explains why I am now traditionally the father of my siblings. The thesis is godfathered by Asah William Ndem (my sister's husband), who is more learned in tradition than the moneyintriguist called Peter Ngunyi Asahchop, who will even be going around ordering or *ultimatuming* the Fon of Nwangong. Yes, Pa Asah Ndem, you correctly addressed me as 'Dear Father-in-Law' because, having succeeded our father, I am now traditionally the father of my siblings. Back now to the Household and Akana whose My-Son ignorance called for this requisite African Culture Lecture from Ekona Town – one of the most engaged and engaging places in the AWOL. *Ekona, your place dey ooh!* Moreover, being a village-born like me, Akana (unlike the coast children of the household) should have been the one to better appreciate my situation when I had arrived and to give me the required support for 'soft landing'. On the contrary, he championed the onslaught of the trauma that, paradoxically, aided me not to partake in their fear of papa that prevented them from dialoguing or reasoning with him on issues.

There was much potential for my siblings *of* the household to pick up a lot from me, especially the girls (who were all born while I was already there and) who always called me 'Brother'. But it seems they were soon prohibited from too much association with the "outsider". To concretely illustrate, there was this tendency for them to answer "Sir" when papa called. One day I sat Maurine down and inquired from her why she addressed her father 'sir' instead of papa. She did not seem to see the importance of the 'baffling' question but said it was the way everyone else answered him. I asked her if that 'everyone' included me, and then she remembered and admitted that I always used "papa". I then asked her which of the two was more appropriate. Before I could even complete the question Maurine was all thanks for the eye-opener. As soon as she began responding "papa" when called, everyone else followed suit and it became the norm at home and quickly spread out to other households in the quarter. Imagine for yourself the future of these children if the definition of family was different and truly inclusive in the household.

Figure #22: Maurine & Momany during his 1993 marriage –
Maurine being the only Momany-sibling, blood or no-blood, at
the marriage
Source: Photo Dave, Yaoundé

Figure #23: Bernard & Marie-Claire during birthday
celebration at my residence in Yaoundé in August 1990
Source: Photo Dave, Yaoundé

As for the two young boys *of* the household, they also did well in school in some sort of competition with me, which I found good and progressive. Like Marie-Claire, Bernard also made it to university graduation and beyond. But it appears like Bernard has been unable till date to shed off the shell of Mamiteelization, as portrayed in some of his 'incomprehensible' letters to me in the context of my efforts to work towards (educational) progress for all. As soon as I was out of the country (both first and second times), I always tried to work together with my siblings and other family relations in order to ameliorate the lot of the entire family. The very first letter I wrote to anyone when I got to Calabar, Cross River State of Nigeria in the early 1980s was to Joseph. This is someone who left Cameroon for the USA in 1985 but had never written a letter to me until his death in June 2007. Like Ayabacholization, I have always been desirous of working as closely as possible to alleviate hardship in the family without distinction as to who is blood or no-blood this and that to me. But I always have met only with this inexplicable leg-dragging comportment (like Dr Liberator is meeting from the IG-Care Entitlementalists). Listen to Bernard himself on 18 April 1997, for instance, to concretize the theories. His letter of the said date told "Hi Cinq" (his preferred nickname for me) that:

I regret the fact that I couldn't reply to your letters before today. When I received them, I had to travel to Yaoundé for my University transcript and this process took me about two weeks. I also went to the Canadian Embassy in Yaoundé for some enquiry; all I need now is the admission letter and the immigration form for, as I was told, I can't do the medical test without the admission letter. I have also sent letters to Sweden for admission letters before writing to the address you gave me for scholarship.

I am first interested in the McGill autumn session before seeing how Montreal winter session can look like. It was not possible for me to get my transcript from Buea because they could not lay hands on our Year 1 marks. Maybe the former disgruntled Deputy Director went away with them, but I hope with the transcript for Ngoa Ekelle you can obtain an admission letter for me from McGill so that I can begin the other procedures at the Embassy against the fall session. Hope to receive it as soon as possible. Accept greetings from Takwi Caroline. Everybody is fine both in Limbe and Yoke. I wish you the best.

Ben Fosungu (cited in Fossungu, 2016: 141).

Well, Bernard's first apology-seeking letter (that I have styled *The Child-Complication Message from Douala-Wourizone*: see Fossungu, 2016: 141-43) had a lot of persuasion as to why he never responded to a lot of the time-sensitive opportunities and my letters generally. This time around: it is a doubtful mystery as to just what held Bernard back not to appropriately react to two letters again. The issue of transcript-issuing is surely a very thorny one with Cameroon universities and we all know that. But, for anyone really bent on getting admitted to a university programme out there, there will always be a way out. And that way out is all the making of the determined person. Before and even during Ayabacholization, are the nay-sayers not still in total disbelief that Ambazonia could have an army, let alone beat LRC in war hands-down? We Ambazonians are so so proud to have someone with this man's courage and ingenuity in these matters. Amba is forever indebted to hum and his team of fearless liberators. To concretely illustrate in the other field, take my attempt to study for a Master's at the University of Windsor. I created two important documents that tore down the two Hercules (1) of academic references and (2) of transcripts emanating directly from the University of Yaoundé (UNIYAO or Ngoa-Ekéllé). Let us have just the shorter second requirement concerning which I told the Windsorians through my write-up, titled *"Why Transcripts Cannot Be Coming Directly From The University Of Yaoundé"*, that:

By this note I wish to let you know that transcripts of my studies at the University of Yaoundé cannot be "official"; with official meaning that these documents are mailed by the institution directly to you; that the documents have never been handled by me, a friend of mine, a relative, or any other individual I know personally; and that the envelope they come in bear proper seals, signatures and postal markings. As you can see from the <u>Nota Bene</u> (N.B.) at the foot of the institution's transcripts that I enclosed with my application, "ONLY ONE COPY OF THIS TRANSCRIPT SHALL BE DELIVERED. IT IS IN THE INTEREST OF THE OWNER TO MAKE AS MANY CERTIFIED TRUE COPIES AS HE/SHE MAY DESIRE."

In addition, the University of Yaoundé in which I studied (1984-1989) is no more, having been replaced by two separate universities, namely, University of Yaoundé I and University of Yaoundé II.

I hope the copies of the transcripts that were included in the application will serve the purpose. Or, should I have them certified before sending to you again?
I requested those from the University of Alberta, McGill University, and Université de Montréal; and I am sure you have already received the transcripts from them directly.
Thanks. Signed. Peter Ateh-Afac Fossungu (ID# XXXXXXXXX) (cited in Fossungu, 2016: 143-44).

This endeavour (like the Liberation Tax from Ayabacholization) is what I would call self-help, something unknown to nonoselfists, aka entitlementalists, who sit in

Mutengene and fantasize being in bed with Beyouncé during the night but cannot challenge Jay-Z in the morning. Would I have been admitted if I stayed uselessly crying over the UNIYAO's unusual and dragdownist academic politics? Would the miserable Two Cubes of Sugar still be in existence today without the wise creation of a liberation army, the ADF? NO, NO, Absolutely, says even Joseph especially who, for some exclusionist reasons, did not take advantage of my presence in the household. Otherwise, how else would you explain his being barred from entering the UNIYAO because of his lack of Ordinary Level English (not to even talk of mathematics and French) when he grew up in the same home with Mr. English? Most often when Joseph wanted to know anything from me at all it related solely to how to *cockler* a girl. Cockler was generally used in the community, but I heard it for the first time from Joseph who had a nag for creating his own words or phrases and for giving people nicknames from nowhere. I remember asking him how he came about the word and he described it to me. You know how a cock does when it wants to mate? I got it right away because for the first time I saw *cock* in the word. I never got to know how Joseph came about *ekapulapong* that he often employed to demand where others have put their brains. He would, for instance, ask a sister like Quinta (who he nicknamed *Quintoko*) who has done something wrong whether she has any *ekapulapong* in her head. The term is now generally used, especially in Yoke where John Azimbe still lives.

John Azimbe, nicknamed *Money-Hard*, was then also living with us. I do not know the exact nature of the relation, but Money-Hard's father seemed to have been either papa's maternal cousin or uncle. They were living in Yoke in papa's house, part of which someone was using to operate the only bar then in town. When we moved to the Powercam Camp from Victoria, Money-Hard started visiting, then staying the night sometimes, and finally became part of the household, an act that was duly ratified by his moving to Kumba with us when papa was transferred there.

Hardworking on the farm as well, Money-Hard's main problem was that of not admitting that he had a long hand even when he has been caught red-handed. In the household we always ate to our full but Money-Hard was never getting enough as far as rice goes. He had this habit of always sneaking back to the pot and scratching rice off as if a rat or something else did it. Akana wanted to solve this rat-and-no-rat mystery and set himself to work. He caught Money-Hard in the act but the latter was still denying. This coupled with Money-Hard's way of always swelling and murmuring things when Akana was beating him up, to earn him Akana's incessant wrath. The latter interpreted the former's comportment as challenging him and the more he beat the more the swelling and murmuring, and the more the beating. I once advised Money-Hard to learn to take his punishment without provoking the hangman. But he would not listen to advice; instead counter-suggesting that we both team up to beat Akana up. I asked him if he reasoned with his head or with his anus. Akana was a bully for sure, but I cannot enumerate how many times Money-Hard himself unnecessarily called for trouble from the bully. Akana was a real bulldozer on the farm and after returning from it, he often dozed off and slept so deeply, snoring heavily and with mouth partly open. Money-Hard would on many occasions put some large amount of salt in his mouth and then make some very loud noises that would get him up. You can imagine the rest of the scene.

Money-Hard was a very good footballer and surely would have gone places with it had he reached class seven or even college in the household. Around class three or four, he absconded when we went to Yoke for holidays, never coming back to

Kumba with us as usual; preferring to remain there, doing his sand work. The altercation with Akana is largely the cause of Money-Hard leaving the household despite that (unlike other "outsiders") he had all the chances of smoothly progressing there. For illustration, as Money-Hard was not a 'hated' Fossungu, he was not regarded as any threat. Again, he was younger than Joseph in age and school standing and generally not as attached to the household as I was. When we usually came down for holidays he stayed with his parents in Yoke and not with us in Muyuka (as was the case at the time of the *muhicosy*). I suspect his mother did not give him the kind of advice my birth mother gave me. But I think all largely depended on John knowing who he was and what he was up against. These are things he did not seem to know when, because of Akana, he refused to return with us to Kumba, where my goals were palpably threatened by the challenges in CCAS because of which the shortcut to university education was effectively hatched..

Chapter 4

University Education, With Or Without Money: The Fight For And In CCAS Kumba And The Manjo-Canada Dueling Strategies

Of course, most of us, hisofeans, who have regularly been to musician Longue Longue's Afrikentication School long enough are able to easily know how hypocritical we, the living, often are with the dead. That questionable mind-set is never on the table of straight-talkers or crisebacologists who tell you what they think, whether you are alive or dead. Calling a spade a spade is civilization's definition (Fossungu, 2023: 28).

On 9 October 2021 Maitre Peterson Tesi of Toronto (on learning of the publication of one of my 'controversial' books) declared in a text message to me that "Peter, I really like your attitude. You are a really mentally strong guy. You are courageous and firm. You have a strong psychological power, and you believe in yourself and ability. You are a never dying man and have fought fiercely against many odds in life. You are stronger mentally and have faced these odds with your desire to move on and challenge anyone or thing that has challenged you. Keep it up." You just can't 'keep it up', as advised, if you fear politics or controversy. In this Chapter, I anchor and dwell mostly on my fight for and in CCAS Kumba, with a slant on the duel and strategies of Manjo for getting to the UNIYAO in time before I could be barred by the age politics to university education in then Cameroon. Both of these processes, of course, are the result of the exclusionist definition of family and of child, not leaving out the desire to have an ideal marriage and family.

It seems to me that people with the kind of outlook on life as mine often, if not always, end up with the kind of marriage mess like mine. Because they idealize the institutions of marriage and of family in a world where self-centredness has become the rule rather than the exception; where take and take and take (onesidetakism or entitlementalism) has long replaced give and take (giveantakism). When I talk about ideal marriage and family, I am simply referring to three things at least; namely, (1) that both parties do share or learn to share the same or similar perspectives on as many domains as possible; (2) that both parents be there together to bring up the children and advance the family; and (3) that the marriage decision should be that of the two persons concerned. All the three requirements combine to bring about the ideal but sometimes only a few are present for a start, with the others being developed as the parties go along. Although "being there together for the children" is not just physical presence, the fact that I hardly know my birth father long led me to vow never to leave my own children with a similar "legacy". This could explain why I started wanting to have children only when I thought I was ready to be there (in all its forms) all the time for them. But regrettably, it seems that the unwanted birth-father legacy is exactly what my kids are headed for even as (unlike my biological father) I am not yet dead. All this is because of my failure to avoid having a narrow-minded spouse like papa had – thanks very much also to the UNIYAO, the short-cut to which was also unnecessarily elongated. All these issues and more are interlocking and hidden in the Manjo brain-busting year. Knowing all that, I will set the issues of Kumba, Canada, and Manjo rolling by conversationally getting into the mind and ways of the big-hearted man (that I am) through the aid of Solomon Enoma Tatah, my bosom friend who once described me accurately as 'a man of many'.

Solomonizing the Powerful 'Man Of Many' (Momany) and Shaming the Quebec Bar of Liars

146

Solomon must have done his homework well because I have *many* of almost everything, including fans and nicknames. Being one of my many fans, Solomon is the one who coined the *Power* nickname. The General Certificate of Education (G.C.E.) Advanced Level was normally acquired in then Cameroon after two years in high school. But I obtained it in 1981 after 'less than one year' in CCAS Kumba. Three years after this academic accomplishment, I met and knew Solomon in the UNIYAO. First excitedly introducing himself to me, Solomon lengthily narrated his elated experiences when he got to first see me in November 1981 in CCAS Kumba. That was after having heard so much about me and even read some of my test scripts that had then become standard materials for the high school's G.C.E. hopefuls, not leaving out the commotion and admiration my arrival there had caused. Solomon was right. At the time in Douala and still uncertain of my academic future (as you will more elaborately see in Chapter 6 and which is captured by Figure #24 below), I had learnt that I had some money to claim in CCAS Kumba in connection with high school entrance performance. I got there only to realize that I was the talk of the day, with some of the newly arrived students like Solomon then having the chance to meet me, their hero and mentor. It was undeniably nothing short of a star meeting his or her fans. You could sort of analogize it with the Ayabacholization Bloc-By-Bloc powerful and unscripted performance in Washington DC, after Chris Anu's crowd-pulling introduction of the Chosen Leader of the AWOL. Coupling this with what also took place at the UNIYAO Solomon had then concluded that only a very powerful person like he thought I was could accomplish such feats. And, therefore, *Power* was the only name that, in his estimation, befitted me.

Figure #24: Somewhere in Douala in 1981 searching for my
future
Source: Momany Fossungu's Album

Solomon and I just happened to have been renting in the same
student residential apartment (*mini-cité*) in Ngoa-Ékéllé. This is
the quarter in Yaoundé where the UNIYAO is located.
Listening to Solomon and the way he articulated both his
points, and his English told me a lot about him, and we
immediately clicked in. Very frank, open and a fire-brand
straight talker, Solomon is the kind of person you can easily
learn a lot from even while cracking jokes. I particularly
commit to memory this joke he started one day regarding my
not respecting the UNIYAO tradition of few or no *mentions*
(honours). That is, by obtaining so *many*, always having one in
all the examinations I took there. This accomplishment,
Solomon thought, was quite unusual especially for an English-
speaking in the vastly mono-cultural and French-speaking
UNIYAO. I then playfully but seriously explained to Solomon

that tradition is made (for better or for worse) by someone like me. I, therefore, do not see why I cannot then also be making tradition by doing what I do. If *many* more people should start doing it the way I do, then a new *mention*-having tradition would be here to stay. This, I concluded, is the way a society evolves. You can see that this talk about making tradition by breaking tradition was obviously digging into my listener's flesh and bones just like the smile of the Yaoundé bone-digging virgin did to me.

Figure #25: Solomon Enoma Tatah in the 1980s

Ayabacholization would never have seen the light of day by continuously remaining within the ranks of the nosifean proponents of the "The Force of Argument" fancy words: Yes ou Oui? Oh! This 1972 Referendum Response! How I just love using it with Hisofeans! Nosifeans could not divine it in 1972, but not quick-learning Solomon who stared at me for a while, admirably, before bursting out: "You see? I call you *Power* but I think your powers are so limitless and amoeba-like that you are always breaking virgin grounds, sometimes without even realizing it yourself!" I curiously asked Solomon what he was implying, wondering to myself whether Solomon was entailing my being a sort of the "virgins' man". "I simply mean," Solomon elucidated, "that maybe I should not just be calling you *Power* but must also describe you as 'a man of many rare talents'." Solomon was obviously making quite some sense but I kept wondering to myself if Solomon's virgin groundbreaking theory could be behind my virgiluckism (being as lucky with virgins as I have been)? Did the virgins have a unique way of recognizing that I was better at virgibrookism (the 'breaking' of virgin grounds) or what?

"*Power!*" Solomon interrupted the virgin lingering, asking to know what other virgin ground I was about to break. Ayabacholization would obviously answer the question with the historic inauguration of the Liberation Tax in mid-August 2023, which is truly the inventive 'Final Solution' to quickly unpacking LRC out of Ambaland. Many nosifeans/traitors are still to imagine how to effectively reverse the way the bulk of Ambazonians are happily lining up to pay for and participate financially in their own liberation. I just love the dialogue between Mamie-Achu and Mamie-Koki on the Ambazonia Communications Network (ACN). Very inspirational! Anyone who gives any excuses whatsoever for not paying this very moderate contribution (just $100US for the entire year for Diasporeans outside Africa) for having a free Homeland, does not deserve to be an Ambazonian and/or live in a free Ambazonia. That is/should be the logical inference from this crucial *Law of the Land* by which Africa-Diasporeans are required to pay $50US/year while for Ground-Zero it is 10000 FCFA/year for Men and 5000 FCFA/year for Women. ADF Logistics Chief, Pascal Kiki, and ADF Mama Wally (OGC – Overall Ground Coordinator) have explained and emphasized the issue and how to pay at www.atla.africa more than enough for anyone to still be claiming ignorance about it now. Spokesman Lucas Asu (whose official contact points are public information) is also always available to guide anyone not able to use the online portal, especially on GZ and other such places, on how to pay their Liberation Tax. It is currently the authentic passport/ID card for Ambazonians. HAVE YOU PAID? Having already enthusiastically paid my DiL Tax (the Diaspora version) and feeling and walking around with much pride and pomp like Mamie-Koki, I did simply insist in response that Solomon too was just as powerful and must also be called *Power* in return. Solomon laughed and said it was not true. After I had lined up just a few of Solomon's own many academic and other achievements, Solomon suggested that he would be legislative while I be executive power.

Solomon is, of course, implying here that I am still more powerful than he is: as evident even in his letters to me, always opening with "The Most Powerful". It derives, no doubt, from the perception of the almighty position of the executive branch in Cameroun particularly and (Francophone) Africa generally. This is an issue that is further portrayed and explored by Fossungu (2013b) and Pratt (2007); with Ayabacholization astutely decrying noise-making lawyers of such a setup: "They should shut the hell up. They should shut the hell up. They have shown themselves as inadequate. Read the Cameroon constitution, which some of the lawyers there are looking at it as the basis of law of a country. Where executive power, you know, even overrides legislative or primary legislation or even secondary legislation. The president rules by decree, passes ordinances, you know, to override primary law. He oversees the Legislature; he oversees the Judiciary. What are they doing?" (cited in Fossungu, 2023: 227). Like the AWOL Leaser, I also told Solomon that he was talking nonsense because power is power and if he wanted to separate it the way he was going, who then was to be judicial power? At this point Solomon could not resist disclaiming the name completely and reverting to his virgibrookistic postulation. He was only converted by my sapient indication that if he would not be *Power* for any other reason, he had to be for the mere fact that he has also had to be a well-known girlimelighter (a man in the glare of publicity for many women) but has no wife fiasco like me.

Figure #26: Henriette Flavie Bayiha in 2010 in Montréal
Source: Photo taken by Momany Fossungu

Talking of wife flop, I must immediately also admit that I often go to Canadian Family Courts. For instance, I was in court in May 2014. Not to argue with the law but solely to assist the law (on which the judge is an obvious expert) to reach a just decision; one that places the paramount interests of the children above all machinations from whatever source (see Fossungu, 2015b: 2-4). By children here, I do not mean just the two kids named in Henriette Flavie Bayiha's *wholly unnecessary* suit. For these children's interests to be appropriately guaranteed, therefore, it was my view that the Court was entitled to (and had to be given) all the essential facts, not the appearances. Thus, I wasn't there to argue with the law that the Quebec and Ontario Bars have shamelessly told me I don't know enough about. Nyamefukahs! Hearing them say that I doubt what you are here making of the Canadian universities in the Law Schools and Faculties of which I have arduously studied – University of Alberta, McGill University, and Université de Montréal. The Quebec Bar even went further to talk of my not being vest in Quebec's Civil Law, and therefore asking for my taking courses in any of the four universities recognized by them (McGill University, Université de Montréal, Université d'Ottawa, and Université de Sherbrooke), two of which I have already actually studied in! You would also wonder with me at this point if they were even aware of then Cameroon legal/judicial system that was predominantly, if not completely, Civil Law. Ambazonians, am I not correct? Oh, these Quebec Gang of Lawyers (or did someone just say Liars?)! They should simply have been frank enough to say they didn't want me anywhere near their Bar because I am too qualified and savvy for the liking of the 'charge and bail lawyers' that the bulk of them are. Full stop!

I like the OQ (Overqualified) reason that a few Canadian employers have used to justify not hiring me. That is more truthful, although that also means that some qualified persons like me would never work anywhere almost, not even in MYR. Thank you very much then "Mario Richard, propriétaire," who has in no insignificant way motivated (albeit unknowingly) the writing of my unique books. You should note that in the place of Mario here, Africans (with their incredible love of fabulous titles) will instead say, for example, 'Kadji de Fotso, Président-Directeur-Général'. In Cameroun's Garoua I also encountered 'the crime of being very intelligence' (see Chapter 6). Some critics would argue, of course, that the 'OQ lovers' are afraid of being sued by the candidate after employment for being underpaid. Is that so? I would then simply be a simpleton or nosifean to voluntarily apply for a job meant for Master's holders and then sue to be paid as a PhD holder. I guess such easy-way thinkers are waiting still for the day I will be suing MYR for hiring a PhD holder as a *débroussailleur*? Order! Can we now leave these *gros titres* and get back quickly to Your Honour's whitewashing court, please?

As I have said, I do not go to argue with the law in court. I am just too much for that. Petit Canadian *experienced* lawyers (like the one representing Flavie in her 'Money-Only' sole custody case – see Fossungu, 2015d) are better placed to do that. I usually do not also have a lawyer. The women always go there to demand child support and I just cannot unwisely afford to pay the two. But I surely would be told by other Canadians that there is legal aid. Yes, of course. But we all know that legal aid has its own limits and limitations. It has failed me before at a moment when I needed it the most (see Fossungu, 2015d). But that is not why I don't like having a lawyer in my family matters. Not having a lawyer or arguing with them in court might not be a big issue because I don't really need a lawyer to tell me how to tell the truth. Telling the truth is a thing I have been doing from when I tumbled out of Mamie Regina's womb. Better get used to it, Canada, before asking me to bring Canadian experience to Canada! (see Fossungu, 2015b: chapter 4). For now, let me fly you back to Africa and to Solomon who, convinced as he was, insisted all the same that I was 'a man of many'. Truly, it was largely thanks to my being 'a man of many' (disciplines) that the CCAS challenges failed to put an abrupt end to my destiny with many.

The Challenges of CCAS and the Manjo Duel: Age Politics in University Education in Cameroun

The Kumba and Manjo combats and strategies are so intimately interwoven (and also knotted to the Montreal effect) to the extent of being inseparable. But I have tried to tear them apart just for convenience and manageability, having to examine some of the roadblocks to these strategies for the UNIYAO from the backstabbers, as well as from the pressures relating to the quest for an ideal marriage and family. Contrary to the thinking of a lot of people there, my one academic year in Manjo was not the bed of roses and of charming girls. Most people that knew me in that small Wourizonian town would find it hard to believe my realities in Manjo just as some others would to my realities in Canada. Because I have learnt not to carry my problems on my face, even the Manjo students themselves would find it hard to believe that I then had some real and devastating issues that were constantly with me. The greatest of them that almost tilted the balance against my returning to Cameroon from Nigeria, and which guided my approach to all the others in Manjo, was that of how to get to the UNIYAO the following academic year. That is, before the twenty-five-year age-limit condition could bar me. I necessarily had to get enrolled in the UNIYAO by 1984 or never do so since thereafter I was to be twenty-five and above (things have changed today, of course?). How was I to meet with this objective? And what about resolving the case of CCAS Kumba?

CCAS Kumba must have been considered by the opposing forces to be the furthest I could ever go, crowned especially with an unsuccessful completion of its programme of study. This was surely the end of the end, as they did happily muse about. Although I excelled in both, when I went to CCAS Kumba, I was a student more of the sciences than of the arts. A day student for the first time, I was living in a room in our house in Bamileke Street in Fiango and attending school in CCAS which is situated on Buea Road. It is by all means not a walking distance. It is also not a one-drop taxi affair (the taxi concept in then Cameroon and most of Francophone Africa not being the same as in the West). This would no longer be the case in Ambazonia since Ayabacholization has been assuring citizens of the possibility of even residing in Abakwa Town in Mezamzone and working in K-Town in Memezone. Meaning that transportation facilities would be topnotch in Ambazonia. I do believe that promise would be delivered because this liberation organization or movement has delivered on its promises even during the hard period of liberation and despite all the multiple dragdownist forces. There is no reason to contemplate the contrary at a time when they would have the Nation's varied resources under their stewardship. Because of the new student-life style in K-Town, I actually began better appreciating the fact that I had not been admitted to a government *lycée* after my go-getting performance in the Common Entrance and First School Leaving Certificate. That failure thus landed me in Sasse College where the lump sum payment of one's school fees would include everything (like sets of uniforms, and books) so that whatever one was given as 'pocket allowance' was in fact just pocket allowance.

While in CCAS, my allowance for each term (three months) was ten thousand francs CFA. The popular justification was that I did not have rents to pay. But the many imponderables far outweighed the rents that I was not paying. Some required laboratory equipment, for instance, cost about fourteen thousand francs CFA. Was I ever going to make it as a science student without the necessary study tools? Was this not the certification of failure that some forces (both inside and outside the household) had for so long been ardently working for? Was I to capitulate and let them have easy victory? What were all these unannounced visits to Kumba by papa for? A similar quandary presented itself in Manjo three years later. The town of Manjo is very critical to my UNIYAO bid. This is a longing that was being timed-out by the age-limit bar for university enrolment in then Cameroon. The town is also very intimately tied to the second signification of "idealizing marriage and family". That is, that both parents should be there to bring up the children. These two principal considerations, exacerbated by the Anna-fiasco (that is epitomized by the Yoke Conspiracy), created a real duel for me there, turning the year into a make-or-break one.

For the answer of the make-or-die questions in CCAS Kumba, I drew very heavily from my first schoolteacher who meant (and still means) the world to me then – Miss Mandengue. I had to say YES to not persisting in beating competitors over her to avoid dismissal from the snake-beating male teachers that were hovering all around her. But this time in CCAS, NO was the answer to capitulating because I badly needed to obtain the G.C.E. Advanced Level which I saw then as a sort of window to the world and the success that Miss Mandengue herself had predicted for me. I never mutually got her overwhelming love but from her lap-lecture I got something so precious that none of the snake-beating teachers could ever

157

come near to taking away from me. I had, therefore, to step up the Kumba fight that began with (1) the CCAS admission itself as well as (2) some other earlier educational admissions

The CCAS Admission and the Other Earlier Educational Admissions

The almost intractable financial and associated problems in CCAS were not the beginning of the battle because even getting admitted into CCAS Kumba had been a lone and personal fight. High school education seemed to have been put beyond my reach when the list of admitted students to Cameroon College of Arts, Sciences and Technology (CCAST) Bambili (in Mezamzone) had come out without my name on it, despite my having nine Ordinary Level papers with good grades. The forces I was up against had seen this as the clean and clear end of the road. (Didn't the LRC leadership also naively see the unseasoned creation of the IG in Nigeria and their subsequent abduction of its leaders as the clear end to the Liberation?) I was shocked (like Ayabacholization was about the IG creation in Nigeria against all sound advice) but kept my calm. When you define yourself through objectives such as I have, you tend to have a globavillagist look of things. For example, if I am telling my story to (the world generally but) my wife and children particularly, it is not to gain their pity or sympathy. That, I never would need. As Ayabacholization has put it, "When the Defense Chair made the solemn declaration to commission our forces to war, it was a phase when Cameroun had declared war on us from the tarmac of an airport. It was not meant to showcase AGovC; it was not meant to showcase Ayaba. It had nothing to do with Sisiko; it had nothing to do with the IG. It simply had something to do with our people" (Fossungu, 2023: 151). Thus, telling them the story is principally, if they learn to be Hisofeans (that every African is supposed to be), to let them be able to correctly appreciate not only who they are and who they have as

158

husband/father, but also to be pleased about all those who have shaped my life in one way or the other. In that way, they could better value Mamie Thecla (for example), because, without her role, I am not sure I would be married but to their mother and that they (as they are) would actually be the ones I call children today. In the same way, the *delayers* of Amba Freedom have played a somewhat valuable role that has helped in filtering out and exposing those who, according to Ayabacholization, simply "saw Cameroun being cloned in Ambazonia; where they can have political opportunities, financial opportunities; they attacked nationalists, try to destroy everyone" (Fossungu, 2023: 228). That is the science known as HISOFE! How could a Hisofean ever be dejected? I am sure I hear CIC Julius Malema well also.

As a farsighted person or hisofean, you thus move from small ideas to big ones; not the reverse. You tend to pioneer bigger things and to easily surmount obstacles that are on your way to becoming better; most often being guided by the knowledge that panicking at every obstacle does not help. As Ayabacholization would have it, "they know the struggle is more important to me than to them. They know the failure of the struggle is something which is unacceptable to me. I have no choice, there is no option" (Fossungu, 2023: 151)..
Hisofeans thus confront narrow-mindedness with progressiveness, not with the same. Otherwise, you never can advance. What I was confronting before and in CCAS Kumba was obviously the handiwork of small minds and I understood that meeting small-mindedness with small-mindedness could not lead me anywhere further. Hail Ayabacholization!

The next day (following the CCAST list), therefore, I quietly went up to Buea (the capital of Ambazonia) to put my case before the regional (then provincial) delegate of education. As fate would have it, that same day the principal of CCAS

Kumba was right there at the delegation compiling his own list of admitted candidates. The delegate quickly sent me directly to the principal. Just imagine that I had panicked after the CCAST list and stayed crying uselessly in my small room or packed and left the household like Marie-Claire wanted to! Has Honourable Julius Malema (the predicted next President of SAF) not sufficiently told the Fighters in Johannesburg that, as the Doctors of society, they must not cry with the society but instead seek solutions to the crying? The CCAS principal was very impressed with my results. Of course, I was not receiving the high-school-entrance money mentioned earlier for nothing. But he had one small preoccupation, namely, why I had not chosen his college (but CCAST) as first choice. I had to quickly improvise and explained that I had been ill at the time of filling the forms and my friends had made the choice for me, knowing that I was more a sciences-student than an art one (what a beautiful lie!). The CCAS principal told me there and then that he was admitting me to his college but that I would not have a place in the dormitory. No problem at all: Just have your presidency and let us (Nationalists) have the peace of mind and time to effectively prosecute this Amba Liberation, Ayabacholization told the entitlementalistic Cameroun-Cloners *noh*? Thank you all so much AGovCists and ADFers! I also thanked the CCAS principal, reassuring him he would never regret his decision, like I had also done to the principal of WWMSS-Mpundu a year earlier.

The Certificates Story: The CCAS Kumba fight obviously taught me so much about obtaining not only academic admissions but many other things on my own, which would all be tied to the description of "a man of many". The main academic problem with me – just like with the Amba Liberators – has just been the financial means (and/or the bribery requirement, for Cameroon). Take admissions into study programmes of universities. Most people consider themselves extremely lucky to be admitted to a study programme in a university. I easily had it with the following: Master of Arts (M.A.) in Political Science, September 2013 to December 2014 @ University of Windsor, Windsor, Ontario, Canada; *Doctorat en Droit* (LLD), January 1997 to December 2000 @ Université de Montréal, Montréal, Québec, Canada; Master of Laws **(LLM)** (Air & Space), September 1995 to February 1997 @ McGill University, Montréal, Québec, Canada; Master of Laws (LLM), September 1991 to November 1992 @ University of Alberta, Edmonton, Alberta, Canada; *Diplôme d'Études Approfondies* (D.E.A.), October 1988 to September 1989, *Maîtrise en Droit*, October 1987 to September 1988, and *Licence en Droit*, September 1984 to July 1987, these three being @ Université de Yaoundé, Yaoundé, Cameroun.

The foregoing cases are those that I enrolled in, completed the programmes and obtained the degrees and certificates. But they are not all because also worthy are: Master in Public Administration (MPA): admitted July 1999 @ School of Public Administration, Dalhousie University, Halifax, Nova Scotia, Canada; Master of Arts (Public Policy and Public Administration): admitted August 1997 @ Concordia University, Montréal, Canada; Magister Juris in International Law: admitted July 1995 @ University of Malta, Msida, Malta; Master of Philosophy (M.Phil.) in Criminology: admitted February 1995 @ The Institute of Criminology, Cambridge University, Cambridge, United Kingdom; *Maîtrise en Droit de la Santé:* admitted August 1992 @ Université de Sherbrooke, Sherbrooke, Québec, Canada; Master of Arts in Personnel Administration/Industrial Relations: admitted July 1992 @ Graduate School of Industrial Relations, Saint Francis College, Loreto, Pennsylvania, USA; and Master of Business Administration in International Management: admitted March 1991 @ The Centre for Management Studies, European University, Montreux, Switzerland. While the CCAS battle

161

prepared me well for other academic battles ahead, its own success cannot be dissociated from (1) earlier admissions struggles and (2) the short-cut decision to leap from lower sixth form to university.

The Other Earlier Educational Admissions: The daunting challenges for and in CCAS would be appreciated through looking at similar earlier events that had groomed me well for victory in CCAS. I will thus be examining admissions (1) from primary school to college and (2) from Sasse College to World Wide Missions Secondary School (WWMSS) Mpundu, Muyuka. I passed out of primary school in high-flying colours but my high-powered performance did not secure me a place in a government Lycée "due to the very corrupt demeanours of [especially public] school administrators and most teachers who are members of the educational community" (Fossungu, 2013a: 183). Not being admitted like this has become normal in Cameroon when you don't go through the back door. Very upright in a time and place where most people regard crookedness as the rule, this 'back door' business is something papa would never do or countenance. The proof is with Uncle Anamoh's bid for an office job that, as you already know, ended woefully. This non-admission also was supposed to be the stop point to secondary education. But, unlike my tree-top uncle, I had personally 'climbed through the tree trunk' by finding the way to Sasse College all by myself for the college's own interview. The small private "messages" from Mamie Regina were aiding very significantly. It was then that I really understood her insistence when I had told her not to worry sending these "messages" to me but to concentrate more on Dieudonné with them. She had said she could not listen to me on that score, stressing that if I thought I did not need her "messages" I still had to accept them from her "and then perhaps pass them on to any beggar at the side of the road, if you like." What a mother! A sure Hisofean!

The crooked nature of the country's public school system thus landed me in one of the most prestigious Harvard-like secondary schools, Sasse College. I remember the then Sasse College principal (Reverend Stumpel) expressing shock that, with the kind of results he had before him, I was not admitted in a government college. He also told me there and then that I was already a student in his college. What I consider as really sending me to Sasse College (quite apart from Mamie Regina's timely "messages") is the fact that admissions lists to all their colleges were always posted in all the Catholic Mission churches around the country. My name conspicuously featuring on those lists (Sasse College's for that matter) was just too much of an embarrassment if I was thereafter actually not attending Sasse College. After four years in single-sex Sasse College my destiny with *many* refused to be put aside for secondary schools.

The Sasse College admission did not end my pre-CCAS admissions woes. The Sasse College administration had dismissed our entire class during third term in 1979 and required re-application through coming together with father. That was to have been the end of my secondary education and, therefore, the end of the academic road for me because, for one thing, papa was never going to go with me to Sasse College for whatever reason. He did not do so for the initial admission, and it was not then that he was to do so. The class dismissal was even looked upon in the household as if I was the only one involved, not "the entire class as he is trying to fool us with." Secondly, I do not know how others (without "four eyes": nosifeans) saw it; but, to me, the then African and non-reverend principal (known to us as Pa Ngando) was a bully-like one. I have my way of not giving bullies the chance to exercise their calling on me; and this because I know that fear (a one-way street) is not the same thing as respect which is a reciprocal affair. "Yeah, that is fossungupalogy, Doctor Liberator! Only the truth can liberate us. Bullies of any sort must not be tolerated in a reworked Africa!" (Fossungu, 2023: 148). As I have said before, anyone who grew up with my father and did not fear him would scarcely fear other people especially when it comes to reasoning with them. I will draw few examples from across my various professions to buttress the Sasse palaver.

The Graduate Teaching Assistant Browbeats the Bullies with an Expibasketical Racial Profiling Case

I was then one of the *Chargés des Travaux Dirigés* (Graduate Teaching Assistants) at the UNIYAO. This is precisely 1990 I am talking about. We had this problem of not being paid for the work we were doing, and we went to see the dean about it. The Faculty of Laws and Economics Dean (Professor Paul-Gérard Pougoué) began threatening us, saying that we were lucky to have been given that favour, with a monthly amount of sixty thousand francs CFA; that if we continued joking around (by making our demands) the favour would be withdrawn, etc. The few of my Camerounese colleagues that had even ventured into the dean's office (a lot of them could not even come near it) had already vanished when he had begun his menace. I just could not swallow all the unnecessary lies and threats and had to cut the dean short with my own lecture to him (to the consternation of the few colleagues and the dean himself):

Mr. Dean, with all due respect, first, I do not see the favour you are talking about. Second, you do not have to threaten us and think that will resolve the problem of our unpaid services. Third, you talk of the monthly sixty thousand francs *bourse* as if that is the payment for our services as *Chargés des T.D.*, pretending to forget that every *doctorat* student (whether *Chargés des T.D.* or not) is entitled to that monthly *bourse*. And fourth, if you think the *Chargés de T.D.* thing is a favour, then I (I do not know about the others) am demanding that my name be taken off it right away.

By the time I had finished saying all this (in French, since I wanted it to sink well into his skull) everyone still in the dean's office was fixated because no one had been expecting anything of the sort. I had to remind the dean (after some minutes of his saying nothing) that I was done with what I had to say. It was then that he got out of his absorption and said: "I will look into your problem, thank you." When we left the office and met the others anxiously waiting, Camerounese colleagues who were present explained it to the others: "That Anglo is something else! You need to have seen the way he was talking to the Dean, not at all afraid. He actually gave the dean a lecture that the dean who was very menacing at first ended up comprehending very well. The problem will obviously be solved." It was by acclamation that the group then made me their spokesperson. But for their acclaimed stupidity and power-drunkennes, why then are the entitlementalists still asking if Ayabacholization has legitimacy? It is very clear he does not have only that but, much more importantly, also the people's welbeing at heart. *Go for before Tara* Ayabacholization, real Ambazonians are ALL behind you following *man wey e know correct road.*

I have had similar encounters with managers and supervisors where I have had to work in Montréal (Canada), notably, Lockwood Manufacturing Limited (see Fossungu, 2015a: 45-49) and Rossy Inc. Most of these people confound fear with respect. The latter, as I have said, is a two-way street. They tend to have this feeling that everyone should be shivering when they come around; and if they find that you do not behave as such, they jump to say you are disrespectful. When I then give them my usual true and bold lecture, they often go nuts. In the case of Rossy Inc. Dollarama, the manager's going nuts got to a point where I actually threatened to take the manager and the company to court for racial profiling and the upper echelon of the company had to step in to quell things, as you can read in my very lengthy letter of 31 July 2006 to Mr. Brian Rossy (the owner of the company). Containing many points of interest to this discussion of boldness and racism in North America, it was titled "A Complaint Regarding Constant Workplace Harassment and Racial Profiling" (see Fossungu, 2015: 36-41).

Perhaps the Sasse College principal must have interpreted my fear-free comportment wrongly (just as the supervisors and managers in the course of my many professions that confused fear with respect), placing me on the blacklist of ringleaders of a class action that was clearly spontaneous and leaderless. Viewing the entire situation from the perspective of a farsighted person, the double jeopardy in going back to Sasse College (with or without my father) was unmistakable. But I had a year of college to complete and complete it must be. This is where the religion of the household (farming) has been a very handy tool to both sides – to the dismay of the other side that (like those confounding fear for respect) saw only the one-way of it. It was because I was not bitter and was still there in Yoke practising the religion during school period that the unexpected occurred. It all happened again (before and) in Manjo too in the form of the information and intervention from God, which you will get below after the Yoke one.

This is where not getting bitter as a result of being open-minded was again serviceable. Looking at the larger picture of things can be, first, a device to avoid despair and move on; second, a means of achieving what you set out to accomplish; and, third, a way of correctly analysing a situation to appreciate

166

what the alternative event would have meant, just as my analysis of the double-jeopardy in the Sasse re-application; all of them being linked to one another, of course. When you define yourself through objectives such as I have, you tend to have a largeyedist picture of things. Farming (especially alone as I was then doing) has always been an invaluable occasion for serious thoughts for me. I had already concluded on the farm that I was going to sit for the G.C.E. Ordinary Level as an external candidate. But let us get back to the narration of the unexpected that put out the external candidate thing. It has to do with my very cordial relationship with my then nauseating sister, Josephine, and especially with her husband (Monsieur Philippe Kamdom, the college teacher and our Yoke tenant who had impregnated her) and his own brother, Monsieur Jean, who owned the only Francophone professional college in Yoke. The school proprietor, my *moyo* or in-law, was surprised to find me in Yoke farming at a time when I was supposed to be in school in Sasse College and I narrated the story to him. It was, therefore, Monsieur Jean who took me to see "my Bamileke brother" (his words) who was then the WWMSS-Mpundu principal, for a place in form five in his college. I got the place there despite that I did not return to Sasse College to write the third term examination to pass to form five. My first and second term report cards were convincing enough. Monsieur Jean was thus very helpful, and I remember telling both principals, when everything was done, that "You both have just made history by doing what you have just done." I also heard Monsieur Jean, who I did not know knew me as much, telling the WWMSS principal (in French) that "if my school had an English-speaking section, I would not have brought him to you, because I know he will bring you and your school a lot of publicity with his performance." Monsieur Jean was certainly correct, and I did not fail him. All these past struggles then came flashing back as I was thinking of what the next move in CCAS Kumba will be, that would not also fail the

167

principal of CCAS as well as me and Miss Mandengue. The first and persistent thing that presented itself was the idea of "a man of many" forgetting about aeroplanes and medicine (like Ayabacholization) and leaping from the lower sixth form to university by switching to arts.

Not Agreeing Just to Avoid Disagreement: The Great Leap to University Education from Sciences to Arts?

It was about three weeks to first term examinations when I had decided that I was spending only one year under the unbearably tough conditions in Kumba. These are conditions that could not be justified in any conceivable way other than the sure certification of failure. It is not like my father was poor and financially unable to cater for me there. He did more than that while I was in Sasse College for four years. As Joseph himself has even told you in the Josephizationing Letters (see Fossungu, 2015: 76-79 & 106-109), Papa was very wealthy but preferred to live simply, investing a lot in houses, farms, and his *birth*-children's education and future. I am very certain that any of his birth-children who wanted and was willing to (like I was), could have gone to any university in the world without any money problems. For instance, in 1985 he single-handedly sent his first son, Joseph, to the USA for undergraduate studies and beyond. It was thus clearly not the issue of lack of means as that of the forces opposing my advance solely because I do not come within their definition of family and of child. I quite remember that the defining conversation with papa (noted in Chapter 2) took place in Kumba when I was in class five. I recall having talked about it to Rita Njunkeng who "really want[ed] to meet that father of yours who must surely have passed on his whole head to you." Here then was I in CCAS Kumba, about eight years later, trying to be better than my father by advancing academically so as to better help the greatest number of persons possible, and being tied down by papa himself? Surely not him that I must have to thank in the only manner he likes, which means not agreeing just to eschew discord.

To solve the problem being forced upon me in CCAS (and thus thank papa like he never ever imagined), I requested a switch to arts from the head of department and the vice-principal, just like Ayabacholization. Let's hear the fearless and savvy liberator fossungupalogistically addressing not only the priority changes even against the storm but also the confusion-generating question while further cutting the fearful politickerizers into swallowable bits in one of the paragraphs of his HISOFE Messages:

Yeah, one of the reasons I abandoned mathematics and computer sciences [like Momany in CCAS] and opted for human rights law and international relations was because for 30 years that I joined this struggle and sat in there with ambassadors, all these doctors they made these things so complicated. And we were always attacked as lacking understanding of these issues. Of course, we had no knowledge since we had not studied any of these things. We attacked Britain; we attacked everyone else and never held ourselves responsible. We never asked ourselves how is it that Foncha stopped the Brits from participating in post-plebiscite discussions. Because Ahidjo had manipulated him, while Ahidjo was receiving support from the French, he manipulated Foncha. We never questioned ourselves. And all along we did have some deep feelings that you can't simply believe in fighting those that believe in the use of arms with fancy words. I remember I had a meeting with John Fru Ndi and we discussed these things and I said 'Pa, we can't keep going this way'. I had a meeting with... [several others]. That was in 1997 when they manipulated the 1st of October. Please, listen, we could use different methods to challenge Biya. Yeah, I travelled from Bamenda to Yaoundé on their call. I came there to Yaoundé...to undertake an operation to destroy the printing

169

press to stop the elections. I made all these people scared. Sani Ahladji, I sat with him in the hotel, and he was scared like a sheep. And they aborted that operation because John Fru Ndi was coming to Yaoundé for a press conference, and they were all scared. I left from there,... met Siga Asanga, sorry, Asonganyi. I sat there with him to go for the next operation. I discovered all these men really wanted action, but they didn't have the guts. They didn't want to leave the comfort of their homes and stay in the bush. But all of them wanted action. We went for action (Ayaba, 2021b).

Yes, firm action speaks louder than just fancy words. But granting my simple request was not quick in coming because the sciences head of department (HOD) thought he could convince me to stay on, even wondering aloud to me: "If guys like you, with five Ordinary Level science subjects among nine are leaving to arts, who are those to stay in sciences?" That was a very poignant question that would have easily swayed anyone that was just trying to follow the breeze without any sense of direction or purpose like the social media noise-makers that Ayabacholization has asked to "shut the hell up" and "depart from the system and join the fighters on the ground" (Fossungu, 2023: 227). Until this time, it had become almost instinctive for me to say NO ("shut the hell up") to or resist anything that meant NO to my academic progress. I would thus use some illustrations here which also make NO an answer to any attempt to make me capitulate from what I believe in, as well as hinging on the somewhat "typical" African family definition and/or roles.

The Research Assistant and Christickinology Define Family Roles in Kananaski

The love science of Christickicnology is godmothered by charming Christine Nyaka (Christine), who I met in early 1984 in Manjo where I was then teaching. She is a tall and well-built light-skinned splendour with a uniquely charming way of walking (that very strikingly resembles that of Anna Ngomateka Bilong (Anna) who you will be meeting later). Chrisrine has this air of retention about her that is kind of very standoffish and truly menacing. Her seemingly unapproachable composure obviously quickly drew me to her, because of my bigimprizism (my love for always going for the big or somewhat impossible prize). But I got really hooked once I got to know and be with her (see Fossungu, 2014: 51). You will be learning a lot in this book (and others) from this special Camerounese Mbo lady who is herself also a clear victim of the irresponsible definition of family in the household. For now, here is her essential message on the 'not agreeing' issue at hand. I had a pregnancy dialogue with Christine in September 1984. The plan was to get her pregnant before I leave Manjo for Yaoundé where she was to later join me.

Describing Christine as my "younger identical twin-sister" would be the best way, I think, of saying that both of us shared so much in perspectives and scope to the extent of seeming to share the same clock-ticking head. With Christine, I never had to do too much thinking before presenting any idea to her because she did a lot of thinking (or christickinologizing) herself on whatever issue we had on the table. And this is where Christine was so very special to me; never just agreeing with me simply to avoid disagreement. Christine did not only reject my point but also was very clear on and extraordinarily convincing in her point. "Chéri, you know as much as I do that it is great joy for me to be both your wife and the mother of our children. But I do not want it to appear as if you are tied down to me just because I am carrying our child. Go, my love, and when everything is in place, as you say, come and see my people and get me. I will always be waiting for you. Moreover,

171

I think it is best for our children to come when we are both together and ready for them, what do you think?"

I did not say a thing for quite some time, just staring at this young and beautiful wisdom-box and highly wondering if leaving for Yaoundé without Christine was worth it. I have known so many women that would talk to the father of the baby they are carrying, referring to the baby as "your child", never "our child" as Christine did. Even the wife I eventually ended up with (that is Scholastica) uses her most domineering and possessive "my children", while all the other women I have children with would talk all the time of "your children" rather than "our children". As I tersely noted to the London court in Ontario, Canada:

I have always wondered why the only time the Applicant talks or acts in relation to these children as if she is not their only parent is when finances are being demanded from me. And I would be in deep shit (while we were still living together) should I not be able to meet any of these financial demands: occasioning most of the verbal and/or physical provocations that are at the core of the various moving outs.... Examples of this one-parent demeanour of the Applicant can even be seen in her always referring to them in her *Form 8* as 'my son', 'my children'; in her taking them away from Quebec without any discussion of the matter with me, in her not giving these children the chance to have their own father (who was willing to) drive them to London when they were leaving [Montreal]; in her registering our son in basket ball courses....[with her own family name and not mine]. (I discovered this during the long weekend of 8 April 2006) (Fossungu, 2014: 93 n.11).

Wasn't Christine then simply out of the ordinary? Of course, many women would also have interpreted my silence as anger for the rejection of my proposal. Not Christine who was waiting patiently, knowing fully well that I was merely marvelling at the depth of her uncommon *sagesse*. My long-awaited response was: "Christine, dear, I just wish I wasn't leaving, and also not knowing exactly what lies ahead: I would have gone right away to see your parents now and thereafter either stay-put or only leave here with you." Now, to the experts to find out: was leaving Christine, Manjo, and Ndoungue behind in October 1984 for the UNIYAO a sensible idea on my part? Whatever those specialists may find the case with Christine to be, the plain truth, from my perspective, is that child support would never have come about with Christine as my wife since she seems to be the embodiment of an ideal spouse for me and especially regarding her emphasis on both parents being there for and with "our children" (see Fossungu, 2014: 92-94). As I said earlier, much more enthralling lessons in Christickinology awaits you in this book, but let's examine the equally riveting Kananaski case now.

As a graduate student and research assistant at the University of Alberta, I met and made a lot of amazing friends from various parts of the globe. We went to the Kananaski resort in 1992 for a graduate seminar weekend together with other graduate students from other Canadian universities in Manitoba, Saskatchewan and British Columbia. It was looking very promising and hectic. In total there were five African students (Blacks) in the lot, three Nigerian guys with me from Alberta and one Ghanaian lady from Manitoba, I think. The first evening the film shown for discussion touched delicately on racism. We all watched and thereafter the discussion began. Participants said whatever they felt like saying about Black people, with the five of us there and participating and following the dialogue without losing our composure. Remember that we are graduate students from Civilized Africa, most of us very ripe and more than mature.

173

The second day the film and topic were on the sexes or what some would refer to as feminism (for a lengthy critical discussion of which, see Fossungu, 2015b: chapter 4). Indeed, the feminists seem to overdo it because, as most of the critics would agree, "Men and women are biologically different [and] Although obvious, the social implications of this simple fact have been the subject of enormous controversy" (Brooks, 1996: 327). Yes, Dr Stephen Brooks, you are exactly right. Feminism began denying the natural differences between the sexes, and thus gave the homosexuals some ammunition to carry the denial to its extreme conclusion. That is, both groups want to eat their cake and have it at the same time; the feminists wanting to have their exclusive world that I may venture to call *Feminista* while still living in *Masculinista*; and the homosexuals theirs of *Homonista* while still inhabiting *Heteronista* (Fossungu, 2015b: 123). Yeah, North America! Your religion and same-sex marriage puzzles are only beginning. Oh, Natural Sweet Sex! Where Are You? Here is a WhatsApp conversation on 07 April 2021 that I had with my wife (or "conjugal partner") who is still stuck in Ambazonia till now because of Canada's funny immigration policies that would prefer that Ernestine be an Ernest instead:

Peter: I wish you were here right now so we could make love.
Ernestine: Yeah, I wish so too. I would have given you hot and sweet sex now. Or just give you some nice kisses.
Peter: My love, it's just a matter of few months. Every time I look at you I know that is exactly what we have in store for each other.
Ernestine: And spend good moments too. Yes, it's true.
Peter: Of course, my wife. I found the wife of my dream in you.
Ernestine: Yeah, no doubt about it.
Peter: Everything will be fine soon. Trust me.

But I was totally wrong to ask for her trust on the matter. Trust me instead that my "conjugal partner" would have been in Canada long ago if it was another man like me! Tuffiakwa! Because, according to Immigration Canada, absolutely nothing prevents us from legally marrying inside the ravaging war in Ambazonia or elsewhere than in Canada! How clumpsy, this Canada that I took refuge in! It is surely another form of the West's pressure on African nations for the legalization of homosexuality, a thing that was initiated by feminism. Just boldly tell these feminists that they can't simultaneously live in both worlds, and they will tell you that it is sexism. These feminists do really complicate our understanding, as even the Kananaski film and discussion also portray.

The film depicted a man battering a woman; the root cause of the altercation being who was to do the dishes due to the *Umogorey Equalness* (see Fossungu, 2015b: 130-31). You would not imagine enough just how red most of the female participants had become even before discussing the film had taken off. Emotions were really running high, and a lot of the male participants were finding it awkward to even say what was on their minds. The ladies had obviously taken it too personal, and I was truly amused at their charging when I took the floor to contribute to the issue. I prefaced my contribution with the fact that I was surprised to be witnessing the kinds of emotions that were being brought into an academic discussion as this. The redness was growing with every word that was coming out of my mouth. But that was no reason to shut off "*The Truth Machine*" which "does not succumb to censorship, its source notwithstanding" (Fossungu, 2015c: 80). An utter war (like Paul Biya's on Ambazonia in 2017) was considered declared when I pursued: "Where I come from there would not even have been a problem at all, because there the majority of women would even get very angry just finding their men in the kitchen, let alone doing the dishes...." I do not think I even finished the sentence because hell had broken loose with sonorous calls from the feminists for me to apologize before the class could continue. Retaking the floor after the noise had died down, with everyone waiting for the infamous apology, I stated very clearly and loudly: "When we are mature enough to

175

continue, we shall continue. But, if an 'apology' from me (for what?), is what is necessary to continue, then we had better begin packing our bags and heading back to our various destinations because, as far as I am concerned, there is absolutely nothing to be apologizing for." Did the IG-Care know what for and why they were apologizing to Yaoundé "when our forces assaulted the enemy" (Fossungu, 2023: 151)? That is precisely how the four-day seminar ended on the second day, despite the all-night behind-the-stage attempts from the coordinator (who was from my university) to get me to "just apologize so that we can move on." Were we there to learn something new or just to move on? Why were we, Africans, there if North Americans could not learn *anything new* from our being there? Do African voices ever matter to the rest of the world? Why is the IG-Care that denounced and distanced itself from self-defense then claiming today to be in the Ambazonia War of Liberation? Haven't Ambazonians seen enough of their doublespeak to still even be listening to and following them?

Figure #27: Cathy & the Four Africans (Sam, Victor, Peter & Lawrence) at Kananaski in 1992
Source: Momany Fossungu's Album

While the Ghanaian woman from Manitoba had openly denied that there was any iota of truth in what I had said, the Nigerian men were very pleased with my performance. But they kept worrying about how we were to ever get back to Edmonton since the three of them were not sure Cathy (the White lady in Figure #27 who had travelled with the four of us in her station wagon) was going to still ride with us. I told them to grow up and/or follow me. Spotting Cathy, I inquired if she had changed her mind on travelling back with us because "my friends here were worried." She was kind of surprised that there was such worrying and simply enjoined: "Why wouldn't I want to return with you guys? I have learnt a lot about Africa just during this trip. And you, Peter, what do you intend doing after you graduate?" I caught on the chance to crack jokes with all the ladies she was with by stating that "I might be tempted to stay on if any of you beautiful ladies here has enough habitable space in your heart that could conveniently accommodate me and my bitter truth." Meant solely as a joke, this response seemed to have opened the floodgates and I was almost inundated later by the fast-rushing waters, almost like the rush to declare me their spokesperson after the encounter in 1990 with the UNIYAO Dean. The message is clear enough. People who succeed are those who not only know themselves but also have a good grasp of what they are up against in attaining their goals. Such persons do not just follow the wind but chart their own path, even against the storm like Ayabacholization. Thus, when the sciences HOD had finally realized how adamant I was with my switching to Arts, he let go of me when the first term was just two weeks to go and I went into the inquisition in arts.

Chapter 5

Divine Intervention Classics and the Drama in the Academic Inquisition in Arts: The Unexpected Dividends of Teaching and Learning Excellence

Ambazonians are a great and innovative people. Make no mistake about that. Only amazing and inventive people like us could be able to rise and never to fall again the way we have done after the international conspiracy and betrayal, coupled with the sixty-something years of brutal subjugation that we have been (and are still going) through (Fossungu, 2023: v).

When I arrived in the arts department, its own head tried to make a mockery of me in his English literature class. It was the first I was attending in that department. The HOD started by announcing that some losers like me think that the arts department is a dumping ground for those who cannot make it in sciences. Everybody laughed and booed. Next, he demanded the secondary school I was from, and I said World Wide Missions Secondary School Mpundu, Muyuka. The booing went even louder. By the time it died down he stated aloud that he knew I must be having four miserable papers at Ordinary Level. I knew it was my time to throw the ball back hard at him and I said, 'Absolutely wrong, Sir'. Everyone was now quiet and he asked "How many then?" I held them in suspense for a while before declaring: "Nine, sir; and, if you want to add the Religious Studies from London, say ten." There was stark disbelief in the faces (in like manner as Ayabacholization's 'leaked' showing up in Dadi, Ambazonia, to officially launch self-defense) that someone from WWMSS-Mpundu had those results.

Yes, people often attach so much or so little to the name of an institution or affiliation than to the product itself. This attitude is also seen in how many academic journals and book publishers have often accepted my manuscripts but later refuse publishing them on learning (from the footnote material they thereafter request for inclusion on author) that I am not then affiliated to any university institution. They just do not seem to believe that someone "unaffiliated" could have produced manuscripts of such quality. Didn't the naysayers/nosifeans fill social media up with claims that the Ayabacholization Dadi Appearance occurred somewhere else and not actually in GZ? No value at all is attached to having even been affiliated to the UNIBU, whose authorities "are champions in fighting for their stomachs rather than the welfare of the leaders of tomorrow" (Nyamnjoh, Gram & Konings, 2012: 203).

For the one academic year I spent as a lecturer at the UNIBU, I never succeeded in being able to see Vice-Chancellor Dr Dorothy Njeuma. To see the woman was even more problematic than seeing the Etoudi Palace Emperor called Paul Biya. Yet, this is supposed to be an 'Anglo-Saxon' environment for promoting academic excellence? These are the types of things that could never have appealed to free thinkers like some of us, quite apart from the low or no pay. This thus pushed some of the best brains from lecturing to joining the Exodus, just as most of our students also have since been clamouring to leave the Disgusting Hole. You would better comprehend why some Africa-loving academicians like us even had to join the exodus out of the rubbish country when you hear the testimony of some employees of the G.C.E. Board itself that should also aid your comprehension of the Dioh-Education Subvention palaver (see Fossungu, 2013a: 98-99).

Beautiful and intelligent Odilia Nkweteyim (as she then was) supported Dioh's theory in a way when she went on in her mail of 26 June 1996 (to me) to exemplify her own thesis on the Cameroon disturbingly deteriorating socio-econo-political atmosphere (or quagmatickism) with "A place like the G.C.E. Board" which many people had considered to be a "heaven" and which is gradually collapsing (like Cameroun itself is doing right now: thanks enormously to the Ayabacholization Economic Sabotage); how its workers have not received their salaries for a couple of months and "it seems more problems are ahead." The paradox of the situation, according to Odilia, being that the Board's workers put in so much, working their asses to death "for the past three months" and "working for at least 15 hours a day and it seems it is not being appreciated." What makes the case pathetic relates to the rudeness of the bosses who are well known for treating the workers "like school children. You know that nearly all of them were teachers. They work [here still] as if they are in the classroom with their students." AEB is certainly taking stock here, I should believe *noh*? Let's now re-bring in one of their real CCAS students then that they are bullying into narrow-mindedness/submission while AEB gets the opportunity for assembling more corrective/reformation notes! Educators too already have the number of miserable G.C.E. papers they associate with certain academic institutions, clearly failing to grasp with President Nelson Mandela of South Africa (as quoted in Fossungu, 2013a: 176) that "It is what we make out of what we have, not what we are given, that separates one person from another." The students in the CCAS class from Sasse College then began claiming that I was not a product of WWMSS-Mpundu but of Sasse College and went into the chorus of "Figaro Cinq, Figaro Cinq", with a later CCAS chorus being "read this classic paper", "read this classic paper."

Figaro Cinq Reading Classic Papers of the Academicshatterer

How Figaro Five became like my first and surnames could be a whole book of its own, but I will try to summarize it here. To begin with, it is not quite clear which is first and which surname, especially as in then Cameroon there was just no order in the order of names. Ambazonia, are you going to continue with this mess or do something innovative, meaningful, and orderly about it? In Sasse College the general trend was for the person to be identified more with the surname that was placed first. Bravo Sasse Collegeans for putting Africa first for once! Thus, we would there say Fogam Edwin Khebila, Ayah Paul Takha, Tabot John Enow (popularly known as Bucaro), Arreyngang Walters Bullivant, Anusiem Celestine Ihenacho, Fonjock Cornelius Ekenya, Ejuba Wilson Ejuba, Kalu Oscar Embola, Nanji Henry Sako, etc. In this book that cuts across continents, I have preferred to use the Western name format of First, Middle (where applicable), and Family – an arrangement still defied by "Figaro Cinq".

The story of the first name would come before the most interesting story which relates to the 'surname' that is still used by my brother, Bernard (aka Coastman), to date, as seen in Chapter 3. Figaro is a 'beautiful-lie' show-name I had myself chosen for two reasons: distinction and camouflage. It had to set me apart from all others bearing Peter in especially night clubs and football fields, as well as other social milieus. No "chick" or 'nga' (as we used to refer to girls: don't I also hear Ngong-Dog Capo Daniel's leaked womanizing Bangkok audios well?), for instance, had to be in any doubt as to who was being talked about. The name did not only sound good and attention-pulling but also unique to a unique guy. Remember that I was at the time a 'college boy' and, though in Sasse College, was making a lot of waves especially in Cameroon Baptist Academy in Muyuka with fellow Sasse College and Yoke mate, Celestine Ihenacho Anusiem (Anusiem). Imagine my father sitting in a gathering there and hearing this talk of Peter being in Muyuka during the weekend whereas he never saw me there in the Farm Capital. He would surely want to ascertain by asking if it is "my Peter" that you are talking about. That would clearly not be the case if the same people were talking about Figaro, who is indeed the same "my Peter". But Figaro became so popular that the cover behind it was almost instantly blown. How could it have been otherwise when Sasse College friends and others would always come to our household asking not for Peter but for Figaro Cinq? That was as far as the first name goes but the most interesting story relates to the 'surname' (Cinq) that is still used by many to date.

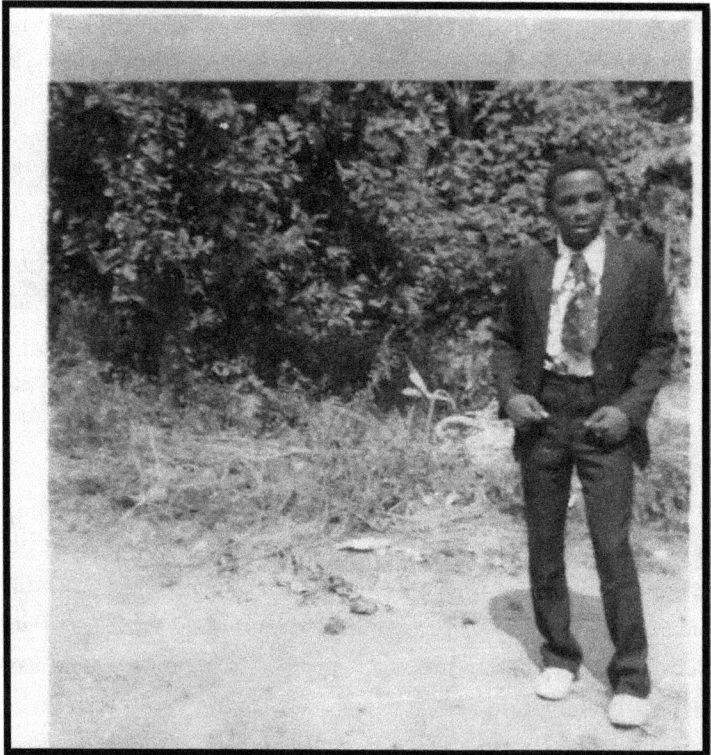

Figure #28: "Figaro Cinq", the teenager and 'college-boy' *posteuring* in Yoke in the 1970s
Source: Momany Fossungu's Album

I seem to have something very special with five. That cannot simply be because I have five children (three handsome boys and two pretty girls who are seen later in Figures 36-39). They were not there then even though I always knew I was going to be father to that number of children or more (although not in the least that they would be from three different mothers – thanks again so much to the household's definition of family). My batch in Sasse is the 1975 Class, a class like no other I have been part of. It appears as if all the Mr. First in Class from all the 'Anglophone' primary schools in then Cameroon converged in Sasse that September 1975 to begin a unique and destined journey together. In this batch it was not unusual for there to be constant clashes of wills such as the Fogam-Ejuba one that set almost the entire class into two opposing camps of the 'Cold War'. Backed by my home experience, I was one notable exception of people that conspicuously refrained from exhibiting the camp-toeing comportment that ensued. All this notwithstanding my being Fogam's classmate from the Victoria school as well as his next-bed neighbour in the St. Peter's dormitory.

By: tfofung
File Name: photo.JPG

Posted: Nov 25, 2011
Resolution: 640x478
Size: 132KB

Figure #29: My Sasse College 1975 Batch in Form 3
Source: Titus Fofung

It was also not uncommon in this class for someone who had been last in class (even without failing) in the first term to fight his way to the first position and vice versa. No one was immutable. In this class of the best no one was able to monopolize any position in examinations except Figaro with the fifth position successively. That is how the Cing got stuck to me in the first place. The Five was then confirmed in the soccer pitch. I have always used both hands and legs a hundred per cent until high school; although, ironically, I do not know how to swim. I had to drop out of most of these things I am gifted at solely because of the CCAS challenges, occasioned by the untoward definition of family. Ambazonia, please take the necessary steps to prevent such Talent Waste in your children, who should also truly be the real Leaders of Tomorrow (see Fossungu, 2021 & 2015d for some further sane suggestions).

That loss of mine in CCAS is the shrimp bending its back again to counter adverse and menacing conditions, as I have said. Until then, you could not easily tell the difference between my two written samples, each done with a different hand.

The only position in the soccer field that I have never taken up is that of goalkeeper. This is most probably because, first, it involves more use of the hands than legs; second, it is very associated with swimming (diving); and third, some beaten goalies often talked of seeing but spears (for example) and not balls coming at them – being witchcraft issues that are also scattered all over this book. Anyway, as troublesome to defenders as I was with my double-legged play, I was also one of the few defenders (number five) that often stopped equally double-legged nightmarish attackers like Bucaro and Bibum Mbock (both examples being from the same 1975 batch). Although I excelled in many other positions, I became more and more identified with the number five position. Some French language lovers in class (and probably also knowing Figaro to be the name of a French magazine, and, perhaps, also influenced most likely by the subtle name-assimilation tactics) turned five quickly into cinq that has since sent the English version to the background. It is thus Figaro Cinq (not Five) that reached the college in Mpundu, whose results were in doubt in the department of arts in CCAS – thanks very much to my never losing sight of my objectives. Ideals that were largely behind my then being in the Academic Inquisition of the Arts HOD who grossly mistook me for a loser.

The Arts Department Head, apparently still trying to recover from his puzzlement, then demanded my grades in the A3 combination that I had opted for, beginning with his subject, English literature. I told him I did not take it at the Ordinary Level (since it is either physics or literature, not both). That, again, gave the class reason to laugh. Anyway, he said, you must have done English language at least; what grade in that? I saved his further questioning by simply stating: "English Language, A; History, B; and Economics, B." I was then welcomed to the class, with most of the girls offering me a seat near them, like Rita in SHS Fiango Kumba strategically did. Being barely two weeks in that class, I took the eighth position with an average of 10.48 on 20 in the first term examination. There was a gapping leap forward in the second term examination, not having to write the third term since I was taking but the G.C.E. Advanced Levels then. Like Ayabacholization does all the time, I was looking further than my contemporaries were, which explains why 'Read this Classic Paper' soon became another nickname of mine in CCAS.

In the UNIYAO, 'read this classic paper' changed into the *Professor* and *Lord Denning* nicknames due to the amount of stuff pouring in so many booklets whereas most of my classmates would hardly be able to fill one booklet answering the same questions. The UNIYAO scripts were not only classic but also very lengthy and tight in ideas and flow that they became some students' unique study material. One of my UNIYAO lecturers once commented that (but for the fact that he knew me quite well and was in the examination hall seeing the booklets being handed to me, one after the other) he would have doubted that I had produced those answers only in the hall and within the time allotted for the exam. Yet, none of these UNIYAO lecturers was willing to act as my supervisor, an indispensable condition for entering the Maitrise programme! It was thanks to then newly arriving Maitre Dr Diane Acha-Morfaw that this collectively placed roadblock was invalidated. Talking of supervision and the unbelievable attitude, they are also seen in the Université de Montreal. The distinguished members of Jury of my Defence Committee were gleefully shocked to learn that the research in the dissertation before them had been carried out without even a single trip to Cameroon. And yet it was as current and well documented as it was? Impossible! Some of them just could not even begin to think of trying to start believing that 'no-sense-making' nonsense! Luckily, the supervisor of the work (Professor André Tremblay) allied the fact that it was factual: since, because of the desire to finish in record time and "be back home with a Golden Fleece", I was meeting with my supervisor almost daily and there was just no way I could have even sneaked my way out of Canada to Cameroon without the supervisor being aware. How did I achieve such a feat then? I hand that over to Scholastica and Barthelemy Dongmo Jiomeneck who are both well placed to tell you through their endless communications to/with the academicshatterer (see Fossungu, 2016: 38-50). Let me take you out of the formal classroom momentarily to demonstrate how Hisofeans always think, using the CGAM experience.

Figure #30: Barthelemy Dongmo Jiomeneck
Source: Barthelemy Dongmo Jiomeneck

Four-Eyesism on the CGAM Faulty Argument against Progress

First, let's have a little background on the Montreal-based Ambazonian Association (it would be AGAM if formed after 2017, of course). As a 'four-eyes' person, I would say Scholastica is one of the brains behind the CGAM. Not only because she was one of the thirteen founders but also largely because of her myopic refusal to run a restaurant despite the suggestion from many, including me. Many in the community wanted a point where they could be meeting regularly for good Cameroun/Ambazonia-type food and socializing and Scholastica's restaurant seemed the perfect place because her cooking compares to none. It had even become habitual for her dishes to vanish before the food of any other lady could be touched in gatherings. Her refusal here was truly myopic or narrow-minded since she saw only her going to school and thereafter getting "a good job" as the singular way "to be able to help my brothers, sisters, and parents." That is the kind of unthinking 'postcolonial education' Africans are given! This is someone who came to Canada with a first degree (BSc) from the UNIBU. Scholastica's narrow-minded attitude pushed open-minded and farsighted persons like some of us to look for other means of reaching the same or even bigger goals. Trademark of Hisofeans for certain. When the CGAM was created in July 2003, the majority of the thirteen founding members were Bangwa. It would have been so easy (as some of them were even hotly suggesting) to simply form a version of the home Bangwa meeting in Montreal. That was just too limiting as would have been my encouraging those passengers not to board the vehicles of the other drivers on the Douala-Edea Road in Cameroon (examined in Chapter 6) – simply because it was working to *my* selfish advantage. As far as I was concerned, the capital idea behind the CGAM project was to especially provide 'soft landing' (something I never easily got on arriving in Montréal) to as many Ambazonians as possible that were coming into Canada generally and to Montréal (the entry port) in particular. Even though created by English-speaking Cameroonians, it was not limited to that community but extended to every "Cameroonian of goodwill" and anyone having Cameroon familial connection, by marriage or adoption.

Goodwill Montreal (as the CGAM is also popularly called) went places, setting the bar in community activities, with previously existing ethnic groupings (of Camerounese origin) copying its statutes and constitution that provided for extensive "social packages" to members and the community at large. These "social packages" included things like financial aid

189

and moral support to those who: are bereaved, get married, are blessed with births, fall sick for a protracted period, etc. But all these go-ahead projects began dropping when small-mindedness set in with the multiple creations of small village groupings from West of the Mungo River ('Anglophone Cameroon'), a process that was spearheaded especially by Lebialem or Bangwa. The IG is now about seven IGs for precisely the same dynamics. Loud-mouth Pastor Anu owning and heading one of these IGs is also Bangwa, don't forget. Imagine that in 2007 a CGAM founding member was nominated to run for the presidency of the CGAM but he turned it down, justifying his refusal on the lack of time, etc. Thereafter he immediately went and formed the Lebialem Cultural and Development Association (LECDA) Montreal, being its first president. These *oversabi* Bangwa people! Other ethnic groups followed suit. The amazing thing is that all these mini-groups simply took the documents of the CGAM and replaced 'CGAM' with their various appellations and then most of their membership come to the CGAM and argue against the continued availability of the social and other packages that they maintain in their ethnic mini-associations.

I truly tend to dislike small-mindedness, although I still work hand in hand with small-minded people. I do not need to belabour the point by saying that I would not be where I am today if I did not learn very early to do so. Of course, I have learned to dislike lies without disliking the one telling them. But some people tell lies so much that they become the embodiment of lies; making it hard to see how in such circumstances you can actually detest lies without disliking the person. When you have objectives in life like mine, you learn to dislike people's ideas; not the people themselves, because they are enclosed in "the greatest number of persons possible" that you want to ameliorate things for. Of course, again, a lot of short-sighted minds would certainly be wondering why I did not react differently to the scheming comportment of Scholastica and her parents. Farsighted ones would know that it is because I am not like them. As already noted above, confronting narrow-mindedness with the same can never get you anywhere away from it. Because of my life objective, having a largeyed view of things has largely been the driving force behind all of what I do (including those in regard of Scholastica *et al*), as it is behind the CGAM and other projects that I also pioneered.

When you have a zoomedeyed look at things, you visualize them more clearly than those looking at the narrow. I have often seen many persons with whom I had heatedly disagreed (say, during CGAM meetings) express surprise when I later say hello to them. This is usually because most of them fail to see that my disagreement with their idea expressed during those discussions has nothing to do with their person or character. They sort of fail then to see the zoomedeyed picture, namely, that my disaccord with their postulated idea might be intended to make the Association even better so that more and more persons (including them) could benefit from the amelioration. Most of the points being made would be better understood, for example, from the following proposals I made in the CGAM Forum on 19 November 2006, titled "My Idea of A Cameroon Goodwill Association of Montreal (CGAM) End of Year Fund-raising Party: Suggestions" in which I lengthily argued:

Hello Goodwillers, let me salute you all with this idea of mine that no idea that is aired is useless. What I think is unfruitful is an idea that is not aired or made known. Sometimes (if not often) it takes a small or little idea from one head to provoke or nourish a grand or big idea from another head. So, fellow Goodwillers, never think that your idea regarding how our dear CGAM could be made even grander (or on any issue whatever) is not big or important enough to be aired.

Of course, not all ideas that are aired would end up being acceptable to all and sundry. But that is quite a different matter from saying that only ideas that are to be acceptable should be put forward. How on earth are we to know whether or not an idea is to be welcomed favourably except by tendering it?
It is only normal for an association that has distinguished itself the way our CGAM has, to organize an end of year party. It is

even more crucial when such a party is fund-raising inclined. It seems to me, from the lengthy discussions during our last CGAM meeting of 11 November 2006 that we have collectively missed a lot of things regarding the specifics of the type of party we are planning for the 30th of December this year. There are other pertinent issues that I would like us to review with the view of rendering the CGAM even more effective in attaining its noble objectives. While touching upon some of these concerns here, I would like to anchor everything on and around our end of year fund-raising party.

1. The Party Organizing Committee (POC)

That the General Assembly of CGAM found the organization of this party very important in its bid to have finances available for the accomplishment of its goals, can be evidenced by its Resolution that also gave birth to the Party Organizing Committee (POC). Here are some recommendations in regard of this POC. First, let us make this POC a permanent organ of CGAM. By 'permanent' here, I simply mean to say that the POC should be an all-year-round functional body that shall be responsible for the organization (in liaison with the host, of course) of all CGAM parties (such as born-houses, baby-showers, marriages, meeting-hosting, Children Christmas, etc), including – but not limited to – the grand end of year one. Second, the POC should have mandate at such functions to take stock to ensure that members honour their responsibility (such as paying the required dues, bringing along a reasonable quantity of food or drinks, as the case may be) so as to make the occasion at hand the success that every CGAM event ought to be.

Third, this POC should be able to return to the venue of such ceremony, on the matter-of-course invitation of the host, and collect all returnable bottles (I can already see some of you laughing here, but wait a minute!) and exchange them for the cash that the treasurer will put in what I will like to characterize here as the End of Year Party Fund (see #2 below). Just imagine (conservatively) that there are a hundred of such bottles after every CGAM event or party and then do the arithmetic yourselves, considering *en plus* the regularity of such events within the CGAM circle. This is just one of the myriad of very efficacious means of raising funds to facilitate the realization of some, if not all, of our well-intentioned goals and objectives while at the same time sparing members of the need to contribute – at that time of the year when, as we all know, the financial pressure from back home is at its peak – toward the organization of the end of year party.

2. The End of Year Fund-Raising Party Fund (EYFPF)
Let us give Goodwillers a break in the usual all-year-round contributions to this and that. Let us strive for means to make CGAM and Goodwillers mutually respectful of each other. I am therefore suggesting here that we create the EYFPF like what we now have as the Emergency Fund (see #4 below). Every member (new and old) should be required to pay the totality of these two Funds before their admission or renewal of membership at the date of application or in January of every year, as the case may be. Since this might be coming very close to the January line, it could be that we make an exception for 2007 (should we decide to institute it) and extend the deadline to about March for the January Option (old members). Of course, this will apparently be burdensome initially and at first look. But the institution of this EYFPF will not only free most of us from the aforementioned peak period financial pressures. It will also ensure that our POC can strategically plan for and organize the grand party and, consequently, we will be able to generate more resources that can enable the speedy realization, for example, of our dream of having our own hall and meeting venue. A typical explication will suffice here. With the funds readily available at the beginning of the year, the POC can (whenever it finds beer, wine, and other liquours on sale) buy large quantities of them and stock. It can as well use this stock of drinks to generate more funds even before the grand party by reselling (at a little less than the current prices but more than its purchase price) to any Goodwiller who is organizing a little or big "something".

Goodwillers, let us look around us and try to see what we have so far not been seeing, not because we cannot see but simply because we refuse to see what we should see. Only the sky will be the limit to us if we not only pool our resources together but also think big and open our eyes wide enough to perceive what is going on around us. Not to sound like belittling the fun-having side of CGAM, I was amazed by the amount of dollars that our last financial report indicated we had spent for just entertainment alone. I was amazed because, for almost the same length of time in its operation some years back, the defunct Cameroon Investment Club (CamInvest) could not raise up to five thousand dollars ($5000.00). It had degenerated so much into a "Big-Talking" Club rather than an Investment Club that its spontaneous death came as no surprise to some of us that had become so disillusioned by the wrong direction the Club was taking. Maybe the time is now right to reinvent something in the nature of CamInvest? There is nothing that stops the CGAM and CamInvest (if we care about its rebirth) from going along hand in hand.

3. CGAM's Non-Profit Status
This hyphenated status has been raised, on countless occasions, to stop CGAM from levying one or other interest rate on its generous loans to its members. We must henceforth desist from burning our candles from both ends. This notorious argument has led several members of CGAM to stop participating in the savings part (a very crucial part) of CGAM and the result we all know: empty bank account whenever a member desperately requires a loan. It is not surprising. No one will need to be an academic economist to comprehend that the very idea of savings imports that of interest returns. The higher the rate of interest returns, the greater the motivation for people to save their money and the easier it also becomes for those in dire need of the loans to get them. It is a win-win situation and should remain that way: Say goodbye to the hyphenated word argument for another reason.

The proponents of this hyphenated status theory have often indicated that CGAM cannot charge a higher rate of interest because it is a non-profit organization as per its by-laws or constitution. If we must stick to this definition of non-profit association, then there will be no need for any interest rate at all, whether 5% or 0.0005%. No non-profit organization, I believe, could function if that were the right description to be attached to it. True to say that CGAM is a non-profit association. But quote me anywhere at any time if you like, a non-profit organization is not prohibited from raising funds to meet its objectives. It is rather proscribed from being solely profit-making inclined. How, for example, is CGAM going to "promote socio-economic and cultural values" of its members without the financial means to do so? If CGAM were to raise enough funds today to be able to purchase some apartment buildings from which it gets money (in the form of rents and tax returns) with which it fosters solidarity between, and easier integration of, members of its community, would CGAM have ceased to be a non-profit association and become a profit-making organization?

Brothers and sisters, let me seize the opportunity here to tell you that the objectives of CGAM are broad and extensive enough to allow us the legal leeway to do the things that we intend to do. To be able to do these things, we need money; and to get this required money we need to do a lot of things. All these things we can simply not be able to do, or even attempt doing, if we let Mr. Timidity take the better part of us. We must have to put ourselves in a position that is comfortable enough to easily confront events before us, be they planned and long-awaited such as births and other joyful occasions or emergencies such as deaths and other crippling accidents.

4. The Emergency Fund
There has been a stark difficulty with this Fund this year, contrary to expectations. Why? There may be several causes, but I will tell you one thing that is for sure. We have rapidly been using this Fund very inappropriately. That is to say that we have developed this odd habit of employing this Fund to

things that are anywhere but near emergency. I do not think that births and marriages, for instance, are emergencies. Let us henceforth strictly restrict the dipping of hands into this Fund for emergencies. The birth of a baby into our CGAM Family is not an emergency, no matter how largely we try to expand that notion. We can generally prepare well in advance to dip our hands into our respective pockets toward this event, especially after the Baby-Shower (if there is one) or the traditional announcement of delivery. After such breaking of the good news via e-mail, what we should be doing (rather than filling the group website with myriad of congratulatory messages) is to see the Treasurer/POC and pay the stipulated amount of contribution needed for the born-house. This is what we should do while sending the congratulations to or through the couple's private e-mail address or phone that we all have. The same goes for marriages and others.

Fellow Goodwillers, the CGAM has, within its short period of existence, attained heights that are yet to be reached by similar very long-standing associations of Cameroonian colourings. This is largely due to the fact, as Mr. Martin Mpana [then Cameroon Acting High Commissioner in Ottawa] rightly put it [during their Recognition and Honouring event by the CGAM], that we are very well organized. I will here implore that we do not limit our renowned organizational ability to receptions and parties but carry it (through those) to the 'Outer Limits' of investment and business. In view of CGAM's status within our larger community, our End of Year Fund-raising Party, if very well planned and organized, can provide us the Gateway to the "Outer Limits".
Thank you for your time. Long Live CGAM!

These are suggestions based on a farsighted view of things that would scarcely be adequately grasped by small-mindedness. Narrow-mindedness will obviously preclude you from serving in any capacity in the administration of your successors. That is totally out of the question when you have objectives that are grounded in the larger-picture and by which you define yourself. It somewhat explains why then CGAM President conferred the first "President Award on Dr. Peter Fossungu In recognition of your devotion and dedication to the cause of the Goodwill Association and for outstanding service rendered to the Association." Noting the recipient's versatility of character which is both complex and simple at the same time; the CGAM president particularly mentioned how, after handing over the CGAM presidency in January 2005, Dr. Fossungu continued serving in other capacities such as cameraman; even combining this with Chief Whip in Ayah's second term in 2006.

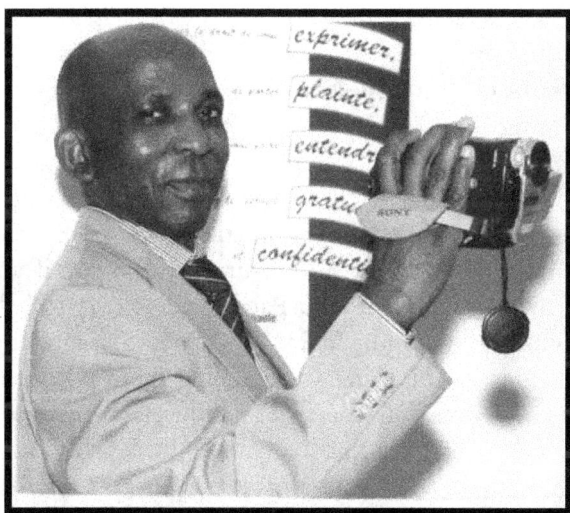

Figure #31: Dr Fossungu, the CGAM cameraman in action
Source: CGAM

If CGAM President Ayah in December 2005 put it in terms that would require a lot of brains to grasp, another CGAM President (who came one president after Ayah) simplified the matter in August 2008 when "Dr. Peter Fossungu Is conferred the title of President Emeritus In recognition and appreciation of his exemplary leadership as pioneer president of GOODWILL." As CGAM President Folefac also noted on the occasion, "What I find particularly unique to Dr. Fossungu is

197

his ability to so comfortably deal with or relate to people of diverse and differing educational levels and backgrounds, not to leave out their ethnic and cultural surroundings." The world would surely be a better place if people generally are truthful and look at the largeyedist picture of things. For instance, it is the Hisofeans that, as the CGAM presidents, have left some positive milestones in the history of the association.

Paul Ayah took over from me and carried the CGAM to a different and unprecedented level; largely using the internet in its management and operation, the scope of the association also being enlarged and modernized. I vividly recall how his progressive proposal for CGAM recognition and honouring of some diplomats at the Cameroon High Commission in Ottawa met with stiff opposition from the bulk of the members, most of who could not then look at the bigger picture and accused Ayah of using the CGAM for his post-hunting in Cameroon. That is clearly the mentality of post-hunters! Are those who are effectively working with the enemy LRC not the same people out there loudly accusing the Nationalists of working for Caneroun? It should not at all be surprising to you if you have properly mastered 'The Two-Pannelles Theory of Traitors Recruitment' (Fossungu, 2023: 172-86).. Disagreeing with someone's idea is one thing and libelling them is another, and the line had obviously been crossed. Ayah came around swinging when he gave the CGAM a bit of his impressive curriculum vitae in a subsequent meeting. It appears that many that had been going around with the stupid suggestion had not done their homework (just as the twisted-minded school authorities in Bamenda – see Chapter 6) to know exactly with whom they were dealing because thereafter the opposition had a glimpse of the zoomedeyed picture Ayah was eyeing. After serving for the two terms maximum permitted by the CGAM constitution, Ayah handed over in January 2007 to Hans Najeme.

It had become almost given that each president served the two terms permitted as they were usually returned to office unopposed. That was not the case with the Najeme administration. Ayabacholization wouldn't fail to agree and emphasize that an open-minded person hardly respects a tradition that is not progressive. The Najeme administration (like the IG Entitlementalists) seems to have indulged in what is now known as the Pepper Soup and Heineken Syndrome; draining the CGAM coffers dry, and generally not paying attention to what the general membership was saying. Fidelis Folefac (like Ayabacholization) was obviously settled on replacing Najeme after the first term and to once more bring honour to the CGAM. He planned far ahead (like Ayabacholization's creation of the ADF) by astutely recruiting a lot of members from his 99-sense Bangwa community into the CGAM. Najeme on the contrary failed to look ahead to see the approaching storm (or Biya's genocidal war) despite that Dr Folefac (as he now is) had made it clear to him that he (Folefac) was bent on booting him out of office in the following elections period, naively believing in the traditional return for a second term.

November 2007 saw another milestone in the CGAM's history with the crushing thrashing of Najeme (LRC) and the rise of the exceptional phenomenon called Fidelis Folifac (Ayabacholization). CGAM (like Ambazonia) moved yet to another level under this gentleman's presidency, revamped and fortified with the unparalleled visibility in the LaSalle Borough (international community) that the Association thereafter acquired. In short, Dr Folefac's community engagement through the CGAM earned him the Moulin d'Or Prize from the LaSalle Borough. The new bar set by Dr Folefac has practically made it very hard for those immediately following him successively (Edward Takang, Florence Nankam, Ignatius Mbeng, Caren Ayah) to really shine in the spot, despite their various efforts to stay away from the Najeme Administration's syndrome and to make the CGAM better and better.

Positive CGAM (like Rising Ambazonia) resulted from a negative answer to a restaurant (Force-Argumentalism). As a Hisofean, you also define yourself with what you want to achieve, not with what you do for a living. An open-secret ingredient of success is open-mindedness or farsightedness. For example, in the CCAS class the teacher has taught, say, Milton's *Paradise Lost* up to chapter two but I have already read the entire book. He sets his questions and while the rest of the class is answering based on knowledge of the first two chapters of the book, I am answering based on knowledge of the whole book. Of course, it is only normal that my script would be outstanding. In CCAS it was a general trend with every subject. It became traditional for teacher after teacher, after distributing marked test scripts, to say to the class regarding my script: "If you want to know what was required of you in this test, read this classic paper." This learning excellence goes hand in hand with teaching distinction that is attested to by more divine intervention classics of the Manjo year.

The Information from God and the Blessing of the Football Field Mishap

In Manjo, providence seems to have had its unique way of readjusting Mr. Bangwa-man's negative-backstabbing balance through Unexpected Dividends of Teaching Excellence. In Collège de l'Unité de Manjo I was on a monthly salary of thirty-five thousand (35,000) francs CFA and it was obvious that with just that UNIYAO was kind of receding from view. To ensure that I did not have to spend more than one year in Manjo before enrolling in the UNIYAO, I tried to acquire as many teaching opportunities; and this, as far as Nkongsamba and Loum, with Manjo being the mid-point between the two. Apparently, unknown backstabbers are gratuitously following and eating with me everywhere and every day. Inside Manjo itself, I had great chances with the only other semi-private secondary school called Collège Nlonako. One Bangwa man I met in Manjo was the senior English tutor there and it was to him that the Nlonako administration obviously turned for aid as to my employability since they do not quite understand 'Anglophone' certificates. Even Collège de l'Unité had to seek the views of the junior English tutor (John Teupuoh, from Cameroon's Savannazone) before finalizing my hiring. At Collège Nlonako, Mr. Bangwa-man (I will prefer to call him like this) just did not want the man he calls all over town "my brother" to be anywhere near Nlonako. He, therefore, told the college administration that my certificates were faked. This message was also passed on to the principal of Collège de l'Unité, who then tried to threaten/blackmail me with exposure. Because of "my brother", I was never hired by Collège Nlonako despite that I and my teaching style had already become the talk of the day in and around Manjo.

I do not usually go around nosing for information about people. But whenever having that information about them is essential to have in order to aid me in treading carefully, it often miraculously comes to me. The information from God is what I have called it here. You will be having several cases of the back-stabbers in the next Chapter and I will here just relate it to Mr. Bangwaman. I only had an idea of what must have happened in Collège Nlonako after I had stopped in Douala (to see Uncle Ngufor) on my way to Limbe for Christmas holiday of December 1983. I cannot exactly recall how the discussion led to Mr. Bangwaman, but I think my uncle asked if I had met any Lebialemzonians in Manjo. When I mentioned his real names (as he was known in Manjo), Uncle Ngufor could not believe what he was hearing. He explained that the real owner of the names was long dead and that the person at the time in Manjo (whose actual names my uncle gave) was merely using the dead man's certificates and passing as him, concluding that the bogus guy "does not even have the First School Leaving

Certificate." I was not at all surprised by the revelation, because I used to wonder a lot just listening to Mr. Bangwaman's language. I am not the spiteful type but just imagine his lot if I were. This information from Uncle Ngufor was, however, timely and very helpful for two especial reasons. First, I was able to clearly see where and how the counterfeit certificates story emanated in Manjo; and second, without it, I should have been going to the devil for help regarding a Manjo 2nd-term pregnancy issue, a thing which would simply have been like jumping from the frying pan to fire.

Like the CCAS Kumba and other detractors, Mr. Bangwa-man thus closed the Collège Nlonako 'quick door' to the UNIYAO. But my way of doing things helped. Anything I do that would directly or indirectly bring more happiness to the greatest number of persons possible I do with excellence, even if it means pioneering it. "I have fallen for you not because you are teaching English. But I am sure your way of teaching it has made many of us to come to like the subject." This is again Christine's thesis from the first conversation I had with her. Her truthful postulation during that enamoured tête-à-tête immediately reminded me of my first economics tutor in Sasse College who we nicknamed *Gentlemen,* because almost every phrase or sentence from Mr. Etta (a Manyuzonian) began with the word. I certainly defied pigeonholing into sciences or arts, but I fell in love with economics (taught from form three) because of the way *Gentlemen* introduced the course to us. "Gentlemen, six blind men went to see the elephant. The first approached from the side and shouted, 'I have seen the elephant, it's like a wall!'; the second, from the ear, said it is like a leaf; the third, from the tail described it as a rope; ... Now, Gentlemen, which of the six blind men saw the elephant?" As we were all happily and noisily debating the answer, *Gentlemen* cut in with "Gentlemen, as you can clearly see, all of them saw the elephant but none of them saw it intact. Gentlemen, economics is like the elephant...." That was extremely captivating for an introduction to the subject, an appeal which rightly, in my view then, deserved my paying great attention to *Gentlemen* to visualize this 'Elephant' intact.

Yes, AEB, I must emphasize to you especially that a teacher's presentation of the subject, especially in the first few days, matters a lot. The charming Manjo student was indeed quite right and truthful. Christine was not just speaking from the standpoint of someone who was so deeply in love with the senior English tutor in Collège de l'Unité de Manjo. Quite apart from being Mr. English, I am someone that does not usually get into doing a thing unless I intend to do it to the best of my abilities. A Must-Be Trademark for ALL Ambazonian educators and other professionals, as per the MISSG in Chapter 1, for the effective and concrete delivery of the Anthem Promise. Ambazonians, you must always remember therefore to always have both your *Prayer Before Meal* (Fossungu, 2023: v-vi) and the MISSG in mind at all times in order to guard against incompetence in Governance. Traorélization has also given a huge Thumbs-Up, *no bi sooh*? YESOOO, says the UNIYAO, where my tutorial classes were always jammed with non-group students who came to imbibe the "stuff" dished out in a way not common in the milieu. At the UNIBU, my law of tort lectures were often attended by non-law students. Most of them simply came to *"chop* Christmas with my own eyes". Teaching is a thing that comes so naturally with me. But you must already know, by now, it is not the only thing this 'Man of Many' does well.

Second term in Manjo phenomenally changed the dynamics of almost everything, including even my girlfriend! I remember fondly the drastic cuts in my monthly expenditures after the first term holiday. It is January 1984 I am talking about here. Most Manjo parents were not willing to sell anything anymore to "Teacher" (that is the way they called me). Why? The stories are endless but one or two will suffice here. On the first market day after Christmas holiday, I was there to get the usual foodstuff and other items. A mother from whom I usually bought a bucket of Igbo cocoyams already had a bag waiting when I approached her shed. She handed over the bag but refused to take payment. Three or four sheds away a father shouted: "Teacher, don't forget to come for your packet of beans, it is ready." It was like every parent in the market already had what I usually bought from them waiting for pickup; every one of them similarly refusing to take payment. As the cocoyams mother joyfully explained, her son had had to write the *Brevet* (BEPC) four times without success. (Now, also begin to visualize this coupling with the university-entering age-limit nonsense then in Cameroon!) But he had come home one day and very excitedly told them that he was having that certificate that academic year (1983-84) because of his new English teacher who had arrived a few weeks before. The tangible evidence was also in his first term results in which he had an overall average (*moyen général*) of 10.5 on 20. Therefore, the mother had concluded, "when I say I am not taking money from you for the cocoyams, it is my way of saying thank you very much for the good work you are doing for the future of our children."

I tried to explain that I was already being remunerated for the "good work" and did not need to be paid twice for the same job and I got an eye-opener when she retorted: "Who said I was paying you? I simply said I was showing my appreciation!" Wow! Wow! Wow! Just all what I could then say before yet another voice cut in with:

Teacher, please, don't you tell us not to appreciate your marvellous job because the college is paying you. Was the college not also paying those who were there before you but not helping our children the way you are doing? As for me, I am not selling but buying. I would, however, like to invite you to come and have lunch with us because my daughter is so certain of making her *brevet* this school year, and has since been speaking only English to us at home. For the first time, she has had an overall average of 11 on 20 in an exam, telling us that English that has this far been her greatest nightmare is now within her control.

Knowing and Mastering the Problem with Language Lessons of Globavillagism

Both of those students were right indeed because I (who had never been to any 'School of Education', the so-called teachers' training colleges known as *Écoles Normales Supérieures* – E.N.S.) understood the problem well and tackled it as well with innovative techniques. In then Cameroon's French-speaking educational system students do not pass in examinations by minimum number of subjects passed in with the minimum score as the English-speaking system warrants. As Professor Carlson Anyangwe duly explained it about five years after my Manjo stay, "One contrast between the *Brevet* and *Bac* examinations on the one hand, and the G.C.E. O' & A' Level examinations, on the other hand, is that in the former, in order to obtain a certificate the candidate need only score an average of 50% on the aggregate of the marks for the subjects taken; whereas in the G.C.E. he must score at least 50% in each of the required number of subjects" (Anyangwe, 1989: 199 n.6). Having taught in both 'systems' of education in Cameroon for a couple of years, I had several opportunities to listen to French-speaking students' admiration and yearning for the "*système anglophone*". But they are condemned to live with what they do not like simply because parochialism on the part of their 'tomorrow-yesterday' leaders would not permit 'copying' from *la minorité*. They persist in this in spite of the great harm that not doing so brings to young French-speaking Camerounese. Let me explain further.

I have used the concept of globavillagism to describe a rare genre of open-mindedness and foresight. The critics of Cameroon's 'bilingualism in French' (what I call Ngoalingualism) are correct and I have personally had to listen to the experiences of some Ambazonians like me (who have studied in Quebec's French-speaking institutions) that would speak volumes to the blinkeredness of Camerounese (see Fossungu, 2021b: 88-92). Swisselgianism that I must keep submitting persistently to the UDA (whose sure birth is being reinforced not only by the Sahel Alliance but also the 19 December 2023 Ambazonia-Biafra Alliance Briefing), could have greatly remedied this situation happening in the Manjo school and market. There is no doubt that disciplines like English, French, and mathematics were compulsory in both educational systems in Cameroon. But a student could still easily make the G.C.E. certificate without *all* these compulsory subjects. For example, you know my brother, Joseph, made his G.C.E. at both levels, although he could not register in the UNIYAO because he did not have any of the three. The important thing though is that he obtained his certificate with which he moved on to further his studies in the USA. This is not the case with the *Bac et al* methodology where there is a pronounced debilitating handicap that the authorities perpetuate without *seeming* to realize. Does the Yaoundé Thugtatorship even care one bit about the population's welfare? The compulsory English language subject alone, for instance, could and is well known (from the two Manjo students just noted above) to stand in the way of most Francophone students for years, through dragging down their *moyen général*. As the politics in place also did not encourage these French-speaking students to consider English and anything associated with it as important, that system of education then kind of imprisons most of its students. The English language-*moyen général*-reducing thesis being criticized here could duly explicate why most of these French-speaking Camerounese students do prefer to cross to neighbouring French-speaking countries – Central African Republic (CAF), Chad (CHA), Congo (COB), and Gabon (GAB) – to take the *Baccalauréat* examinations there. Dr. Christopher Nsahlai,

206

Cameroon's ambassador to the first of these neighbouring countries, clearly made the point on the mass border crossings in an interview in 1996 carried in *The Herald* N° 322 (24-26 June 1996) page 6. Understanding the problem is easily solving it.

Some Methods Employed for Diagnosis: Crisebacology Teaching English in English

My task then in Manjo (as well as in Institut d'Études Commerciales MATAMFEN in Yaoundé, etc.) was to aid these students to score not less than an eight on twenty in English. To accomplish it, I devised lots of unique teaching techniques that were wholly revolutionary. Ground-breaking in the sense that these students began skipping other favourite courses to *voler les cours d'Anglais;* that is, attend my English language lessons not normally scheduled for them. The techniques included things such as putting some salient distinctions (e.g. hard & had; walk & work; thought & taught; were & where) in class-beginning songs. An example is this one (the chorus being general/constant to all the songs):

As John was *walking* to school this morning, his head was *working*
Because he *thought* all along about what the teacher *taught* in class yesterday
Until he got to *where* the other students *were* assembled
And told them English was not as *hard* as he *had* imagined
Chorus: I love my English lessons and I am going to pass my exams this year

It is not just my teaching style that makes me a successful and well-liked teacher. The Ritaian crisebacology also plays a very noteworthy role, as well as my refusal to teach the English language in French. The application of crisebacology has not been limited to my own student years (male student-female student relations) but extends as well to my relations with those I teach. With me, the only advantage my student girlfriend, for example, has over the other students is the fact that I am available 24/7 to explain or answer questions on anything she does not understand; never to accord her undeserved marks. Manjo's Christine was so very special to me and when she said she did not fall for me because I was teaching English, she was very serious. She shared this same teaching/learning philosophy, as many of my other perspectives, to the extent that I sometimes wondered if she was not my younger identical twin-sister.

Figure #32: In the happy company of some of my
MATAMFEN students of both sexes
Source: Momany Fossungu's Album

This crisebacologistic skill in teaching has proven to be one of my strongest forces in the domain, setting me apart from the "marks scewers" and "money harvesters," and winning the trust and admiration of both male and female students as Figure #32 above can duly attest to. One education critic in 1998 told the story of the "non-doctorate doctors [in the

UNIYAO who] work as a team", one of whom "boasted around Bonamoussadi [the student residential quarters] saying, 'I have the fate of 300 students in my hands' and in this position, he collected ten thousand [CFA] francs (10,000) from each student who wanted a score of 12 and above on 20. Shame! You probably heard of this other one who, given the chance to scrutinize the files of freshmen for admission, admitted students who had neither French nor English – a prerequisite for admission. It was not an error. He did this by harvesting twenty-five thousand francs from each of the students who lacked this criterion" (Sheradin, 1998: 4). I vividly recall the hullabaloo that went around when my sister, Marie-Claire, failed the tort law examination that I graded at the UNIYAO. And also, when my wife's best friend (that many in the UNIBU mistook for my lover) failed the same when I taught there. Many just could not figure out how that can be normal in an environment where the twisted is the norm (should I not say, 'like father like son'?).

No one brings the incomprehension out as well as a student in the UNIYAO who I briefly dated. Rosemary came home one day after test papers had been distributed and she did not score well. She was very respectful as usual in public, never addressing me by my first name but by "Sir" (and "Dear" in private). But not so on that day. "Peter, I cannot believe that you failed me in the test. What's the matter with you...?" I had to cut her short, making things as clear as they should be. First, I told her, "I do not fail any student. If others do that, it is not my way. You fail because you do not merit passing. Second, you should be asking what the matter is with you, not with me." Rosemary was certainly not taking it in when she asked: "Why then am I your lover? What for, Peter?" I looked at her angry face for about two minutes (wondering why Christine could not be there at that very moment to address her for me) before telling her to tell me when her anger was gone so that I could then respond to her queries.

When Rosemary told me she was ready, I demanded if she had just dropped into town when she decided to go out with me. She said no. "Then you must have at least had an idea of who I was, or didn't you?" I asked. As she was saying nothing, I added: "Has someone sent you to come and change me then?" It happened as if it were Sam's Mother hammering the truth nail into Sam because Rosemary startled and said "How did you know?" before trying to retract with "I mean how do you mean?" There is a lot of force to the revealing Startling Thesis here also from PM Dion Ngute's popular 2022 Transmission of the Head of State's Freedom Message in Bamenda after his close-range encounter with Amba Fire from the Boyses in the Bushes. As for the UNIYAO Lover, I did not press further except to pick on her first question which I interpreted to her as meaning in effect that she was a lover to all those lecturing courses she passed in. She left my home together with the relationship. But not with my teaching practice and principles that dated back as far as Ekondo-Titi in Ndianzone (NDZ), Bamenda, and especially Manjo, where I also refused teaching English in French.

Another important tool I employed in Manjo (as elsewhere) was something that initially irritated most of the students – my firm refusal to teach English in French. It worked very well because many of them got the impression that I was null in French and thus began struggling to express themselves in class only in English, with the opportunity of my correcting them as they went along. I recall the first few days in one class when a student put his hand up and was given permission to talk or ask a question. He instead made the following comments in French: "Our English teachers have always explained things to us in French. I don't know how you are going to teach us when you cannot speak French." I perfectly understood him but seized the opportunity to send a very clear message when I turned to the best English student in class called Elizabeth Mbomgning, to explain to me what he had just said. After her explanation, I addressed the entire class in English, of course:

Listen to me carefully. First, this is the first and last time anybody will act as translator in this class. Second, I am here to help you obtain your *brevet* and any of you who would pay attention to my English lessons can already consider that certificate yours this school year. I know what the problem is and, working together, we will fix it. That is what I have been hired to do; not to learn French at your expense like your former English teachers. Let those who want to have their Brevet this school year put up their hands.

Everyone's hand was up. Collège de l'Unité de Manjo's Brevet results were far better than previously. When I returned there to teach in September 1984 in order to collect my holiday money, Collège Protestant de Ndoungué (near Nkongsamba) came knocking with a hefty job offer. The salary there (sixty thousand francs per month) was almost twice what I was making in Collège de l'Unité de Manjo, plus a big and spacious two-bedroom house and other amenities. This was a mission institution with a high school section as well, and I could also have combined its junior English tutor position with the Collège de l'Unité de Manjo position. But the call to university education was far too loud and pressing, the more so after what I had had to do to overcome Manjo's obstacles and other objectives clashes. I left for the UNIYAO, converting from teacher to student to continue authoring more unbelievable feats.

This unbelievability is also seen in how detractors (that hardly know me well) have attempted to frustrate my advance, just like most of my CCAS detractors must have been in disbelief hearing my name as the GCE results were being aired in August 1981 – thanks to *The Blessing of the Football Field Mishap*. I remember the McGill University LLM programme for especially an occurrence that reminded me a lot about my CCAS Kumba battles. During the first lecture in his course, this lecturer (a holder of an LLM) wanted every student to introduce self and what he or she had been doing prior to beginning the programme in McGill. Once this guy knew that I had not only been a lecturer like himself but was there for a third master's, he felt threatened (for what reason, I do not know). This thing went overboard when he further learned that I intended to proceed to the doctoral level. He openly told me that I was "overly ambitious." I did not see anything wrong with being that ambitious until when I (with a series of As in the others) scored an F in this guy's course which, by the way, was "open book" like all the others. The damage was already done because, by McGill policy, no one with such a grade can find himself or herself into their Doctor of Civil Law (DCL) programme. Of course, when you are a visionary person, you hardly carry all your eggs in one basket. The McGill professor had succeeded in barring me from the institution's DCL but not from the doctoral programme generally.

Yes, the McGill Air and Space Law lecturer foolishly thought I was easily stoppable. This is just like my detractors in CCAS Kumba who thought they had barred me from excelling (in their limited class examination) by reporting this and that. My CCAS Kumba second term results (even with the zero on twenty in manual labour) were so dazzling that some of my detractors (championed by Boh Herbert and Biga Emmanuel, if I still get his name right) thought they were bringing me down by reporting to the authorities that I had never been doing manual labour. This was at the beginning of the third term, and they were quite right. When I had transferred to

Arts, I left behind the manual labour patch that had been accorded me in the department of Sciences and was never accorded one in Arts. I did not worry about asking for one since it was not any part of the G.C.E. that I was preparing for. Their reporting this was simply what Sam's Mother would describe as petty jealousy because I was earning no marks for what I was not doing. But the CCAS Vice-Principal did not look at it that way and ordered that I must take care of clearing half of the school's football field. He provided my name to every tutor, with firm instructions for them to only allow me into their classes on provision of a note from him. The detractors were very happy that this misfortune had befallen me. They were going around saying "we shall see how he will perform as well in the next term examination now that he has been barred from attending classes until half of the field is cleared." They were even doubly happy when they checked every day and found that I was not on the field clearing it.

Unknown to them, however, this mishap was a very timely blessing to me. In fact, my 'one-term' high-powered success in CCAS seemed to be tied to double blessing. While it clearly limited my actual studying in the CCAS Arts department to just two weeks plus one term, there was a double blessing in the CCAS Football Field Mishap. First, it permitted me to put the finishing touches to my G.C.E. readiness with ease and without the additional distraction of further lectures and class attendances. Second, I had a perfect cover that prevented anyone in CCAS from even surmising that I was writing the G.C.E. My absence from the class examinations (which CCAS makes sure always coincide with the G.C.E. timetables to discourage anyone from writing both) was interpreted solely as tied to the fact that I had not yet cleared the half football field. It was a perfect cover, and it was not until August 1981 with the airing of the G.C.E results that they knew I had written it. I made it flying very high as usual because, as I will keep

213

emphasizing, your therapy begins with you understanding yourself and situation. BKF Captain Ibrahim Traoré, *Me I di hear you well well for 'Waga' nooh*? In my case in CCAS that necessary comprehension was backed and fortified by Anna's singular love and understanding. Most of the CCAS girls that were throwing themselves all around for me (thus invoking the jealousy of 'the reporters'), to no avail, just could not comprehend me. The CCAS battle had been won through a shortcut, thanks to Anna (then my wife-to-be). But that for acquiring university education would largely be responsible, in an oxymoronic way, for the loss of Anna. Because it took a very surprising turn, meandering through what seemed to be a dangerously elongated and snaking double-segment path. The second part being in Manjo that has already been partly examined here, the first segment (the roaming days) is studied in the next Chapter.

Chapter 6

God Proposes But Man Disposes: The Great Trek Roaming From Wonderful Bad News Bombshell And Elongating Shortcut

I know some readers are finding the question baffling, so let me quickly footnote the theory involved by deciphering what is actually at stake in *non-glacé* Africans drinking *glacé* garri in Douala, Cameroun! *Upsidedowning Africa and Downsideupping Europe!* Are you still wondering how? Figure this out again then. Cold Europe drinks hot coffee (that is exploited, just not to say savagely stolen, from civilized Africa) to keep blood warm for an ameliorated thinking capacity. But hot Africa, instead of drinking warm or hot liquids to keep already naturally warm blood even hotter for more improved thinking capacity, uncritically goes for cold drinks that would stifle thinking capacity altogether: simply because Europe has to sell its appliances called refrigerators, colonial education for "service disciplines", etc. (Fossungu, 2023: 92).

Half-heartedness on papa's part has always characterized my leaving one-level to another in academic progress and may largely belie the bombshell success. After obtaining the G.C.E. Advanced Level in the lower sixth form in August 1981, the idea was that of using Wednesday, the Yoke Market Day, to compile my file in view of registering for university studies in the then one and only UNIYAO. Therefore, before he left every Sunday for Limbe, papa would give money for the certification of some of the necessary documentation on the following Wednesday. (It is not like all these documents could not be certified in one-shot.) This happened for two weeks, and the file was almost complete, requiring just another week to be ready for the journey to Yaoundé. Like Anna, I was so excited but kept my cool at the same time because I never for one moment forgot what I was up against, especially when it always came to leaving one educational level to the other. The more so because of the manner the news of my success in the Advanced Level had been received in the household in Yoke. As Mamie Cecilia Asongu Fossungu (who was then papa's inherited wife and my mother's *mbanya*) wondered about it, "How could such wonderful news be received instead as if some very important person in the family has died?" I was right. And my correctness will see the dropping of the bomb which would initiate my roaming days that would eventually lead to the Anna-fiasco which itself would worsen the make-or-break year in Manjo two years later.

One major fault I have found in my father over the years is his over belief in those he has confidence in or in those who claim to know things (the experts) that he thinks he does not know. The confidence-fault of papa has worked both ways for me though. Papa generally treated his children without distinction or bias. This could, for example, explain why I did not know that Josephine was not his biological child. Of course, when any of them had won his trust or confidence, it became almost like a sin to the other siblings and my mother. In such circumstances, papa would never stop praising you and constantly requiring the others to emulate you. Take food for instance. He often found something to criticize in it: not enough salt, too much pepper, meat cooked too much, etc. When there is nothing to complain about, he would say this to the hearing of everyone: "I know it's Peter who has prepared this food." This type of praising did not only turn me into the household's sole cook but also enlisted my mother's distrust that dominated her whole attitude toward my continued presence and progress *in* the household. It is also because of his confidence in me that I (unlike many others) was able to even progress in the household until high school notwithstanding the constant tussle with the other forces.

But with this UNIYAO-going inclination, the unfavourable forces in the household realized the battle was tilting away from them and towards my side. As is usual that truth is stronger than lies, some cohorts from the outside had to be brought into play to reinforce the lies. The outside legion, as I later learnt, took the form of some of my mother's relations residing in Dschang who went all the way to Victoria (while we were in Yoke farming) to convince papa that it was an uphill task sending a child to the UNIYAO (but not to the USA where Joseph will be going four years later?). Studies at the UNIYAO were tuition-free and enrolled students even were accorded *bourse* or the monthly stipend that students called *epsi*. Since the talk of uphill task was coming from Pa Martin (as I hear the Dschang man at the centre of it is called), it was simply gospel truth. Papa obviously fell for it. Hence, the following Sunday (13 September 1981) when papa was about to leave and called for me, I was expecting to get money for the last set of documents to complete the UNIYAO registration. Instead, what I got from papa was this shocker: "I don't think I can be able to continue with sending you to Yaoundé; I am tired and there is no money. Go and find yourself a job anywhere." With those words from my father, I felt the world crumbling under my feet. Both papa and I knew that what he was saying was not true but that was not my main problem. It was the timing that puzzled me a lot. Had I been told this earlier, I would simply have gone down to WWMSS Mpundu, for example, where I had graduated in flying colours the year before and easily secure a teaching position for myself. Cameroon Baptist Academy, too, was just a walking distance from our house in Yoke. At that point and date (13 September 1981), no school could still have been without a full staff, with the school year often beginning between 10-15 September. I was truly shocked and temporarily confused but refused to be bitter.

I had learnt at a very tender age to depend on myself and never to be bitter even when I am disappointed or failed by those I love. Remember the 'biting up' uncle's slap in Chapter 2. This should have been one of the very first things that should have thrown me into bitterness, if anything had to. I have narrated my ex-wife's 'take and take and take' attitude in this book to discuss the new definition of family and why bitterness is not in my vocabulary. Thus, it makes no sense why I should have been bitter when papa who (in our own relationship) has been the only giver told me (the receiver) that he could no longer give. Remember also my conversation with Marie-Claire in Chapter 2. Not becoming bitter has proven to be one of my greatest strengths in overcoming adversity in life and moving on. A veritable ingredient of success, it is. Bitterness, for sure, will consume you even before the hardship that you are confronting comes around to do so. I am, therefore, never bitter; only what I say may be bitter (truth is obviously bitter, it is said). I think only those who cannot handle the truth get bitter because if you can handle bitterness, there will be no need for you yourself to become bitter.

And here is a bitter truth I reminded myself of on that 13 September 1981 in the comforting arms of Anna (the woman who is not my wife today, thanks mostly to this bombshell). At this point and level, I sternly told myself, if I fail to advance in, and towards, my objectives, the fault would not be that of papa but solely mine. Second, I must always bear in mind (as I had done till then) that many roads could lead to the destination and do not allow the closing up of one road bar me from getting there. Hence, I must again have to find a way around this particular roadblock. As usual, Anna was more than a 100% in the combat as she told me: "Piero, with you and me together, nothing can stop us. I know it is not going to be easy when you are out there alone. But I also know you know I am always there with you. And this knowledge, by itself, is both our shield and sword for the victory." What better wife than this would any man ask for?

Figure #33: Anna Ngomateka Bilong & Momany in Douala in May 2014
Source: Momany Fossungu's Album

The following Wednesday Uncle Ngufor was on his way to Kumba from Douala and made the usual stop in Yoke. My siblings were all gone by now from Yoke since school had already started. As you already know, Uncle Ngufor too had had his own share of unexpected disappointments, both elsewhere and in our household. He had been very disappointed and left for Douala but was not bitter. Which explains why he was always still visiting us (and bringing some Douala goodies along) whenever he had the chance like on that Wednesday. I told him about the episode of the Sunday before and he was both shaken and reassuring. He told me he does not make much from his job (which I knew to be quite true) but that he would not mind managing it with me, if coming to stay in Douala with him was the option I had in mind. I was so thankful and felt very blessed to have him. As he emphatically added, "you must have to discuss with or inform papa before leaving." I indicated that papa himself had already made it clear that I could look for a job *anywhere*. But Uncle Ngufor still insisted that, no matter what, papa must not only find out that I have left after I have left. Good and timely advice indeed. Explaining why he was topmost in the operation meant to eradicate poverty in the family (see Fossungu, 2016: chapter 3).

The following Saturday (19 September 1981), during our food break on the farm, I informed papa about the discussion I had with Uncle Ngufor. I made it clear that I was to go with him to Douala the following Wednesday when he would be returning from Kumba in the evening "to see what is left out there for me." Until this moment my arrangement with my uncle had been kept private. My announcement on the farm then sort of hit so hard (like the Ayabacholization bold introduction of the Liberation Tax) because, it seems, no one had figured out that I will ever be able to figure a way out of Yoke, the Farm Capital. I was less interested in the reaction of the other adults, paying more attention to papa instead. He seemed to have been turning a lot of things over in his mind. Almost like someone who deeply regrets a decision he has just made but finds that he cannot immediately alter it. Has Lion-Man Biya not now become a useless play-toy in the hands of his own appointees? Post-'Canada Pre-Negotiation Talks' events in LRC would adequately furnish your answer, I guess. I perfectly understood papa's predicament and knew, like Uncle Ngufor had explained, that he was a very good person that was surrounded by a lot of forces that were unendingly desirous of adulterating his goodness. At last he said, almost sobbing, "Okay." But his mood was different for the rest of the day and, but for the fact that I had to necessarily take full control of my future into my own hands (from then on), I would have told him that I had changed my mind. On Sunday, 20 September 1981 before he left Yoke for Victoria, papa handed a parcel to me that, at that time, I could only have compared to what was handed by the Father to his Prodigal Son before he set out.

This is in the sense that papa must have somewhat been thinking that it was the last time he might be seeing me. But, to me, there was no last time with papa whatsoever, even as my roaming days thus began with the ride to Douala the following Wednesday.

Exposing More Backstabbers and Divine Intervention From Douala to Yaoundé via Garoua and Ngaoundéré

Uncle Ngufor drives exquisitely well and the ride to Douala was smooth and enjoyable: except that I did not get to see a lot on the way since we left Yoke at about 8 pm. But the myriad of city lights that welcomed us to Douala was something memorable to someone who would only have been hearing of Douala in stories from the "been to" people, who often add too much salt and pepper to the whole thing. For instance, the impression has often been given that in Douala there are so many companies and jobs that you do not look for the jobs. The jobs instead look for you. Here then was a young man of twenty-one who had been told to go and look for a job anywhere and was just arriving Douala to get those jobs looking for him so that he could then choose the one he likes most. But I cannot even begin to count how many job applications I put in, and the number of companies I personally visited for the purpose. After several months there in vain, I had to move on and Debundschazone was the natural place to return to. I had a teaching spree there (National High School in Fiango, Kumba; a typing institute in Kumba Town; Unity Comprehensive College in Ekondo-Titi); always moving on because of my impatience with employers that do not pay me when it is due.

I then travelled to the then North Province (current Adamawazone, Logonezone, and Benouezone); having become very fearless and not having to think that I have to know anybody anywhere to go there. The journey up north was not through Yaoundé and by train, as most people usually take going there from Douala or Debundschazone. I went north by road, passing through Foumban (Bamboutouszone), Banyo

221

and Ngaoundéré (Adamawazone) to Garoua (Benouezone). This voyage reminded me much of my very first trip in life, out of the village to *ncheng*. As we boarded the same kind of Saviem bus (that I had first seen in Dschang) from Foumban, I was wondering if it was repeating itself all over again. During the long and tiring trip my thoughts were on the backstabbers in the household and outside of it, known and unknown. My brother, Bernard, is squarely at the centre of the Bishop Rogan College (BIROCOL) money affair which kept forcing its way into my head during the long trip north as well as during the one into Nigeria.

The BIROCOL Money Affair with the Njumba and the Bad-Name Giving Loan-But-No-Loan

Joseph was boisterous, very disrespectful, and haughty. But you would prefer dealing with him because you can easily predict his moves, unlike introverts of the household like *Coastman* (Bernard), Annastasia, and Gladys. By some curious ways of nature, the introverts were separated by the non-introverts in their birth positions. You will hardly know what is in store for you from such people until it has actually happened;, making them even more dangerous. Let's first take a very serious case of Bernard's duplicity, namely, the attempt on papa's life at his *njumba*'s home in Yoke. When this happened, Joseph's name was written all over it, with Bernard having thereafter taken off to Wum in Savannazone for holidays at his namesake's. Fon ST Fossungu (our grandpa) had to come down to Yoke to find out what could have propelled a child to such an abominable act. On being questioned by His Royal Majesty, Joseph declared that he had nothing whatsoever to say to anybody whosoever until his partner, *Coastman*, was also brought in. It was only then that anyone outside the duo (or trio?) shockingly knew Bernard had been actively part and parcel of the entire plot to slaughter both papa and Madam Catherine, his *njumba*. At the time of this worrisome episode Akana had been long gone, most probably because his hangman role had been conveniently taken up by the two boys? Perhaps *Coastman*'s

222

middle name, Mbancho (*battlefield* or *battleground* in Bangwa), was very apt?

Bernard was in BIROCOL in Small Soppo, a stone throw from Sasse College where I was. I once had some financial difficulties at school and wrote to papa for help. Since my mother had become a regular visitor to BIROCOL with Bernard there, papa (in response to my need and request) sent some money to me through her. She never came to Sasse College but left the money with Bernard who I saw often when we had outings. No mention of the money was ever made. During the following holiday, papa never heard me thanking him, as usual, for the money sent to me, so he asked what the matter was. Thanks to papa for being the type that speaks out his mind, the smear campaign failed. I am fond of people like papa who speak out their mind when they realize something is not going well. As I always tell people around me, remember always that those who never disagree with you are either your stooges or enemies. These are those that gossip about you since they do not have the courage to tell you what they think about you (or your stance on issues) in your face. That he who listens to gossip and does nothing to stop this gossiping, himself gossips. If I tell you that I saw Yoyo stealing something, the best thing to do is to have Yoyo and I present and then ask me to repeat what I had told you about him. If I cannot then say it again, then it is gossiping that it was, and you would have thereby stopped it because I would not have the guts to come to you again with any more gossips. There are, therefore, two reasons why I particularly like when someone corrects or criticizes my errors. First, I know I am human and, second, I know I am dealing with another human, not a monster that may devour me when I am not looking. That is why if I were Cameroun's President, I would fire all 'collaborators' that never disagree with me; including those that do so only to eschew being fired for not disagreeing, for these are even more dangerous.

Unlike my father in the BIROCOL money case under discussion, Peter Ngunyi Asahchop (my ex-father-in-law) cannot speak out his mind and thus helps in disseminating gossip or blackmail, if not actually creating and promoting it. In October 2002 I lost my father. Friends in Montreal, Gatineau, and Edmonton donated whatever they could to assist me to go to Cameroon for the burial. But my wife (Scholastica) instead lent me a thousand dollars. I duly repaid this loan after my return from Cameroon because a loan is a loan, not a gift (notwithstanding that she was lending me money while still wholly 'parasiting' on me – to use her own words). In view of Scholastica's obstructionist and moneyintriguing comportment, especially as captured in my lengthy Eugenizationing Letter of October 2001 (see Fossungu, 2015: 27-32), it is surely a complete miracle (*The Means of the Divine*) that I was even able to be present at the burial of my dad in October 2002. As said earlier, I could only make the journey, thanks to the efforts of my colleagues in Edmonton, Gatineau, and Montreal who assisted financially as shown in Fossungu (2016: 163-64).

From the above reference, the contribution from my Rossy Inc. colleagues (a few of whom are with me in the picture below) came with "A message of Sincere Sympathy" card that all of them signed which told me that "May the love of those who care, strengthen you during this time of sorrow." In their sympathy card, titled 'Remembering You In Your Time Of Loss', the Whistance-Smiths of Edmonton also wrote to "Dear Peter" that "I hope that you make it to Cameroon in time for your father's funeral. We've enclosed some money as a gift to put towards the cost of your air ticket. With much love, Nancy, Andrew, Greg, Tim & Emily."

Figure #34: With some co-workers of Rossy Inc. in December 2004
Source: Momany Fossungu's Album

Figure #35: The Whistance-Smiths in the 90s: Nancy, Tim, Greg, and Andrew
Source: Nancy Whistance-Smith

From the same point of reference above, you can see that someone like Denis Alem contributed twice (both as an individual and as a member of the group) whereas all what Scholastica did was to *lend* money to her husband (upon whom she was even utterly reliant while taking good care of the Asahchopination with every dime that came her way). But that is not all. Before I had reached Cameroon for my dad's burial, however, Scholastica had communicated with her father, telling him she had sent a thousand dollars (1000.00$) to him through me. I arrived and after the ceremony in Nwangong I visited my parents-in-law in Fontem and spent two or three nights there. All along the house was always full of visitors (their friends and neighbours) that, of course, I needed to entertain; and all along my father-in-law kept saying "we haven't talked". All the time I would be waiting for him to introduce the talk to no avail. I never understood him until I left Fontem and eventually returned to Canada. As already indicated, I repaid the loan to his daughter, my wife.

It was not until June 2004 when I again visited Cameroon (after my father-in-law had died in February that year) that I understood he had been very angry with me, having written to Fon DF Fossungu (the Fon was kind enough to let me have that letter) and bitterly complaining about my disrespect for him and his entire family. Is it not amazing that someone who disrespects you is right there with you, and you cannot tell him that to his face, but wait till he is gone, and you talk about it to others? Knowing me and not believing it to be true, the Fon had inquired to know how I could have been that callous towards my in-laws and my father-in-law then narrated to the Fon the entire story of his daughter sending him money through me and how I never handed it over. What a way to give a dog a bad name! Just how many more of such contrivances are out there around my name and person? The really important question is: Why did Scholastica's father not squarely confront me by directly and cleanly asking for the money that had supposedly been sent to him through me, like papa did concerning the money he sent to me but got no thankyouology in return? Wouldn't that have been what to expect from a bold and truthful father-in-law especially?

Take also my mother-in-law's case since we are now not only talking money affairs and their roles in the definition of family and children's future but also talking about unknown backstabbers. You must have heard Fon DF Fossungu's take on the intriguer's death and burial (see Fossungu, 2016: 89). In the Fon's letter, they were also spending the 18,000 CFA francs, which is normal. But the abnormality is that they were never even told by the man's wife (Elizabeth Asahchop) that I had *directly* sent 500,000 (five hundred) CFA francs to Mrs. Elizabeth Asahchop (née Njuafiac Elizabeth Tendongafac) for the purpose through Western Union MTCN 610-524-1226 of 8 February 2004; agency Doreen, operator 493; the sum being equivalent of CAD $1402.18. This money was not just hidden from the Fossungus but also the dead man's own family members. Again, in the same Fon's letter, Scholastica justifies well her not talking about the marital issue to the Fon of Nwangong. But it also raises stiff questions relating to when 'I was present' when she did talk (lie) about it to her own parents (and other relations)? What was she hiding this time?

I do not usually do anything because I want to go about boasting about it. But, as Chinua Achebe has again said, the lizard that successfully jumped from the high iroko tree said it would congratulate itself if no one else did. The parental role is very important in the shaping of the future of children; being intimately tied to the truthfulness of parents and other relations. That is why I am here talking a bit about Scholastica's mother's back-stabbing attitude that augurs badly not only to the definition of family but also to children's future, using her callous ingratitude generally and her moneyintriguism particularly. Mrs Asahchop is not fit even as a grandmother! Most of you would find it hard to believe that it was only in

Cameroon in 2014 (when I went to bury my birth mother) that I learnt that Scholastica's mother has been living in Canada for years. I could only then divine that this might even be why my calls to London (Ontario) had since never been answered, making absolute nonsense of Scholastica's letter of 10 September 2004 to me in which she clearly indicated in the 4th paragraph that "The children are going to miss you, and please do not hesitate to call them and talk to them. Do not stay away from them because they need you. You could pay them a visit" (Fossungu, 2016: 29). As I have indicated, some people hide their identity by calling *private*, but I never call *private*, having nothing to hide in doing that. Their reasoning must be that if I am talking to them, the children (since children don't usually know how to lie) would let me know that 'grandma' is there with them. Yes! Children don't lie! Who has not heard the story of the debtor, son, and creditor? The debtor hid himself in his bedroom and told the son to tell the creditor that he has gone out. On the creditor's inquiry of the father's whereabouts, the son said: "My father who is hiding in his bedroom told me to tell you that he has gone out." Hearing that, the father had no choice but to come out of his hiding place while creating other schemes to tell the creditor. Did someone not already tell you that schemers are always living in fear, thinking everyone else is scheming to do to them what they know they always do to others? Otherwise, what is it that these Asahchopination people are trying to hide? Even if Elizabeth Asahchop is in Canada illegally, am I an immigration officer or police officer or what?

The significance of these questions is heightened by the following children-father abortive communication that has also enormously given impetus to the writing of this book. On Tuesday, 23 February 2016 I wrote a letter to my daughter and son. I sent it by registered mail to the address of the French-speaking school attended by these two children in London, Ontario. Until today, the letter has not been returned for non-delivery. Yet, I did not hear from the children, in spite of the earnest appeal in the letter:

My Dear Ngunyi and Nguajong:

I write this note to you with a heavy heart. I hope it finds you in perfect health. Please, I just don't know how else to reach you both other than through this medium. I have called 226-XXX-XXXX several times but have never heard from you: despite all the messages I left on the answering machine. I guess you are not aware of my phone calls. That is why I am now trying this other method of getting to you directly through your school address. Don't be surprised that I know where you school. I am your father and, despite that we are not physically with each other, I am always with you both, as well as with your three other siblings – Kelie in Douala (whose photo is enclosed) and Peter & Peteraf in Montreal, who you also see in the photo together. My recent photo is enclosed as well.

My Dear Ngunyi & Nguajong, you may not be growing up together with me and your other siblings, but that *alone* cannot change the fact that you are all *my* sons and daughters. Your senior sister, Kelie, has never ceased sending her greetings and affection to the four of you. She has never stopped wanting to communicate with you directly. She has never stopped desiring to meet all of you in person. I know Peter and Peteraf are still too young to be able to independently communicate with the three of you. But the three of you are now mature enough to do so. Kelie would have already contacted you but for the fact that I don't have your email addresses – the most appropriate means for that at the moment. Please, do let me have your email contact [if available] so that I can also reach you through it as well as pass it on to Kelie. Better still, you can also directly contact your sister by email: ... [omitted email]. Kelie is French-speaking and will be enthralled to read from you. My own contact points are as indicated above, and I would also love to read or hear from you soonest. We have a lot to catch up on.
I LOVE YOU!
Signed. Daddy (Fossungu, 2016: 4-5).

Figure #36: Nguajong, Daddy, & Ngunyi in London, Ontario
in 2018 at Nguajong's graduation
Source: Momany Fossungu's Album

Though sent as a single registered mail, inside it there were two different sealed envelopes, one each addressed to the two children. It is this same letter that you have read that was in each of the two envelopes. But the said sets of pictures in each letter were different. It is a package that, with the necessary modification, would also have been directed to the Montreal children but for reasons mentioned in the letter. They, too, are in the same soup since when their own mother (Flavie) high-handedly changed their day-care and has been hiding them from their daddy (see Fossungu, 2021: 38-47). So, tell me what was/is going on?

Figure #37: Daddy, Peter Jr., & Peteraf in Montreal in 2019
Source: Momany Fossungu's Album

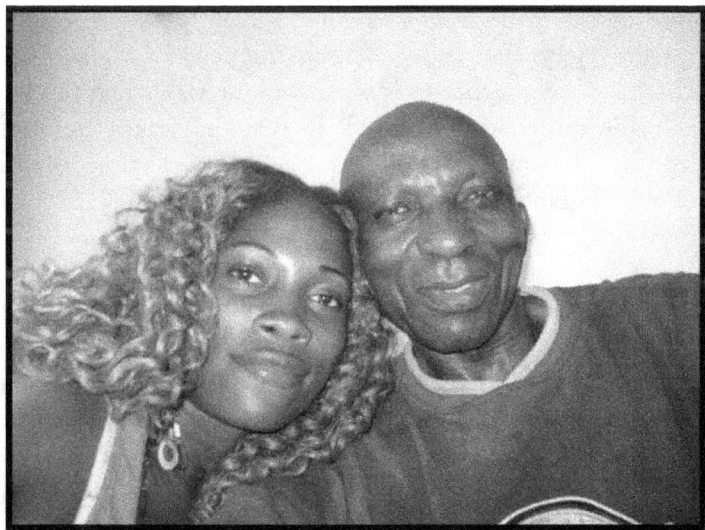

Figure #38: Kelie & Daddy in Douala in May 2014
Source: Momany Fossungu's Album

Let me fasten the Asahchopination case with the five hundred thousand (500,000) francs CFA that I sent to Mrs. Asahchop on 8 February 2004 when she lost her husband. I sent this money to her directly because it was meant to assist in the decent burial of her husband, my father-in-law, knowing fully well what assisting her through third parties (like members of my extended family who have been talking so much about it in their various letters) would entail. I had tried to get to her directly to pass on the information on the funds transfer but for some reasons (of nature) her phone was not going through despite all the numerous attempts. That is when I thought of getting the information to her through Violet Malatey Fossungu (now Fonenge), a cousin who was then studying linguistics in the University of Dschang. Nature alone knows why Scholastica's mother's phone never went through; otherwise, no one would be aware that I had assisted at all in the ceremony since my mother-in-law hid the money; not even informing the rest of the members of the dead man's family of it. And all this even as everyone was condemning the fact that I (as the most pronounced in-law to the deceased) was playing no role in the matter. It was only Violet (a cousin also to Scholastica!) who later brought home the news of the sum that I had sent to my mother-in-law for the purpose when the libel had already gotten out of hand. Is that the way a bold and truthful mother-in-law (desirous of the wellbeing of her children and grandchildren) should comport herself?

Solomon's spouse is one of the few women to whom I would have easily sent my own wife for some marital schooling in view of the high esteem I hold both her and her husband for being role models in many domains, including marriage and family. In 2006 Solomon visited Canada to attend a conference at the International Civil Aviation Organization (ICAO) in Montréal and was putting up with me. On arrival he was so excited to tell me how my mother-in-law was putting up at his residence in Yaoundé and preparing for her visa to Canada. The way he was saying it told me that he must have been in the dark about a lot of what was going on under his roof. I merely informed Solomon that I was hearing about it from him, but it was so hard for him to believe that I was serious. Of course, he is my very good friend. But it is not in my way to call everyone

232

in Cameroon and elsewhere to talk about what was/is going on in my family in Montreal. We moved on to other issues and my friend ate, slept and rested well.

Solomon later called his home in Yaoundé to greet and let the family know he had arrived safely and indicating that he was at my home. He was then shocked to hear his own wife confidentially telling him not let me know about Scholastica's mother being in Yaoundé because Scholastica does not want me to know. "Power, so you were serious when you said you did not know about it! My wife has just been telling me on the phone not to let you know about Scholastica's mother's trip to Yaoundé and I objected. How could Alice of all people on earth do such a thing?" I merely told 'Power Solomon' that I was just as bewildered as he was. No one is saying that Alice Tatah should not help these people that she knows through me. But the fact that she joins the chorus that makes it look like I am such a bad person that would spoil the woman's trip to Canada makes me wonder if it is not the synonym of stabbing in the back someone you are in front calling friend. This was the same thing Mr. Bangwaman was doing in Manjo. It obviously looks like there is a complete 'Asahchop family' plot to disparage me in view, perhaps, of whitewashing gross thanklessness and other devilish schemes. Otherwise, why couldn't my parents-in-law have acted like papa?

When I had told papa I never received any money, the BIROCOL money smear campaign was ruptured because papa immediately called his wife who said she had left it with Bernard. Bernard then went into his box, got the money and returned it to papa. The money therefore never reached me nor solved my problem. But the important thing at that point was the fact that papa knew that I was not the ungrateful kid that his not being bold and truthful would have created of me in his mind. The other important question is: Was Bernard acting on his mother's instruction or merely preventing me, in his own way, from "eating our father's money"? I am not the vengeful type, but Bernard paid in a way for his monkey business, including always making me prepare many dishes at home for no good reason. Coastman is the type that claims he does not eat this or that simply because I would be asked to prepare a different dish that his whims and caprices would choose. One of his favourite 'don't-eats' is *ndolé* (bitter herbs). One day we came back from the farm and mother who had stayed behind had not yet cooked anything. We were tired of "drinking garri" on such occurrences. So, Bernard and I headed to one of those Yoke homes where, for sure, we would be served some food, precisely at Sam's Mother's. It was delicious *ndolé* and boiled ripe plantains that Sam's Mother put before us. After about two spoonfuls, I asked Bernard if he had started eating *ndolé*. He then pretended not to have known and asked if it was *ndolé* and outspoken Sam's Mother quickly and happily confirmed. He stopped eating and did not vomit or have any problem as would normally be the case for someone that has eaten what s/he was allergic to. I thus "wiped" the food alone. My intention was not to deny him satisfaction of his hunger but to have him come clean of his pretence. He chose not to do so and, therefore, bore the consequence of his dishonesty. As Sam's Mother had explained afterwards to me, very happy that I had asked the *ndolé*-eating question just at the right moment, "I think I understand Ben's problem well enough. He is a heavy eater and people like him need much time to do it slowly and surely. This is a thing that he does not get eating from the same bowl with the rest of you. Therefore, he must find a way of having a dish all to himself. But rather than say so plainly, he prefers the dubious manner." This duplicity, I was bound to conclude, had a very big hand in my then going to a strange town like Garoua without money and not knowing anyone there. I was then sitting in the Saviem bus and wondering if something positive was also going to result from the 'negative' of going to Garoua without knowing anyone there.

The Garoua Guinness Job and the Crime of Being Intelligent: From Lecturer to Taxi-Man and Labourer

It was terribly hot in Garoua but I was already there. The question was that of where and how to begin. To others, this may be a very difficult issue. Not to me. Because the decision

234

to even get there is more difficult than that of what to do, being already there. As my desire in life is to better the lives of as many people as possible, I would not bother about the type of job I have to do as long as it helps me to achieve my objectives. I am sure many AGovCists would be surprised to realize that the famous 'Papa Doctor in Canada' (my pseudo-name used by Spokesman Asu) who has been contributing huge sums to the AWOL War Effort is not a millionaire/billionaire but simply a forest worker. The liberation of Ambazonia is to better the lives of as many people as possible. That is why (like Ayabacholization) I have had to pioneer a lot of projects, one of which I will now use to lead you to how I survived in Garoua, as in many other strange places I have been to. The project to be used here is the Douala-Kilometre-30 Road that will conduct you to the Garoua Guinness job that God directed me there to occupy but man stubbornly stood in the way.

From Lecturer to Taxi-man: I had been lecturing at the UNIYAO before leaving for further studies in Canada in 1991. When I returned to Cameroon after my studies at the University of Alberta, the idea was to continue lecturing, either at the UNIYAO or any of the others that had been created while I was abroad (UNIBU, University of Douala, University of Dschang, University of Ngaoundéré) thus helping young students toward a better and brighter future. On getting back, however, those in places of authority thought they could keep me out of the environment, for reasons that only they know. Professor Peter Y. Ntamark, then head of the English law department of the UNIYAO II, kept giving me fruitless and endless appointments in Yaoundé, knowing quite well that I was then based in Douala pending being hired. During a lot of the resources-draining trips to Yaoundé, I was struck by the way people in the villages between Douala and Édea had to suffer just to get to Douala for necessities. There were times that I drove past in the early hours of the morning and found some of them waiting to get a paid ride on trucks transporting wood to Douala. On my way back in the evening I would still see them there. On realizing that the university authorities were

235

just out to play nasty games with my time and resources, therefore, I cut off seeking re-entrance into that milieu and took to the transportation business. I concentrated on those villages about forty kilometres from Douala (on the Douala-Yaoundé highway) and back. I pioneered that road and, today, those people have no more problems getting to Douala and back any time of day or night because there are a lot of other drivers who soon followed in my footsteps.

At the start it was not easy for many of the new drivers who came along. The people (probably as a sign of their enormous gratitude) often refused to board their vehicles, saying they would wait for Peter, no matter how long it took. I had to step in to publicly convince them of the need to travel with whoever was available. I made them to properly understand that my idea of coming to their rescue in the first place was to make life better for them, not just to make money – a goal that is better achieved when many more vehicles are plying the road. After this intervention, things changed for the better for all of us because one or two disgruntled drivers openly made some very revealing confessions. According to them, three of them had teamed up and sent one member to the village to get "something" with which to finish me because they had thought I had used some charm to confuse the bulk of the passengers that were refusing to board their vehicles so that I could be the only one making the money. Just imagine where I would be today if I were that egoistic and narrow-minded. Long dead and buried, of course! Just also imagine where the Ambazonian Revolution would be today if the abducted Nera-Nkoundengui Prisoners didn't hijack a multiparty platform for selfish goals! This KM-30 case has many implications. But I would only highlight it here as a clear indication that progressive persons know (unlike Uncle Anamoh) that their worth is not to be found so much in *what* they do for a living as it is in *why* they do it.

The Labourer and Night-Watchman: Becoming better is exactly why I was in hot Garoua where (for some weeks) I had worked very hard in the seaport during the day and, with nowhere to

236

sleep, spent the nights with night watchmen, taking turns with them while each (including me) slept a bit. If only Uncle Anamoh had objectives with which he defined himself and had begun with the yard-boy position in Powercam Yoke, who knows where he would be today with his objectives? This uncle of mine would certainly be shocked that, then holder of the G.C.E. Advanced Level (a higher diploma than what he came to the household with), I made quite a bit of money as a *chargeur* (loading and offloading cargo) at the Garoua artificial seaport before stumbling upon a job advertisement by Guinness Cameroun S.A. in Garoua that perfectly fit my profile. I went enthusiastically knocking for the position in Guinness. The branch manager then was Mr. Nsoh (an Ambazonian). After examining my credentials, he told me categorically that he was not going to give me the job because, as he put it, "You are too good and intelligent to be 'locked up' here in my company. You are the kind we need in the university and beyond because in all my years I have not seen students like you who have made their Advanced Level in the lower sixth form and I truly do not think I would be doing you and this country any good if I employ you here."

I have never in all my life felt so dejected hearing a compliment like I did hearing those words of the Guinness manager. The praise made me wonder why *he was not* actually my father. It made me want to wish that the Head of the CCAS Kumba Arts Department was right that I was a mediocre student. It made me feel like being very intelligent was an offence. It made me feel like God had directed me to come and fill the position, but man was preventing me. If only the manager could have known what having that job meant to me then! I earnestly tried explaining to the manager how I wanted so badly to go to the university but that I also badly needed the job to be able to raise enough money to do so. He was very unyielding and, instead of offering me the job, he gave me as much money as could permit me to get to Yaoundé and register at the university. He seriously advised me not to waste my talents, stressing that I would be able to manage things out with the *bourse* that the University then accorded students. I was not very satisfied with his withholding the job from me but still thankful for his help, telling him same and leaving.

I still had a couple of weeks within the UNIYAO registration time so I decided not to return to the Garoua seaport (the Guinness incident had truly rendered the city useless to me) but to instead go down to Ngaoundéré (from where I had to take the night train to Yaoundé). The idea was to see if I could find something doing there for the remaining weeks. Every franc was important to me since I did not know what was awaiting me in Yaoundé. In Ngaoundéré, I tried several schools to no avail; also failing to find my cousin, Godfred Tendongmo Fossungu (now Chief Fonenge Godfred). It was holiday time and, being a government schoolteacher, he was not in town. But the search for him led me to Mr. Charles Fonkem, then *Regisseur de Prison de Ngaoundéré*. This Bangwa man is not only good but is also truly blessed with a unique wife. She had just given birth to their first child (a baby girl they named Solange) when I got there. I had not known them before then. But they not only welcomed me into their home with very open and generous hands but, in addition, treated me like the royal that I obviously am but never felt like till then. I was in fact in the position to stay there as long as I wanted. But I had to move on, my life objectives calling hard on me. I also got the family's moral and financial encouragement to pursue further studies in Yaoundé.

A Nasty Coincidence Coupling with the Train and Bus Tickets from God in Yaoundé for the First Time

When I was dropped off at the Ngaoundéré train station that September evening in 1982, hardly could I have predicted anything unusual that could be waiting for me in Yaoundé, the capital of Cameroon that I was then visiting for the first time. I had never been out of Cameroon till then. But I had (since leaving Yoke in September 1981 and searching for my future) developed this habit of carrying my bag the way North Americans go about with their backpacks. This bag contained just a few jean dresses and all my certificates, academic and

238

others. I got to Yaoundé early next morning. Getting out of the Yaoundé train station that morning, two guys in plain clothes sort of sandwiched me and began asking questions in French. I thought at first that these were just people who wanted to be friendly, and I also found this a perfect occasion to start polishing up my classroom French. It all started with a simple *comment ça va* (how are you)? I responded that it was alright, thank you; and what about you? They were fine, but continued questioning: Where I was coming from and where I was going to (in Yaoundé). The first was easy but the second I did not exactly know. At this point there was some kind of discord between the two because one was telling the other "It's not him" with the other insisting "It's him alright".

I knew at this time there was a mix-up somewhere but what it was I could not tell. I therefore indicated to them (this time in English) that it was my first time coming there and I was going to see a brother, Michael (remember my mother's brother, Michael Njumo, I met in the household when I came from the village?). He was then attending university, but I did not know where in Yaoundé he was living. The guy who had insisted I was the one cried out to his partner (in French): "You see? I told you he was the one. Have you not just heard his American English?" Frankly, until I entered the UNIYAO in 1984 (where and when the language corruption began, even English speakers (my classmates and others) often found it hard to follow when I spoke. Quite apart from being Mr. English in primary school, I was also lucky to have had mostly Europeans as language teachers at secondary level. They tended to encourage rather than chastise me when I sometimes baffled even them in the language. I was known in college to read *The Oxford English Dictionary* the same way other students would read a novel or story. It is, therefore, not surprising that an African French-speaker should listen to me speaking English and conclude that I am (Black) American. But his colleague was still not convinced until what happened after the next query.

If I truly did not know where my so-called brother lives, they demanded, how was I going to find him then? I knew quite well at this point that I was in trouble for being a suspected American spy. But I also discerned that lying could not take me very far out because it is extremely hard to be consistent in lies. This is a very useful lesson that many Entitlementalists have not learnt. For instance, my ex-wife (Scholastica) is the very one who went about telling people how useless I am to her and the two children I have with her; doing absolutely nothing for them. But she had soon forgotten this when she called the same people to talk about the monthly child support that "was helping me a lot." I was not there in London but know this because an astonished listener of hers called me to express her admiration that I had been doing all this and yet had been painted as worthless. I simply told Lysly Ako Ayah that it was a good thing that she got both contradictory versions from the same source.

Helpful Child-Support or Supporting Mother's Illicit Money-Grabbing? It could indeed be true that "Someone who has deliberately taken up confusing and manipulating others as her or his profession would often (if not always) end up herself or himself gravely confused" (Fossungu, 2013a: 104). I do not like talking a lot about the divorce because I like to move on in life by leaving negative occurrences behind me. But since this book is also about the definition of family and the future of children and social work, it cannot be meaningful without this divorce that is so intimately bound to the 'new and strange definition of family' in Canada – just like the confusion-filled talk of federalism in Ambazonia/LRC. I, therefore, must be drawing from the divorce proceedings and consequences from time to time. I will presently do so to concretize the confusion thesis with a bit more of what brought about the contradiction, a fact that also addresses the future of social work.

I lost my job in 2006 because of the several court appearances (for child support, child custody, and divorce) I had to make in London, Ontario (which is eight hours drive from Montréal,

Québec: meaning at least about three working days lost every court session). The given reason was "reorganization" since my company could not have openly stated that it was firing me for over-attending to court sessions. Things went from bad to worse on me that, after a long time searching (to no avail) for just anything to do, I ended up on last resort assistance (social welfare). Scholastica's interpretation to her friends (who were knowing only then from her that I had been paying child support) was simply that this was my ploy to make her suffer because the child support "was helping me a lot." Here then are two important questions for Social Work Canada and for sheepish believers in professionals like papa. First, if a registered social worker does not know that social welfare is not accorded simply because you present yourself for it but because, after a keen study of your case, it is found that you deserve it, then who should know? My ex-wife does not even need to be a social worker to have this knowledge because in 2001 Scholastica went requesting for social welfare behind my back and her application was rejected because she could not satisfy the requirements since she was then living with me, and I was working and supporting her. Second, if the *child support* is actually to support the children, then will your not being able to pay it because you are on welfare make but *the children to suffer* or their mother? Yet, I have had to pay the arrears of child support that accumulated during those years I was unable to find a job and on government assistance. This is largely because Scholastica and her moneyintriguing parents do see child support not as a responsibility (that I have towards my children that are not leaving with me) but as a source of enrichment and/or some sort of punishment for whatever crime they pin on me, including my being truthful about my children – with and without her. As you can then see, lies are never consistent; only the truth is consistent.

241

Avoiding lying, therefore, I had told my Yaoundé questioners that I had to go through some other person who was to take me to Michael's home. To the question regarding where this other person lives, I was, again, oblivious but had to go to the person's office to meet him. And where is that office? American Embassy was the response. What a nasty coincidence! The insistent guy was now more than triumphant while the other was convinced. The next thing I heard was their call for the policemen in uniform to *"amener ce gars au poste."* I was locked up without further ado for about two days and all the money I had worked so hard for, as well as that contributed by the friends in Garoua and Ngaoundéré, was seized (stolen) by these rogues in uniform. When I was finally released, all I got was *"Tu peux partir"*. When I asked about the money and other items they had taken from me, *"de quel argent parles-tu?"* was the question to my question. And these are the supposed "peacekeeping" officers of what kind of *peace?* I left the police *poste* of the Yaoundé train station very determined to get out of that city; although how, I was still to figure out. I had no money but money, I reassured myself, is not all that there is to success. That is cleanly a Globavillagist's way of life. In my place there at the Yaoundé train station a narrow-minded and money-focused person like Scholastica would surely be so confused and perhaps desperately die because of the lack of money. I am clearly not like that. I am sure I was even released from the train station cell solely because my story was found not to be inconsistent or bogus.

I began finding my way to the American Embassy to meet the only contact I had in town. I inquired from one person how far the embassy was from there and was told it was farther than I could imagine and that I needed to catch a cab to get there or take and connect about two or three city buses. The second person said it was just around the corner and I, therefore, approached a third, who happened to be English-speaking. The Ambazonian had more patience in directing me how to get there, indicating with approximate traffic lights how far to go on a boulevard or street before meeting this or that other street and turning right or left, etc. I quickly scribbled all this down and, although it was quite a trek, the helpful guides shortened it considerably. I finally reached the Embassy of the United States of America about an hour and half before closing time. Mr. X (another Bangwa man whose names I have long forgotten) came down to see me and asked me to wait until closing time when he would take me to Michael's home. At last, I was feeling like something good was happening in Yaoundé. We got to Total Melen where Michael was then residing. Finding that he was not in town but elsewhere on holiday, Mr. X (who had been duly briefed of my train-station ordeal) abandoned me there, boarded a taxi and took off. What was I to do? Luckily, I have learnt not to despair in such circumstances but to wisely ask questions. I stopped a passerby that I had staked from a distance and asked where the university was. The man pointed over a hill from where we were standing, and I demanded further how to get there. He said I should go through Château. In my later years in the UNIYAO I realized that it was about five to ten minutes' walk passing through CUSS (the University Health Sciences Centre) that was on the other side of the road. Being new to town, I had to take the long way through Carrefour EMIA to Château and down to Ngoa-Ékéllé. It was September and there were students on campus to re-sit the subjects they had failed in during the June session. I was moving with ears wide open for anyone speaking English or Ambatok since, it seemed then, they were proving to be more helpful to me in this 'crazy' city. Without knowing, I was already around the student residential area (hostels) when I heard some Ambatok in one of the stairs. I followed it until I knocked at the door, and they opened it.

I was a bit relieved but extremely hungry and tired. I narrated what had happened to me on my arrival in town about three days before and asked if they had anything to eat. Much as they sympathized with me and, above all, very glad that I was very fortunate to have been released and still alive, they, unfortunately, had no food. But, unknown to them, they instead offered me something that was far more important than food – post-dated student train ticket to Douala! My hunger and fatigue suddenly varnished at the mention of the ticket even though they indicated that I could only use it in a few days' time, not immediately. I asked for the ticket and how to get back to the train station that same evening. One of them, seeing how determined I was to get out of Yaoundé, also offered me a bus ticket, explaining in detail how and where to connect. His task was made a lot easier by the bus experience I had acquired in Douala while desperately job-hunting there. I thanked them plentifully and said goodbye. Without the bus ticket, I obviously would not have made it to the train station in time. The controllers in the train had signalled that the problems attached to my post-dated ticket would be looked into at the Douala train station. Recalling how these Camerounese presume guilt before anything else, I wisely avoided those other Douala-train-station troubles by jumping out of the moving train when it was somewhere in New Bell, Douala – some distance before the final station in Bonanjo, Douala. At this point my mind had crystallized on leaving Cameroon for any English-speaking country. Nigeria was the natural choice since it was the only such bordering country, and I also did not then have money and travelling documents.

Money Is Not All There Is To Success in the Long Trek into Nigeria via Bamenda and Back to Yoke

After a week or so in Douala, I left for Bamenda where I unknowingly entered a tiger's mouth. But my instincts got me out in time before it could gnaw – all thanks largely also to my belief that, as crucial as it is, money is not all that matters for one to succeed. Arriving Bamenda and having nowhere to stay while waging the "becoming better" war, I naturally navigated to Mile Two Nkwen. I had learnt that one of papa's co-workers from the Yoke Powercam Camp was then residing there. The homeowner first suggested that I go back to Yoke and manage his sand business there, giving me the freedom to do whatever I wanted to with money from the business. I had not shown any interest in this proposal. My reasoning had been that, if that was such a great opportunity, why was this man's own son who had obtained the Advanced Level the same year as I did,

244

not running his business that he so liberally wanted but me to run? Good critical thinking! It was only after my return to Yoke from Nigeria that I learned that everyone that has been that connected to the man's sand business has had to die mysteriously. Finding the sand business thing not to be catching my attention, my host began insisting that I go hunting with him in the night. I never obeyed my host's demands and left for my own place: even as things were so hard on me, still believing strongly that money alone is not what is essential for success. Ferguson (2008: 26 & 29-30) would even go further to argue that "Money is worth only what someone else is willing to give you for it" because "money is a matter of belief, even faith: belief in the person paying us, belief in the person issuing the money he uses or the institution that honours his cheques or transfer." This segment of my roaming days is dominated by the money idea, a handmaiden of which is that the gift may be little to the giver but may mean the world to the recipient.

The Interviews of the Constuction Worker and the Twisted-Minded Individuals

Two factors had particularly propelled my decision to perch at the home in Mile Two Nkwen. First, the madam of the house is such a nice, understanding, and selfless woman that I have often wondered why my mother was not like her. Second, their first son (who was by no means the eldest in the house) was in CCAS Kumba with me, being one class ahead of me, though we had both obtained the G.C.E. Advanced Level the same year. He was a boarding student in CCAS and was doing the same A3 option as me. Because I could not afford going home for the *midi* break and then coming back for the afternoon session, I used to stay around his bed while they were taking siesta. At such times, I often read some of his books since I could not afford to buy all the books then. I saw this Bamenda stay as a perfect occasion to thank him for his help, unwitting as it was. But the Clement Kenah's reaction simply told me that, had he been in the least aware of my G.C.E. bid, he would very well have hidden all his books from me. For example, he

245

had secured a teaching position with Our Lady of Lourdes College, Mankon (Bamenda) after the G.C.E. results. At the time I was in Bamenda, he had passed the Sonel examination into the corporation's training school, and I asked if he could recommend me for his Lourdes position. He flatly told me that the place had already been filled. It was a plain lie as I later discovered on going there by myself. In Lourdes I was made to understand that he had abandoned the position and never responded to their repeated requests for him to bring along someone to replace him. They had thereafter contacted a former student of theirs (who had enrolled in the UNIYAO but was contemplating abandoning it) to see if she could come and fill the post. Nevertheless, they asked me to come back in two weeks by which time if the former student had not shown up, they could offer me the position, the absent senior Sister also to be around by then to make the decision. I kept my fingers crossed and continued teaching economics and English language at Progressive Institute of Stenography (PIS) around the Pharmacy Junction, having already been there for close to two weeks before the close of the month. I was hired there on a monthly salary of fourteen thousand (14,000) francs CFA. As soon as I received my dues for the first two weeks there, I got a place for myself around the Bamenda General Hospital, despite that I so badly needed to save as much money for the Nigeria Trip, a thing to be easily and quickly done by continuing to stay at Mile Two Nkwen.

But whenever my instincts (or the small but clear voices inside my head) come calling I scarcely hesitate in answering. This has proven to be a unique ingredient of success for me. It was precisely because of the swift answering to the call, for instance, that I also stumbled on a Muyuka acquaintance at the University of Calabar (UNICAL) in Nigeria, at a time and place when/where just meeting someone I know was so critical to surviving. As a construction worker and spending the nights in the tools and materials compartment on a construction site in Calabar (imagine the high exposure to being killed there by thieves!), I had this strong feeling one evening that I should visit the city's university to have an idea of what the milieu looks like. I was planning to enrol there after finding my feet in the place. You can imagine what most people in my shoes here would do: work every hour and day to make the money first and as fast as possible. Not this guy who almost always answers to his instincts. The next morning as the others arrived for work, I approached the supervisor who immediately asked: "What now, Cameroon boy?" That is the way everyone was referring to me because my intonation is something I just cannot hide or change. From day one, as soon as I opened my mouth to say anything, "Na Cameroon boy be this" was always the general observation. To date, a lot of people even doubt (my being from abroad) when I am in Cameroun/Ambazonia and some relatives keep proudly introducing me as their "brother from Canada" because of my unchanged Cameroonian/Ambazonian inflection.

Anyway, I had explained to my construction site supervisor that I needed the day off to take care of some pressing issues emanating from home, then Cameroon. His hands were obviously full, and it was so abrupt. But the brusqueness coupled well with the fact that I was not known to be the off day taking guy to make my case very compelling. He gave in and I took off, not even knowing exactly where I was going to. I was only propped up by the reflection that if I had made it to Nigeria and down to Calabar with almost practically no money, what was there to keep me from finding my way in Calabar then when I even had some money? I was just as marvelled at the UNICAL campus (comparing with what I had seen in the UNIYAO in Cameroon) as I had been at the roads leading out of Takum, the first bordering village town (by Nigerian standards) but more than a city by Cameroonian scales. In fact, if I had not actually entered Nigeria trekking through the border, but by air, I would have plainly disputed that I was still in the Africa I was (until then) used to, let alone in neighbouring Nigeria, which is denigrated by Camerounese as 'Biafra'. The difference was simply staggering. What could be responsible for such gapping differences between two neighbouring African states? Could it be attributable to the disparate colonial legacies; to the federal nature of Nigeria; or to what else? As I was swaggering around that campus, lost in thoughts and totally oblivious of the suffering at the construction site (the only Calabar I had known till then), I was startled by a voice calling out "Figaro!" Who could be calling 'Na Cameroon Boy be this' in Nigeria by that name? I thought I was dreaming, not just daydreaming and had to slap myself hard to wake up. But there he was, smiling and saying "It is not a dream, it is not Muyuka, it is me, Vahid, and we are both in Calabar, Nigeria, now. What are you doing here?" The feeling was just awe-inspiring. I recognized Vahid Ashu as the Muyuka boy living not far from the Catholic Mission church and school in Strangers Quarter. But I did not know his name until then. Did I have a short and precise answer to Vahid's question like I did to the Lourdes Sister's?

I had excitedly gone back for the Lourdes rendezvous after the two-week period. The lady they had been waiting upon had still not come and I had a small chat (or should I say interview?) with the sisters. As you know already, I am not the type that would camouflage who I really am just to obtain someone's favours, let alone what I know I merit acquiring. Staying true to self has been another indispensable ingredient of success and of failure of mine, both in and outside the household. I think I got that also from my father's training. Papa was very organized, disciplined and disciplinary; wanting all his children to learn to be responsible both individually and collectively. Thus, when his return from work approached, no one was at ease at home. Just don't be the first person he encounters at the scene if, say, a pan is not in the right place. Just get the pan to where it is supposed to be and never say 'I don't know' to his question 'Who put this pan here?' If you do, he will counter: "Good Gracious! You don't know! So, who should know? Or, if it is a spirit that put it there, did you not see it, and why is it still there?" As noted earlier, some people who do not like strict people would jump to describe papa as 'wicked' because his love for following rules and for hardworking folks was hardly turned over.

During the Lourdes interview, one of the sisters (as I suspected, the senior one) asked what I must have been thinking appearing for the appointment the way I had. I was not going to pretend that I did not get her point to be asking for further enlightenment as she had expected. She wanted me, in brief, to come in a way that would give the impression that I was someone that would not be interested at all in dating some of the female students I was going to be teaching. Much as I was then not even interested in any other woman, and much as you know I needed that job, I merely pointedly asked back: "With all due respect, Sisters, which is more dangerous dealing with – a wolf that openly comes to you as a wolf or one appearing in sheep skin?" With this question-response, I heard the former student tale all over again. I knew right there that their promise to get back to me was mere hypocrisy passing for politeness. It is just as then principal of Bopson Comprehensive College in Nkwen, Bamenda, who (from my understanding of his funny behaviour) wanted me to come and "see him with oil for his unstable mouth" before I could fill the vacant position in his college. This Bangwa man called Thomas Ajamah (who, by some later strange happenings, has one of the aunties of my ex-wife as wife) just did not know the calibre of the man he was dealing with. Imagine (from Chapters 4 & 5 above) the great things that some of the students in both Lourdes and Bopson missed from me just because of a handful of twisted-minded individuals.

But those twisted-minded people were not the only that made my Bamenda passage both difficult and memorable at the same time. It was in Bamenda that I also reunited with Dieudonné, after about sixteen years of growing apart. Dieudonné had just completed primary school and (because there was no one to send him to college) was in Bamenda, living with a maternal relation and learning tailoring and bricklaying, successively. It was supposed to be a real splendid moment and time to catch up on the lost years. But it did not turn out to be so because of the 'becoming better' pressure I was under. By this time, I had moved back to Nkwen where I was putting up with Uncle Gabriel Nkwetta Fossungu (in Figure #40) who I had met during the many visits to Bopson Comprehensive College, where he was then studying together with many other Fossungu cousins.

Figure #39: Dieudonné Asongu Fossungu & his musician friend
Source: Dieudonné Asongu Fossungu

Figure #40: Nkwetta Gabriel Fossungu (middle with 1ˢᵗ child of Margaret Akendung who is on his right, and on his left is Maria Fossungu, Uncle Ngufor's 1ˢᵗ wife)
Source: Nkwetta Gabriel Fossungu

I had a lot of dresses, no doubt. It had even become one of the household's complaints singsongs that I had "things even more than a working class." But at that time, I was not going around with a lot of dresses and shoes but a lot more of my certificates and other documents. Dieudonné is a lot taller than me, but we wear the same shoe size. So, apart from a few bigger and longer shirts, I let him have almost all the pairs of shoes but one that I needed to be using especially when I needed to attend an interview that required suiting up. One day while I was behind taking my bath in preparation for an interview with Nacho Comprehensive College there in Bamenda, Dieudonné came in and, against Uncle Nkwetta's counsel, took away that last pair of shoes, saying "Why is he my brother if I cannot take the pair of shoes?" A male version of Rosemany, you are saying? I do not know whether this was destined. I missed the appointment, not being the only candidate for it as was the case in Lourdes. I was so crossed that when my brother later showed up and was behaving as if it was nothing, for the first time I raised my hand and hit him before I could hold back myself. It is one of those few very devastating things I have had to regret ever doing. It kind of instilled the fear of me and a permanent freeze in Dieudonné that has been kind of difficult to take away, especially as we scarcely had any time together thereafter because I left for Nigeria.

The Positives and Negatives of Not Nosing around for Information

The main things on my mind in Nkambe (as I was waiting to have some Nigeria-bound cross-border traders with whom to make *The Long Trek* and even during the entire trek) were the BIROCOL money affair and this issue of people always nosing around for information about things that do not even concern them. That is why only Uncle Nkwetta knew that, and when, I was to leave Bamenda for Nigeria. These issues dominated my trek out of Cameroon since I was trying to see if my not partaking in the habit could have been costly to my bid for university education. I have this nag for saying things without having any evidence at the time of speaking, with them then turning out to be as if I had the evidence before opening my mouth. Some would call it intuition, and which most of the time (in my case) is tied to ignorance. I am talking about the type of lack of knowledge that results from the fact that you are not accustomed to unnecessarily nosing around for information like some journalists accuse some Cameroonian lawyers of doing. Or what Ivoirians popularly refer to as looking for history where there is no geography ("*chercher l'histoire là où il n'y a pas la géographie*"). For example, what would you say is behind a divorce case (except the desire to extract so-called child support) when the petitioner gets her demands but would continue year after year policing, by nosing around for information in regard of, the respondent and his relationships?

Nosing around for information or being a "curious Johnny" is not always bad though. For example, papa always opened my letters that came care of him. He is not supposed to do that. But on two out of three occasions it was very helpful that he did so. Otherwise, I would have missed the critical employment opportunity in Collège de l'Unité de Manjo. He speedily came up with the letter to Yoke the same day and I left for Manjo, reaching there just in time before the lapse of the offer. Again, I would not have had my acceptance slip for the G.C.E. Advanced Level in time since he was not even aware that I had registered for it. Opening and seeing what it was, he rushed with it to Kumba and I, consequently, got the necessary requirements and headed for Buea where I wrote the exam. I warmheartedly remember papa dissuading me from (and warning about the dire consequences of) taking this G.C.E. Advanced Level in the lower sixth form. He had wondered why "children nowadays are wont to want to fly to Jericho without having first developed and tested their own proper wings." When papa opened the letter my beloved Christine wrote to me during holiday, it was in French, and he could not read French although her enclosed photo was telling enough to make papa's knowledge of *Egytian* irrelevant. He, consequently, only brought it up to Yoke during the weekend. "Curious-Johnnying" is, therefore, not always bad. I even consider it a kind of flaw in me that I do not sometimes do it. A clear instance is in regard of my half-siblings, especially Awandem who even came and lived with us in Yoke, and I could not still divine his actual relationship to me. But, for me, not nosing around has been more on the ingredient of success side than on that of a defect: the revealing pregnancy stories further confirming.

Always nosing around for information, for one thing, can easily instil in you what I call the Loser-Syndrome. That is one of the reasons I dislike it, and tend to consider anyone who does it to be a loser. Of course, I cannot talk about my dislike for nosing around for information with talking about a Bamileke lady in Montreal I met after the London divorce. I had to call off the relationship with her especially because of this trait in her.

Imagine sitting in a gathering with her and being asked whenever someone walks in or out: "Who is she? What does she do? How long has she been here in Montréal?" At the beginning I asked back: "How am I supposed to know all that, Gina?" believing she would realize that I am not interested in that attitude. But it only went from bad to worse. This nosing around is a thing that is mostly being condemned when it becomes a kind of addiction. Or like in the case of Scholastica divorcing me but continuing to nose around as if I am still her husband. So, again, what was the divorce case for, except to extract so-called child support? This duplicity that was so ubiquitous in the household itself, I was bound to conclude, had a huge role in my then arriving in a strange country like Nigeria without money and after spending many nights in an unknown forest. We spent about three to five nights in the forest and when we arrived in Takum I was sort of relieved but very worried. Being new in the affair, the uniform boys and girls on both sides had taken so much of the money I had that what I still had left in Takum was purely insufficient to get me to Calabar. A huge lesson on gifts was learnt in Takum and beyond.

The Philosophy of Gifts and the Defying Definitions of Family

I got the nicknames *Professor* and *Lord Denning* while I was studying in the UNIYAO (to leave out *Read this Classic Paper* in CCAS Kumba) because of the way I usually extensively "poured stuff" in support of my points. I am not about to do otherwise here with the analysis of the new definition of family that is wholly out of place, whether viewed from the African context or the Canadian. This strangely new definition of family is just the tip of the iceberg of the parental spell and scheming to the total disregard of children's future that I am talking about as well as condemning. For Scholastica, this spell was there even at the marriage-decision stage. But it was aggravated and entrenched especially during the four years I was away studying in Montréal, Canada (1995-99); during which Scholastica must have fallen completely under the hex of her scheming parents. So, was it an error for me to have left lectureship at the UNIBU in 1995 for further studies in McGill University? I pose some of these questions because, just like the lay persons deserve to know from the intellectuals (see Fossungu, 2013a: viii-ix), I think a child also rightly deserves to know if, when, and why his or her parents' marriage is not working as others he or she finds around him or her. Parents that conspire not to tell this child the truth (at some point) do not deserve to be parents to that child in the first place. The truth regarding the failure of the Peter-Scholastica (Scholamany) family/marriage, therefore, impels my briefly discussing the new definition of family in the context of the giver-receiver philosophy.

Some of the essential lessons I acquired in Takum are that the Giver's Little Gift Can Mean the World to the Recipient; and that those who can never give cannot quite appreciate whatever someone else gives to them. Get all the appropriate indepth education you need on the issue from a classic 2004 Letter to the Whistance-Smith family in which I wrote:

Dear Andrew, Nancy *et al*,
WHAT A GIFT! I had become almost speechless before this gift's arrival but now I am completely flattened by it. What can I say? Thank You? Would that be Enough enough? What a nice and wonderful way to begin the year 2004 after the likes of 2002 and 2003! Your letter is jammed with a lot of interesting things that have happened to your entire family in the last year or so. But the gift of writing off my enormous financial debt to you has overwhelmed me and I do hope you will understand why I can hardly talk now about any of the other things you have written about.

Despite how sad and heartbroken I have been, especially in the last two years, some small and clear voice inside of me has, of late, been incessantly telling me that 2004 was to be the year that I have been waiting for to "re-blossom". I didn't know, until today, how exactly that was to be. Now, of course, I do know how and why that voice has kept "pestering" me with its unrelenting consolation.

I think I just have to get ready to hang up the heartache of the past two years, gather myself up, move on and start my life all over again. I must tell you this. No winning lottery ticket of any amount of money would mean as much to me as your GIFT. I wasn't expecting it. Yet, I can't say NO, THANK YOU. My intention has always been to honour my word to you by paying back the debt. The only troubling issue has always been WHEN (not WHETHER) I would be able to do so. This issue has been haunting me a lot, considering the predicament I have had to find myself in since Scholastica's surprising attitude began.

Now you have just turned one of my greatest worries into my greatest gifts of all and I think the best way for me to say Thank You enormously will now be to fearlessly move on and not, in any way, let the unfortunate gap created in the last three years stand in my one-way journey. ALL THAT I DO NOW HOPE AND PRAY FOR AS I MOVE ON IS THAT I BE GREATLY INFECTED BY YOUR ABUNDANT GOODNESS.

Sincerely yours, signed. Peter A. Fossungu (Fossungu, 2016: 104-105).

One cannot correctly appreciate this Gift-appreciating missive without the full contents of the gift-making letter (see Fossungu, 2016: 105-106). Put differently, the take-and-take-and-take people, never having been on the giving side, can hardly be appreciative of what they just keep receiving. The 'Four-Eyes' or HISOFE Mathematical Equation in this scenario becomes "Give and Take versus Take and Take and Take". If I, again, apply my knowledge of arithmetic here, one of the three 'takes' on the right cancels the only other on the other side, leaving one side to continue indefinitely giving while the other continues endlessly taking and taking: with an obvious accentuated destabilizing imbalance that does necessarily un-define the other side; and thus also un-defining (and 'redefining') family. That, in a nutshell, describes the entire nature of the relationship between Scholastica and me. Two or three gifts will fortify the point, namely, (1) the Takum gift from God and (2) the Nwangong generator gift of June 2004.

The Takum Gift (and Loan & Flight Ticket) from God: The Yoke Flight Ticket and Edmonton Loan

Calculating in Takum with the traders who were heading to Abba and Onitsha, the money I still had left could take me only as far as Katsina-Alla. Do I know anyone there, they inquired. Good thing I still kept in touch with my Yoke and Sasse College pal, Anusiem, who was then in the University of Nigeria, Nsukka. I told them the only person I knew in the country was in Nsukka and there was some amount of relief on their part. Remember that I only became these traders' acquaintance at the point in Nkambe (Ambazonia, then under Cameroun annexation and occupation) where the trekking started. But they were here contributing some money to permit me reach Nsukka in the hope of meeting Anusiem who was not at all aware that I was coming. What if you cannot find your friend in Nsukka, one of the traders asked. Very grateful for their kind and brotherly gesture, I merely responded: "When destiny calls, I must answer present. I did not anticipate this particular money problem. Maybe if I did, I would not be here right now. But the issue has surfaced stiffly and just see what you guys have done. God should very bountifully bless all of you. I would, therefore, not want to worry about what problems Nsukka has in store until I am in Nsukka. Once more, I am indescribably grateful for your kind-heartedness." This advice then becomes important. Always know that before becoming an expert, the expert was a no-expert, and would obviously have remained a no-expert if he or she never did what transformed him or her into an expert until he or she was already an expert. I must talk of papa's capacity to put money to the service of people when I define money as not just the amount of it that is piled up in a bank account. Let's extensively concretize it now with the loan and plane ticket from God.

The Yoke Flight Ticket and Edmonton Loan: I fondly remember telling Scholastica in Douala in 1994 that we were going to go to Canada and her quick question was "Where would the money come from?" My answer to her quiz was that there are a lot of other things to succeeding in life than just having the money on hand. As a Hisofean, and growing up with papa, I have come to see money not solely in terms of the amount of it staked up in a bank account but mostly in terms of what money can do to alleviate some of the sufferings I find all around me. For instance, when I say papa was very rich, I am not just referring to what he had as money (and he had lots of it too). I also look at his ability to put money to the service of people. In my bid to attend McGill University in 1995 papa gave me the required amount for the bank statement and I was counting on selling my car to obtain the flight ticket. But that did not work even at the last minute because prospective buyers were offering amounts not near the value of the car or the amount for the air ticket (CFA 800,000 francs). The arrival deadline given to me by McGill University was fast drawing near and I had already tried other alternatives to no avail. As a last resort, Scholastica and I drove from Douala to Yoke to see papa who was then retired.

In view of what papa had already done that far, I was not surprised by his indication that there was nothing left in his account. But Madam Catherine (then his legal wife) interceded, pleading with him to help me in whatever way to surmount this last obstacle. Papa said OKAY and went into his bedroom. He was in there for quite some time and my thinking was that he was getting ready for us to drive down to Victoria or to another bank, perhaps there in Muyuka. To our surprise, when he came out, he gave a packet of eight hundred thousand francs CFA to his wife to give to my wife and me to count and be sure that he did not make an error. It was Scholastica who did the counting and confirmed. I would not want to go into describing the emotion but instead just highlight two things that go straight into the basket of the ingredients of success, with or without money. The first is that I was able to overcome this obstacle because I had not taken sides in the domestic quarrel between Mamie Thecla, on one side, and Madam Catherine, on the other. The second concerns my not being bitter after being dropped by papa in 1981 (the roaming days which I am now discussing) – some fourteen years before. All of these could not have been possible if I were not the kind that would always have a zoomedeyed look of things, knowing abundantly well that money alone is not all that is important to succeeding in life.

The Community Benefit Theory: Four years after the Yoke Flight-Ticket Money Incident, Scholastica herself was joining me in Montréal, Canada in April 1999. Where did the money for her schooling and upkeep in Buea during those four years, and for her trip and stay here in Canada till 2004 (when she began working) come from? And was it just the money that really counted? Now, if I say I have a problem with people like Scholastica who cross the river and burn the bridge to prevent other persons from also crossing, a lot of narrow-minded people would restrict 'other persons' here to my own brothers, sisters, and parents. This is incorrect to Hisofeans. I well remember Nancy Whistance-Smith narrating some very negative experiences they had had in Kenya (Africa) and how, because of those, they had vowed never to trust Africans. But that negativity toward Africans, she had concluded, completely changed when they met and interacted with me. That is precisely the reason they had been lending us (Scholastica and I) as much as they have had to in enabling us do all what we have done.

I particularly have no problem with Scholastica's ingratitude toward my person. But I would be lying if I say I do not have one when she extends this to those (like my father and Andrew and Nancy Whistance-Smith) who have so sumptuously helped me to help her and her family (which she has, since arriving Canada and becoming a Canadian permanent resident, defined as composing of only herself, sibblings, & parents). You will better grasp the point if you imagine the great friends I once had in Edmonton (Alberta, Canada) who believed so much in Peter and Scholastica (without even having met her in person). Scholastica and I both know very well that we were supposed to have paid back close to twenty-one thousand dollars (interest-free) that the Whistance-Smiths lent us. This sum includes the one thousand five hundred dollars (1500.00$) they sent to us in 2000 when Scholastica's permanent residence application deadline was proving difficult to meet. But that is not all. But for their generous loan of seven hundred dollars every month plus letter of undertaking, I would never have gotten my student authorization for, and completed, the doctoral programme at Université de Montréal in Canada. Similarly, Scholastica would also never have done same in the UNIBU, let alone join me in Canada in 1999. More than eighteen years since I graduated from Montréal, more than nineteen since Scholastica arrived in Canada, more than fifteen since she began working professionally, we had not yet paid a dime to people who made all these things happened. Yet, Scholastica can afford to own homes in Canada and vacation in Hawaii, Florida, Niagara, etc, while I (who no longer feature as anything in her definition of family) also pay six hundred and fifty dollars (650.00$) every month to her (as support for children that are also not part of her definition of family) rather than to our creditors. If Scholastica considers this fair game, I clearly don't. I wonder whether she has also refused to repay her student loan to the Canadian Government.

Talking of money and scheming cannot leave out the debts I also contracted in Cameroon for Scholastica's benefit. At the time she was studying in the UNIBU Western Union, and other such money transferring agencies were not functional in the "shithole" country and I had to arrange with Inspector Elias Akendung to be providing her with sums of money in emergency situations before I could route monies to her on a monthly basis. I am here referring therefore only to two of the debts we had in Cameroon – one with Inspector Akendung (seven hundred and thirteen thousand francs CFA) and the other regarding the arrangements for Scholastica's coming to Canada via the USA which was contracted through her best friend and my former student in the UNIBU, Edith-Rosa Khumbah, in the neighbourhood of $4000.00 CAD. When Scholastica got to Canada she behaved in a way that meant she had nothing to do with these debts also, not even those that she herself used to collect from Inspector Akendung while filling an exercise book to that effect in her own writing. This book was eventually handed over to me when I had fully paid the loan.

But it is not just about the money that I am talking here. Without these detailed facts provided, most of you would just not want to believe that the Whistance-Smiths had already written off the debt! I am talking more about (1) honouring one's engagement with others and (2) the future of children and social work. Respecting engagements makes life much more meaningful to the many people behind you since you do not burn the bridge after you have crossed it. Come to imagine the number of other (African) persons who, had we already repaid or were repaying the loan, would already have also benefitted from the kind heartedness of this wonderful Canadian family, including those lining up behind them (like Scholastica and her brothers, sisters and parents have been behind me): then you will get the zoomedeyed picture I am talking about (see Fossungu, 2023: 140-47). The Asahchops' predominating onesidetakism and moneyintriguism are two giants which are solely responsible for the excessive lateness in honouring the repayment of an invaluable life-saving loan. I am still talking about the Whistance-Smiths' critically important loan whose repayment only began with my letter of 26 July 2019 (see Fossungu, 2021: 99-100 n.4). "Giveantakism actually means thinking of others in our deeds and is what showing gratefulness really entails and engenders" (Fossungu, 2023: 144).

Also come to think about the future of 'our' children growing up in a two-parent home of a registered social worker as mother and a university law professor (or practising lawyer) as father and you would have adequately grasped the zoomedeyed picture I am alluding to. This larger-picture is a thing that can hardly be grasped by someone who sees only take and take and take as the rule in life; a perspective that obviously does not portend well with the future of children who, moreover, are not part of the outlandish definition of family – *absolument sans enfants et mari!* That being the case, here then is one other essential puzzle for believers in professionals and for Social Work Canada in particular. If a person's definition of family is 'I, my brothers, my sisters, and my parents', I visibly think that person noticeably cannot be counselling people whose definition of family is 'my spouse, our children, and I'. I wonder then whether such a person can be able to correctly divine what would be important in the case of those having a different definition of family. What, therefore, is the future of your children (who are not in her definition of family) if there are some nascent problems in your family and a social worker of this calibre is assigned to your case? What hope for social work with such social workers?

Whatever the case with their future (as I have already mentioned), only givers do truly appreciate gifts as receivers. For instance, being the generous giver that he is, after the helpful counsel he received, relating to the insolent letter from his first son in America, papa wrote to "My dear son" (Momany) in 1999:

I must thank you very much for the two hundred US Dollars, which was 120.000 frs. When I was reading your letter, it was you standing before me. I only pray to Almighty God to bless us to see each other. I thank you for all the advice you gave me about Njumo's letter.

Justine has not done well in this first term examination. She has only 7.9 average, but all the other terms she has been doing well. Many greetings from all the family people to you and I pray that God should keep you well until we meet. Thank you again for the money. Live well till we meet.
Your loving father, Fosungu N. Emmanuel (Fossungu, 2015: 87).

Yes, it is very true that only givers do truly appreciate gifts as receivers; elucidating why those appreciative words of mine to the traders in Takum, coming from the bottom of my heart and watered by the tears of joy that were flowing while they were being uttered, were so touching to one of the traders that he offered me an additional three hundred naira, saying: "Take this, my son. You will surely need it. I have never seen anyone with your courage and determination. May the lord bless and guide you." It was as if he had just opened the floodgates of Kananaski, because the further individual donations from most of them truthfully weighed me down. The feeling I had at that moment could only be compared to the one in Nwangong in June 2004, in another unexpected gift situation that caused me to break one of my golden rules of not making promises beforehand.

The Nwangong Generator Gift in June 2004

In June 2004 I made a short-notice trip to Cameroon to attend to my sick and frail birth mother in the village, at the time living with a younger relation of hers in Nwancheng quarter. During this visit which was in response to 'the health situation of your mother [which] needs your regular calls, contacts and some preparations before it is too late' (Fossungu, 2016: 114), I made a small surprise gift to the people of Nwangong. This is a village which, like so many others in then Cameroon, did not have electricity. Reaching the village, I got the keys to papa's house in Letia quarter from the Emollah Palace. Papa's house is where I usually stayed (till then) when in the village since my own building (on the other side of the road and not far from papa's) was yet to be completed and ready for habitation then. Papa had allocated part of his house in the village to be used as the village dispensary or health post. Many thoughts crossed my mind as I was setting things up in the visitor room. Maybe I should concentrate more on the health post than the generator for the Emollah Palace? There were many more questions on roads and the promotion of youth education and other training. But in the end, I told myself to just do what I had in mind during this unplanned trip and look at the others later.

After I had bathed and eaten next morning, I told the people who had then filled the house to welcome me that I had to go to Dschang, the closest Bamboutouszonian town to Nwangong. When the cab got to Letia in the afternoon and the generator, other accessories (like connecting wires, bulbs and holders, more than enough for all the Palace homes and those in its vicinity), television set and DVD player were being off-loaded, the feast had commenced. The news of it spread like dry season fire. Only four-wheel drives go down to the Emollah Palace. But by the time the numerous spontaneous volunteers transporting the numerous boxes got there, there was already so much singing and dancing that triply augmented at the sight of the boxes. Unannounced as it was, food almost immediately started pouring in from both the Fon's wives and beyond. Queenta (the village nurse from Bafut) was surprised and happy as everyone else but still managed to very competently immortalize the occasion with the aid of the video camera.

Figure #41: Some Nwangongers posing in celebration of the
Palace Generator in June 2004
Source: Queenta Ngum Afanwi

Fon DF Fossungu (like papa in Kumba in 1972) was also
obviously looking at the bigger picture in his 'Thank You'
speech that evening of 22 June 2004. The Fon stated, first, that
a good deed never walks alone, and that he was sure it was just
the start as my example was surely going to be imitated. In
short, he was describing the gesture as a pioneering one that he
was hoping would provoke similar undertakings from others.
Second, the Fon told the people of Nwangong that "other
people would only be entitled to minimize you if you do
minimize yourself." The Fon noted, in the third place, that
when Chief Formbuehndia (papa) was still up and doing, there
was no end of year that people in the village did not "receive
messages" from him. But that it was not a problem even then
that papa was no longer alive, rhetorically asking: "Is what we
are having here this evening not still a message we are receiving
from Chief Formbuehndia who trained and sent Dr.
Nkemtale'eh to where he is coming from?" The others agreed

that it was. "Some years back," the Fon carried on, "who would have believed that today we would also be sitting in this Palace not with bush-lamps but with bright shining electric bulbs hanging all over us?" (Ask the same question with Ambazonians carrying sophisticated guns and making/using IEDs) No one at all, was the sonorous response. It seems that in the village speaking through rhetorical questions is a much-cherished manner of involving listeners who, consequently, follow what you are saying better.

Saying a lot of good things, including the fact that all the receipts, duly handed over to him, were bearing the Fon's names and not the giver's, Fon DF Fossungu then stated that all this was only indicative of the giver's wisdom and farsightedness. For, "with Dr. Nkemtale'eh back in Canada, could we be able to prove, in case we were going to repair any of these items and the police stopped us, that we did not steal them?" How could we, was the general response. As you can see, looking at the globavillagist aspect of things becomes part and parcel of you when you have objectives such as those I have defined myself with. The Fon had then asked that I should come and stand at a position indicated (like Manyuzonian Chiefs did to General Big Number, aka Supreme General Efang) and I think I heard the village nurse immediately saying "Wow! Dr. Fossungu is going to be awarded a medal!" That is exactly what happened (with General Big Number becoming a big Sisiko) and I asked Queenta later how she knew, and she explained: "I have lived in your village for quite long [eight months then] and have realized that your customs are not different in a lot of respects from those of Bafut. The Fon of Bafut does not tell someone about whom he is talking to come and stand here or there unless he wants to confer a medal on that person. And that is not something you see done often. Dr. Fossungu, people like you are rare to come by and I count myself very lucky to be

266

your friend." I had to thank her for both the compliment and teaching on the medal awarding culture.

Figure #42: Mamie Pauline Anangfack Fossungu
Source: Fon NN Fossungu

Personally placing the medal through my head onto my neck and lengthily justifying my meriting it, the Fon tersely added: "What I like so much about Dr. Nkemtale'eh is especially the fact that he never makes promises before doing anything. He just does it when he is ready to do it. This is very good because you can make promises and then find out after that you cannot keep them and thus become a liar." Many other speakers also took the floor (after the Fon of Nwangong) and attested to their gratitude and hopefulness in greater things to come into their lives. Notable among them were the speeches of Ndi Nkem Barnabas Fonge and Mamie Pauline Anangfack Fossungu in Figure #42. The general happiness that was pouring around for and from this little surprise gift of mine was so overwhelming to me that, in my response to the Fon's and other speeches on the occasion, I paradoxically broke the golden rule by making promises, especially to the youths of the village. I advised them to take their studies very seriously because it is what had permitted me to be where I was coming from, promising those who did so some financial and other assistance up to the minimum of high school, beginning the following academic year (2005/2006). My promise to the youths of Nwangong has never happened and I have thus become a liar because of the type of woman I ended up with as wife. The spouse domain is a particular field in which I have always wanted to be better than my father, since it is an area which has been the stronghold of the forces working against and slowing down the advancement in his globavillagist outlook on life. Paradoxically, it seems instead to be the one area in which I have had so many failures and un-defining moments. These unusual moments have, without a doubt, curtailed considerably the number of persons that would by now have made their way into "the greatest number of persons possible" whose lives I would already have ameliorated in ways

268

far greater than the traders in Takum could ever have imagined when they were aiding me to at least reach Nsukka.

Figure #43: Celestin Ihenacho Anusiem
Source: Celestin Ihenacho Anusiem

I spent three nights in the hostel of the University of Nigeria, Nsukka with Anusiem who was simply out of words when he met me. It was really a good break and rest from the long and dangerous trek through the forest. My friend suggested my hanging around Nsukka, but Calabar was the place I wanted to stick it out in, with my eyes set on UNICAL. Anusiem did not only boost me up with financial help but also with a lot of reminiscences. "How is your sister, Josephine? Is she still acting as strange as I used to know her to?" Anusiem was always right about his observations in Josephine's regard because he just could not believe the excitement in his two senior sisters in Cameroon Baptist Academy when we often arrived there from Sasse College. It was the contrary with my sister. He used to complain about something being wrong with

Josephine and I often said there was not anything wrong with her that I knew of. This time in Nsukka I knew what the problem must have been. But I was not going to let the Josephine thing start marring my thoughts, so I answered only the first of Anusiem's queries, indicating that Josephine was happily married with about three children then; and quickly turning the conversation to Sasse College and Yoke or Muyuka generally.

The Significance of Muyuka and the Cameroon-Reversing Chicken Gear

Muyuka has also been so vital in my struggles to advance (as it has been too to the AWOL). Not only because of the concentration there of the negative forces impacting on the definitions in the household. But also since most of the positive movers that have unexpectedly popped up when I have been in some sort of dire strait have been tied to the town. Vahid from Muyuka, for example, had long finished his studies at the UNICAL and had come back there just to get some documents required for his Youth Service Corp that he had been assigned to effect in Benin Kirbi in Sokoto State (as it then was). Vahid did not only give me all the information on how to join him there. He also arranged with some acquaintances of his who were still in UNICAL for me to be spending the nights with them in the hostel until I was ready to make the trip up north. Guess what! One of those acquaintances, Roxton Chukwu, I also met again in Edmonton on my arrival to the University of Alberta in 1991. Sleeping on the floor in a university hostel was far safer and more eye-opening than at the construction site, where I still worked during the day until I left for Benin Kirbi.

In this moderate northern city, I got to really know the calibre of the man called Vahid Ashu. I just cannot describe him

参考

Feynman, R. (1963). 费曼物理学讲义 1961-1963. 第一卷 26-3、32-2、32-4；第三卷 1-1、32-2。Michael A. Gottlieb 和 Rudolf Pfeiffer 编。帕萨迪纳：加州理工学院。https://www.feynmanlectures.caltech.edu

Feynman, R. (1979). 道格拉斯·罗布纪念讲座，新西兰奥克兰大学。http://www.vega.org.uk/video/subseries/8

Polkinghorne, J. (2002) 量子理论：简介。（第 11-13 页）。牛津：牛津大学出版社。https://en.wikipedia.org/wiki/John_Polkinghorne

Steinhardt, P. (2004) 10. 光与量子物理学（第13页）。普林斯顿大学物理系。https://phy.princeton.edu/people/paul-j-steinhardt

Stetz, A.W. (2007) 量子场论简介。（第5页）。https://sites.science.oregonstate.edu/~stetza/COURSES/ph654/ShortBook.pdf#page=5

enough but would merely advise that you must not go about leaving negative trails wherever you pass. If I did so, Vahid would never even have behaved that day at the UNICAL campus as if he knew me. That is exactly what he told me. In this connection, I also recall this young man stopping his car at a bus stop in Montréal where I had recently arrived and was waiting for the bus. Smiling very broadly at me, the young man's face was very familiar but I could not pin down exactly where I had known him when Marcel Ndengue refreshed my mind that I taught him at the UNIYAO and requested that I get into the car so that they (he was with his wife) could drop me off wherever I was going. Would this former student have even bothered stopping if I had been an obnoxious lecturer? You cannot be that when you are a Hisofean with what a Toronto lawyer describes as zoomed-eye view. I have even had to teach former Kumba primary school classmates (and rivals for Rita) in secondary school. Most of them were later again my classmates (or even 'seniors') in university. As Vahid (who was only then knowing my real name) had explained to me in Benin Kirbi, although we never really got the chance to know each other well enough in Muyuka, he always admired the fact that, flying as high as I then was, I was never boastful and mean as most others in my position would easily be. Do I still need to specifically identify that as an ingredient of success? That is the 'letting our titles shine only from under' that I have always been harping on.

Vahid indeed worked as tirelessly as he could to secure me a teaching position in a secondary school in town. It was nearing fruition when the Shehu Shagari re-election strategy of doing away with 'illegal' immigrants came in between. Ghana Must Go! Vahid particularly talked me into staying and sticking it out. But, knowing myself and what I was up against, I persisted and followed my instincts that were pointing straight to a return to Cameroon before things could get out of hand. Vahid

271

at a point wondered if it was "that your black beauty" (obviously alluding to Emelda Tangwa) that was pulling me back to Yoke. Of course, a lady's invisible hand could not be completely put out of the equation, but it was not the main reason for the U-turn. To begin with, there was just no way that I could have successfully passed for a Nigerian (from whatever part of it) like my friend. Second, I understood my new environment (experience also derived from staying in Garoua) to be one where people can be laughing so profusely with you but the very next minute they may be stabbing you. Of course, what is happening in Northern Nigeria (and especially the on-going slaughtering in Plateau & Benue states by 'Fulani herdsmen'), even as I speak, between Christians and Muslims, is not news that I need to be the one to break. And third, the one seeking re-election with the nonsensical strategy was particularly from this Benin Kirbi area, the more reason for a person of the targeted class to be a sure victim there. Vahid might not have been able to see exactly why I was "chickening out". But as I have said many times before, your therapy begins with you first understanding your situation.

The separation was not an easy one at all because Vahid and I had so much in common, being able to discuss academic and other issues very fruitfully despite our level gap. Roxton himself was very surprised in Alberta that I was in the Faculty of Law and not in the Faculty of Sciences, where he would have been looking if someone else had told him I was in the University of Alberta. Vahid and I had simply clicked in almost the same way Solomon and I did in the UNIYAO. But we finally were able to say goodbye and let go. My journey back home followed the same reversed course from Katsina-Alla as the incoming trip. It was kind of easier than the outward one – perhaps because I already had the trekking experience. Or simply because I was going to where I know and with someone there that was always in my thoughts. Just reaching Takum again where the trekking had to begin brought back a positive recollection of all the magical things that had happened from when I left Yoke in September 1981 till then. There were a lot of hard moments too, but I was viewing all those only as blessings in disguise. I was returning to Yoke and farm work, for sure, and to start from scratch without money. But as I have said many times, money is not all that is necessary for success. If it were, then, surely the many lacks of money situations, including the BIROCOL money palaver, should evidently have spelt the end of my road.

People sometimes talk about money in language that would make you think happiness totally depends on the size of it that you have or expend. How much, for instance, did papa need to spend in 1981 to permit me enrol and study in the UNIYAO, compared to what he had until then used up on me? And compared to where the entire Fossungu Royal Family would have been today? Again, how much did I spend on the generator and other items that brought so much joy and celebration to Nwangong during my impromptu voyage in June 2004? Just about three hundred and fifty thousand francs CFA, which would be practically less than eight hundred Canadian dollars (about a month's rent in Montréal for a moderate 2-bedroom apartment). And I did not spend that amount of money simply because I had so much of it but because of my desire to make things better for the greatest number of persons possible. The one person (Anna) who almost entirely shared this perspective and with whom I wanted to work and walk throughout my life increasing "the greatest number of persons possible" was in Yoke to where I was then returning.

I have already noted that as a hisofean, you hardly carry all your eggs in one basket. The many and diverse university admissions noted earlier can demonstrate. From Nkambe in then

273

Savannazone to Yoke in Debundschazone (passing through Bamboutouszone and Wourizone), I made sure I was always occupying a seat by the window so that I could very quickly jot down postal information from the sign boards of colleges as we passed by. Because I have very good sight and write extremely fast, I was able to note down many of them, including that of Collège de l'Unité de Manjo. Back to Yoke and farming, I did not consider it the end of the road just as it had not been after the Sasse re-admission saga. I regarded my being back there as a mere waiting period for the several teaching-position applications to bring up something with which to continue with the quest for university education after the 'wasted' but positively 'maturing' two academic years. But it looks like my being back in Yoke and to farming was interpreted by many (including the parents of my wife-to-be) as the final act; thus, occasioning the 99-sensism events relating to my darling Anna never becoming my wife. It is also amazing that Manjo would come calling only after (and not before) the Anna flop, a debacle that would seem to have catapulted the multiple disasters in the spouse quest (that I was until then no longer worrying about), crowned by the Scholastica surprising family definitional mess in Canada, capped by her pregnancy games that are examined in my next book. This one must then be closed.

Conclusion

The most appropriate conclusion to this book that I would have given, given the opportunity to break virgin ground by breaking long-established tradition, would be to ask you to begin reading again from the first page to this one; or to just repeat here that 'If you are destined for greatness (like Ayabacholization is), the only obstacle that can prevent you from becoming great is you' and that is it. Not having been accorded that opportunity to break tradition here (since I have embraced it by beginning with a traditional Introduction), I must highlight a few points by way of conclusion, knowing still that you are very entitled to draw your own conclusions for yourself. To begin with, I have told this story solely because a lot can be learnt from it by a lot of people, whether they are facing similar exclusionist situations. Those facing situations can also get inspiration while those not, will better appreciate the fact that they are not. Ayabacholization, don't I always speak in the language you have very properly demonstrated mastery of?Impending Administrators of Ambazonia must be Hisofeans. I think the world would be a better place if people generally are honest and farsighted. Visionary people (exemplified by Ayabacholization) are usually those that are better suited to give children, without definitional distinctions, a better or brighter future than what they themselves have, irrespective of the societies they live in. The Ayabacholization Speeches generally, and especially the early one in South Africa (see Fossungu, 2023: 202) would evidence the theory well. Should Social Work in Canada, as in Africa, and the rest of the world, not try to see to it that people working in this domain that has enormous powers to make or mar the future of children in particular be at least people who can truthfully attest to and pass the 'Charity begins at home' litmus test?

275

On Success and the Role of Money: This book has given you some of the 'Becoming Better' battles that I have fought in view of making things better for the greatest number of persons possible: despite the money and other handicaps resulting from some exclusionist definitions of family. Money, as essential as it is, does not become too essential an ingredient of success to those who really want to achieve their objectives as they would still achieve – with or without it. How much money did the AGovC, for instance, have when they recruited, trained and deplored the ADF for self-defense? Answer the question (like the Yaoundé train-station policemen) with this other question: What have the IGs done with the astronomical amounts Ambazonians enthusiastically handed over to them in the name of "War Draft" and "My Trip to Buea"? When I look back, therefore, and see how much I have had to be helped in various ways by several people, some of them being complete strangers to me, I cannot help but be optimistic and fortified that I shall one day (on one way or another) carry my objective of "making life more worthwhile for the greatest number of persons possible" to a much higher level or platform; and this notwithstanding the obstacles so far encountered and those that are still, or will be, standing in the way. Always be grateful and thankful from the bottom of your heart, therefore, for every act of help that comes your way. It is because of this mannerism that I was able, for instance, to extricate myself from the Takum (Nigeria) dire straits. Africans, as the classical thankyouologists that we are, appear to grasp this lesson well, as seen so far

Bitterness that is not born out of the truth will only consume you before the real obstacle itself shows up for that purpose. Once you know yourself and have objectives with which you identify, you will often quickly and almost instinctively find a way to get out of situations that hinder the attainment of your goals. You consequently look at the big picture of things, not the small. That is why the funny definition of family in Canada did not just push me to be reactionary but to continue with what I thought was the best option for the future of the children, including those people that the strange definition was geared toward 'advancing'. The same reasoning applied to many other situations in Cameroon as well as in Canada. My knowledge of some of the things that have enormously aided and will continue helping me succeed in life has been brought about by many people, both within and outside my large and extended royal family. I have all through the longest short-cut to university education and marriage/family highlighted the contribution of the many early influences that have helped in my progress. In the family, I cannot escape specific mention of my two mothers and one of my two fathers, as well as uncles (like Chief Foletia, Ngufor, and Fonge) and aunts (such as Tumekong and Nzouata) and other siblings of the household. I particularly learnt a lot from Therese's tragedy just as I am expecting a lot of people would learn a lot from my story's successes and failures.

When you know who you are and what you are up to and up against, you will often correctly anticipate a problem before it comes and the whole story illustrates that there is nothing as easy as solving a problem that pops up when you are ready for it. What makes a problem scary is when it takes you by surprise and you are caught off guard. And, truly, Scholastica's definition of family in Canada really caught me off guard and its implications would have been even more catastrophic but for the fact that I am a 'man of many' everything and predictive. To a Hisofean, for example, money is not all that is necessary for success; honouring one's engagement with others is also very important since it is in a way making life much more meaningful to the many people behind you by not burning the bridge after you have crossed it. The AGovC has been facing fundraising issues most likely because most

Ambazonians are still carrying the scars and scares of the IGs' scams called *My Trip to Buea*, *War Draft*, etc. In another sense, you also should not let something that happened to you in the past completely determine the present and future because there are many doors to happiness; meaning that when one door is closed many more are still open.

An open-minded person hardly respects a tradition that is not progressive; a trait that largely explains why it is open-minded people who are mostly associated with the breaking of virgin grounds (pioneers). When you look at the larger picture, you visualize things more clearly than those who look at the narrow. Learning early to depend on you and not being bitter when disappointed as I did (as well as Ayabacholization continues doing) has proven to be one of my greatest ingredients in overcoming adversity in life; because bitterness consumes you even before the hardship being confronted can do so. Only those (like the IGs) who cannot handle the truth get bitter because if you can handle bitterness (like Ayabacholization), there will be no need for you yourself to become bitter. These are some of the things that go into the postulation that, if you are destined for great accomplishments, the only obstacle that can prevent you from becoming great is you. It is obvious that I would not have been able to build on what the experiences of the others in the household and other early influences (both in the village and in *ncheng*) provided if I did not know who I was and what I was up to; if I did not have an open mind or look at the larger picture of things; and if I did not have clear objectives with which I define myself (like Ayabacholization does with its Liberation Strategy and Roadmap), thus not knowing my worth and, consequently, was too afraid to break virgin grounds with professions and the Liberation Tax for Ayabacholization.

The Folly of 99-Sensism: As a young man I hardly did fit into the definition of family or of child largely because of the 99-sensical home I grew up in. My whole life seems to have been devoted to having an ideal marital union to eschew these same problems passing on to my own and other children. But that desire does not seem to be realisable because, as a parent, 99-Sensism and other associated -isms catalogued herein would appear to have trailed me, excluding my ever being included in the definition of family even as a spouse, let alone a mutually loved one. Like taunted, sized-up, and hunted Ayabacholization, I then seem to have learnt a lot on marriage and 99-Sensism from many members of my own large and extended Royal Family. But my learning in the fields covered in this book especially did not end with just my extended family; lovers also contributed significantly.

I can surely not leave you without drawing attention to one of the particularly ridiculous and narrow-minded corners of 99-Sensism. People seem to have 99% Senses but lack the most essential one per cent Sense. (Ayabacholization also brings out the folly, using the IG-Care: see Fossungu, 2023: 35.) Find out for yourself what it is by posing these few basic questions. When 99-sensers keep on selling only cocks (for fear of hens producing for the non-99-sensical buyers), do they ever for one little second think of the day there will be no more cocks available to mate with their many jealously guarded hens? They do scholaadelastically-assumed here, don't they? And who, furthermore, would even be the 'buyers' in a world of only 99-sensers? Wouldn't Momany (like Ayabacholization) have then become a better or more sensible Bangwa as ably theorized herein? Does the world not clearly need its numerous Momanys and Ayabacholizalists to be the world, or a better place for all?

279

Bibliography

Achebe, Chinua (1964) *Arrow of God* (London, Heinemann).

_____ (1960) *No Longer at Ease* (London, Heinemann).

_____ (1958) *Things Fall Apart* (London: Penguin Books).

Anyangwe, Carlson (1989) The Magistracy and the Bar in Cameroon (Yaoundé: PANAG-CEPER).

Anyefru, Emmanuel (2013) "The Refusal to Belong: Limits on the Discourse on Anglophone Nationalism in Cameroon" available   at http://www.thefreelibrary.com/The+refusal+to+belong%3A +limits+of+the+discourse+on+Anglophone...-a0279891521 [accessed on 11 February 2013]

Avison, William R. and John H. Kunkel 1992. "Socialization" in James J. Teevan, (ed.), *Introduction to Sociology: A Canadian Focus* 4th edition (Scarborough, Ontario: Prentice-Hall Canada Inc.), 55-87.

Ayaba, Lucas Cho (2021a) Dr Cho Ayaba's 20-minute message of the Leader of the Ambazonia War of Independence (AWOL) to Chadians and to all Africans, delivered on 21 April 2021 on Ambazonia Communication Network (ACN).

_____ (2021b) Dr Cho Ayaba's 'Uncensored Message' to all Ambazonians delivered on 21 December 2021 on ACN.

_____ (2021c) Dr Cho Ayaba's 8-minute "Rare Message to Our Friends of the IG-Care", delivered on Wednesday, 20 December 2021 on ACN.

Beaujot, Roderic (1992) "Families", in James J. Teevan (ed.), *Introduction to Sociology: A Canadian Focus* 4th edition (Scarborough, Ontario: Prentice-Hall Canada Inc.), 285-327.

Brain, Robert (1972) *Bangwa Kingship and Marriage* (Cambridge: Cambridge University Press).

Brooks, Stephen (1996) *Canadian Democracy: An Introduction* 2nd edition (Toronto: Oxford University Press).

Campbell, David E. and Robert D. Putnam (2012) "God and Caesar in America: Why Mixing Religion and Politics Is Bad for Both" 91:2 *Foreign Affairs*, 34-43.

Crehan, Margaret Gram (2013) *The Divided States of America: A Comparative Case Study of Same-Sex Marriage in the United States* (PhD Dissertation, Northeastern University).

Ferguson, Michaele L. (2010) "Choice Feminism and the Fear of Politics" 8:1 *Perspectives on Politics*, 247-253.

Ferguson, Niall (2008) *The Ascent of Money – A Financial History of the World* (New York: Penguin Press).

For-Mukwai, Gideon F. (2010) *Fighting Adversity with Audacity* (Bamenda: Langaa RPCIG).

Fossungu, Peter Ateh-Afac: (2023) *Royal Burial and Enthronement in Ambazonia: Interrogating the Relevance of Postcolonial Education in Africa* (Chitungwiza, Zimbabwe: Mwanaka Media and Publishing).

_____ (2021) *Family Law and Politics with Biology and Royalty in Africa and North America* (Chitungwiza, Zimbabwe: Mwanaka Media and Publishing).

_____ (2021b) *Battling Language Rights Governance in Africa: Swisselgianism, Ubackism, and the Ambazonia-Cameroun War* (Chitungwiza, Zimbabwe: Mwanaka Media and Publishing).

_____ (2019) *Getting Africa Out of the Dungeon: Human Rights, Federalism, and Judicial Politics in Cameroon* (Masvingo, Zimbabwe: Africa Talent Publishers).

_____ (2016) *The Expibasketics and Intrigues of Love* (Bamenda: Langaa RPCIG).

_____ (2015) *Family Politics and Deception in Northern North America and West-Central Africa: Litigating God's Marriage Intention?* (Bamenda: Langaa RPCIG).

_____ (2015a) *The HISOFE Dictionary of Midnight Politics: Expibasketical Theories on Afrikentication and African Unity* (Bamenda: Langaa RPCIG).

_____ (2015b) *Africans and Negative Competition in Canadian Factories: Revamping Canada's Immigration, Employment and Welfare Policies?* (Bamenda: Langaa RPCIG).

_____ (2015c) "African Democracy vis-à-vis Western Democracy: Afrikenticating, Follyfying, Expibasketizing, and Reversing the 'African Democracy' Debate", in Munyaradzi Mawere and Tendai Rinos Mwanaka (eds.), *Democracy, Good Governance and Development in Africa* (Bamenda: Langaa RPCIG), 71-124.

_____ (2015d) *Canadian Institutions and Children's Best Interests: Henriflavipeterism as the Quebec 'Money-Only' Sole Custody Case Meant for the Hall of Shame?* (Bamenda: Langaa RPCIG).

_____ (2014) *Africa's Anthropological Dictionary on Love and Understanding: Marriage and the Tensions of Belonging in Cameroon* (Bamenda: Langaa RPCIG).

_____ (2013) *Africans in Canada: Blending Canadian and African Lifestyles?* (Bamenda: Langaa RPCIG).

_____ (2013a) *Understanding Confusion in Africa: The Politics of Multiculturalism and Nation-building in Cameroon* (Bamenda: Langaa RPCIG).

_____ (2013b) *Democracy and Human Rights in Africa: The Politics of Collective Participation and Governance in Cameroon* (Bamenda: Langaa RPCIG).

_____ (1998) "The ICAO Assembly: The Most Unsupreme of Supreme Organs in the United Nations System? A Critical Analysis of Assembly Sessions" 26 *Transportation Law Journal*, 1–49.

Fozo, Abongwa (2015) "Biya's Fake Homage to Fallen Soldiers: The Embarrassment of a Nation" @ http://bamendaonline.net/blog/biyas-fake-homage-to-fallen-soldiers-the-embarrassment-of-a-nation/

Heum, Audhild Steinnes (2016) *"They Say We Have Peace": Perceptions and Practices of Peace in Northern Cameroon* (Master's Thesis in Social Anthropology, University of Bergen, Norway).

Jumbam, Fr. Gerald (2017) "An Open Letter to the President of the National Episcopal Conference of Cameroon (NECC) – Archbishop Samuel Kleda" (Letter obtained on 8 May 2017 at 12:11 PM from Oben Besong who sent it to the Soba-America Forum) (on File with author).

Konings, Piet J.J. (1999) "The Anglophone Struggle for Federalism in Cameroon", in L.R. Basita and J. Ibrahim (eds.), *Federalism and Decentralization in Africa: The Multiethnic Challenge* (Fribourg: Institut du Fédéralisme), 289-325.

Linker, Damon (2015) "God's Banker by Gerald Posner" @ http://www.langaa-rpcig.net/+God-s-Bankers-by-Gerald-Posner+.html.

Mentan, Tatah (2017) "Shaming Heaven: Peace of the Graveyard in Cameroon" @

http://cameroonjournal.com/2017/04/11/commentary-shaming-heaven-peace-of-the-graveyard-in-cameroon/

Milton, John (2003) *Paradise Lost* (London: Penguin Classics).

Ngefac, Aloysius (2010) "Linguistic Choices in Postcolonial Multilingual Cameroon" 19:3 *Nordic Journal of African Studies,* 149-64.

Pratt, Nicola Christine (2007) *Democracy and Authoritarianism in the Arab World* (Boulder, CO: Lynne Rienner Publishing Inc.).

Randall, Vicky (2010) "Feminism", in David Marsh and Gerry Stoker (eds.), *Theory and Methods in Political Science* 3rd edition (London: Palgrave Macmillan), 114-135.

Reaves, Celia S. (1992) *Quantitative Research for the Behavioral Sciences* (Washington, D.C: John Willey & Sons).

Sheradin, Shey (1998) "Ngoa-Ekele Doctors without Doctorate Degrees" *The Herald* (Yaoundé, 2-3 December), 10.

Smith, Miriam (2005) "The Politics of Same-Sex Marriage in Canada and the United States" 38:2 *Political Science & Politics,* 225-28.

Mmap Nonfiction and Academic books

If you have enjoyed *Ayabacholization Classroom In My Life: The Longest Shortcut To University Education*, consider these other fine **Nonfiction and Academic books** from *Mwanaka Media and Publishing:*

Cultural Hybridity and Fixity by Andrew Nyongesa
Tintinnabulation of Literary Theory by Andrew Nyongesa
South Africa and United Nations Peacekeeping Offensive Operations by Antonio Garcia
A Case of Love and Hate by Chenjerai Mhondera
A Cat and Mouse Affair by Bruno Shora
The Scholarship Girl by Abigail George
The Gods Sleep Through It All by Wonder Guchu
PHENOMENOLOGY OF DECOLONIZING THE UNIVERSITY: Essays in the Contemporary Thoughts of Afrikology by Zvikomborero Kapuya
Africanization and Americanization Anthology Volume 1, Searching for Interracial, Interstitial, Intersectional and Interstates Meeting Spaces, Africa Vs North America by Tendai R Mwanaka
Africa, UK and Ireland: Writing Politics and Knowledge Production Vol 1 by Tendai R Mwanaka
Writing Language, Culture and Development, Africa Vs Asia Vol 1 by Tendai R Mwanaka, Wanjohi wa Makokha and Upal Deb
Zimbolicious: An Anthology of Zimbabwean Literature and Arts, Vol 3 by Tendai Mwanaka
Drawing Without Licence by Tendai R Mwanaka
Writing Grandmothers/ Escribiendo sobre nuestras raíces: Africa Vs Latin America Vol 2 by Tendai R Mwanaka and Felix Rodriguez
Nationalism: (Mis)Understanding Donald Trump's Capitalism, Racism, Global Politics, International Trade and Media Wars, Africa Vs North America Vol 2 by Tendai R Mwanaka

Language, Thought, Art and Existence: New and Recollected Essays and Non Fictions by Tendai Rinos Mwanaka

Experimental Writing, Africa Vs Latin America Vol 1 by Tendai Rinos Mwanaka and Ricardo Felix Rodriguez

Fixing Earth Anthology: An anthology of Africa, UK and Ireland Writers, Vol 2 by Tendai Rinos Mwanaka

Africa Must Deal with Blats for Its True Decolonisation: Unclothed Truth about Internalised Internal Colonialism by Nkwazi N. Mhango

ROYAL BURIAL AND ENTHRONEMENT IN AMBAZONIA: INTERROGATING THE RELEVANCE OF POSTCOLONIAL EDUCATION IN AFRICA by Peter Ateh-Afac Fossungu

SCHOOL BASED HIV EDUCATION AFFECTING GIRLS IN SELECTED COUNTRIES IN SUB SAHARAN AFRICA by Ivainesu Charmaine Musa

HIV AND AIDS IN ZIMBABWE: A REVIEW ON THE RELATIONSHIP BETWEEN PERCEPTION OF MASCULINITY AMONGST UNMARRIED YOUNG MEN AND THEIR SEXUAL BEHAVIORS by Lucas Kudakwashe Muvhiringi

AFRICA'S CONTEMPORARY FOOD INSECURITY: SELF-INFLICTED WOUNDS THROUGH MODERN VENI VIDI VICI AND LAND GRABBING by Nkwazi Mhango

Upcoming

I Can't Breathe and other Essays by Zvikomborero Kapuya

https://facebook.com/MwanakaMediaAndPublishing/

www.ingramcontent.com/pod-product-compliance
Lightning Source LLC
Chambersburg PA
CBHW051955270326
41929CB00015B/2659